Underserved Patrons in
University Libraries

Underserved Patrons in University Libraries

Assisting Students Facing Trauma, Abuse, and Discrimination

Julia C. Skinner and Melissa Gross, Editors

Foreword by Nicole A. Cooke

LIBRARIES
UNLIMITED®

An Imprint of ABC-CLIO, LLC

Santa Barbara, California • Denver, Colorado

Library of Congress Cataloging-in-Publication Data

Names: Skinner, Julia (Julia C.), editor. | Gross, Melissa, editor.
Title: Underserved patrons in university libraries : assisting students facing trauma, abuse, and discrimination / Julia C. Skinner and Melissa Gross, editors ; foreword by Nicole A. Cooke.
Description: Santa Barbara, California : Libraries Unlimited, [2021] | Includes bibliographical references and index.
Identifiers: LCCN 2020020565 (print) | LCCN 2020020566 (ebook) | ISBN 9781440870415 (paperback ; acid-free paper) | ISBN 9781440870422 (ebook)
Subjects: LCSH: Academic libraries—United States. | Public services (Libraries)— United States. | Academic libraries—Services to people with disabilities— United States. | Academic libraries—Services to minorites—United States. | Academic libraries—Services to adult college students—United States.
Classification: LCC Z675.U5 U48 2021 (print) | LCC Z675.U5 (ebook) | DDC 027.70973—dc23
LC record available at https://lccn.loc.gov/2020020565
LC ebook record available at https://lccn.loc.gov/2020020566

ISBN: 978-1-4408-7041-5 (paperback)
        978-1-4408-7042-2 (ebook)

25 24 23 22 21   1 2 3 4 5

This book is also available as an ebook.

Libraries Unlimited
An Imprint of ABC-CLIO, LLC

ABC-CLIO, LLC
147 Castilian Drive
Santa Barbara, California 93117
www.abc-clio.com

This book is printed on acid-free paper ∞

Manufactured in the United States of America

To all library workers, present and future,
who believe they can change the world.

Contents

Foreword

Nicole A. Cooke

Before becoming a faculty member at a graduate library and information science program, I spent almost fifteen years in academic libraries doing reference and instruction and serving as a subject specialist to various departments. When I was a practicing librarian in the late 1990s to the early 2000s, it was very common for me to be the only visible minority in the organization, or one of two or three people. This still happens in 2020, but it is accompanied by much more frustration and discussion. Along with the lack of a diverse workforce (across library types), academic libraries have been slower to consider, embrace, or implement services to diverse populations. Academic libraries have been viewed, internally and externally, as sites of strict information provision and intellectual innovation, but not always when it comes to equity, diversity, and inclusion (EDI) issues. This has resulted in academic libraries being thought of as intimidating and disconnected spaces, instead of warm and welcoming community spaces.

When I worked directly in these spaces, there was no lack of literature (e.g., critical information literacy, critical cataloging), workshops, and service opportunities (e.g., diversity committees sponsored by the American Library Association) that emphasized the need for diverse spaces and a diverse library and information science workforce. There were some EDI initiatives in medical, special, and public libraries, but not as much for general academic libraries, whose role was seen as teaching and facilitating research, not programming (where EDI content often falls). As time moved on, there may have been some EDI "happy talk"[1] inserted into library mission and vision statements, and in strategic plans, but these statements were not actualized into day-to-day operations and services.

To this end, I vividly remember an academic colleague who was amazing at their job and went out of their way to help patrons. However, there was a trans patron coming into the library, and this colleague was exceptionally uncomfortable with them, to the point of leaving the service point when they came into the area. I thought about two things: I was surprised that someone so professional and knowledgeable would exhibit this behavior. I shouldn't have been surprised—we're all human and have implicit biases and room to grow and improve. Secondly, I wished there had been some training provided by the library to assist their staff with dealing with diverse patrons.

With the world as it is today, incredibly diverse but also divided, we need to do more. Academic libraries need to do more when it comes to EDI; the EDI imperative cannot just be for public libraries. This is the approach that I take in my teaching. I teach three classes related to EDI, and my goal is to prepare all aspiring information professionals to become culturally competent, empathetic, and prepared to enthusiastically and compassionately serve people who are different from them. All information professionals, regardless of library type, will encounter diverse and otherwise marginalized populations, and they should be up for the task!

This collection is timely and will provide academic colleagues an abundance of ideas and, more importantly, tangible proof that academic libraries can and should rise to the occasion of proactively and creatively incorporating EDI into their collections and services.

This Collection

The authors in this volume present some of the innovative services and conversations now being had in academic libraries. They are thinking about ways to serve diverse populations, and they are implementing new and customized services, even if they are not initially successful.

Lorin K. Jackson presents her work as an embedded librarian, which allowed her to individualize and customize her services and increase engagement with her patrons. Jackson frames this essay (and the overall collection) well by stating "the unique positioning of academic libraries as elitist repositories of knowledge in a higher education context, as well as how academic libraries are cultural sites of production that can be profoundly unforgiving for underrepresented populations." With this in mind, her work intends to counteract this narrative and assumption by catering to those patrons who have library anxiety and/or a lack of social capital, and those who have limited knowledge of or experience with libraries. Jackson emphasizes the importance of having diversity among the professional staff of libraries—representation matters when working with diverse populations who need to see themselves in their libraries.

Phillip Fitzsimmons and April K. Miller describe their work with international students involved in English as a Second Language (ESL) study. By participating in the production of an ESL newsletter, they exemplify active learning and relationship building with these students and their instructors. This personal interaction also depends on effective communication skills and the ability to work across language and cultural barriers. Fitzsimmons and Miller also stress that learning and growth can emerge from failed attempts at working with diverse populations. The subsequent growth enabled them to develop a collection of diverse activities that built appeal with their students.

Several chapters are devoted to older adults, and the variability of characteristics and information needs that exist within this larger group. Joseph Winberry and Bharat Mehra discuss older adults who face ageism and prejudice, particularly when trying to find employment in an effort to stem economic injustice. Their work highlights the mandate of land-grant institutions who are charged with serving members of the public, many of whom are these older adults who can benefit from both public and academic libraries.

Amanda Roper, Andrea Kincaid, and Andrew Foskey are also serving adults, in the form of returning students through the TN (Tennessee) Reconnect Program. Their services include professional librarians whose work hours coincide with the evening hours that are most convenient for adult students who work during the day. Their library has also considered the enablers and barriers of physical space for this group; they have worked to customize their space to better accommodate these students and their families by adding a family study room.

Michelle Shea works with yet another diverse and adult population in her library, veterans and military-affiliated families. Shea creates displays and specially curated services, spaces, and resources. Her goal is to get to know the veterans, including learning the military terminology they use when describing their needs and experiences.

All of the authors working with adult populations emphasize the need to deeply learn about their specific populations, and the need for academic libraries to have specific policies and statements, outreach efforts, and sincere community engagement.

Several chapters address victims of personal and sexual violence, which is a particularly underserved and misunderstood population due to privacy issues, lack of understanding, and fear (on the part of the victims and library staff). Jinxuan Ma and Lynne Stahl work to promote and distribute information about the prevention of sexual violence through referrals, announcements, social engagement, and instructional intervention. Racine L. Amos focuses on victims of interpersonal violence (IPV) who come into the library. Amos stresses that libraries need to protect the people who utilize our spaces. She says, "academic libraries experience high volumes of people, extended hours, and typically limited on-site security presence. This combined with the nature of collaborative academic work in public yet, isolating workspaces can make libraries attractive venues for those seeking to commit acts of IPV." This is a sobering observation that reminds us that we need to curate safe spaces as much as possible, provide accompanying resources, and support and instructions on how to use them appropriately. Monte-Angel Richardson,

Stephanie Rosen, Marna M. Clowney-Robinson, and Danica San Juan write about trauma-informed practices to support patrons in need. Trauma-informed practices are certainly applicable to IPV victims and patrons experiencing other types of disturbances. The authors detail the importance of consistent and ongoing training for all library staff, regardless of level or function, in order to develop empathy and the skills to identify "the impact of trauma, recognizing the signs and symptoms in patrons and staff, responding by integrating knowledge about trauma into library policies and practices, and actively resisting re-traumatization."

Bobbie Bushman and Dale Monobe encourage readers to thoughtfully consider students who are incarcerated or who have been previously incarcerated. These students have limited experience with libraries and uncensored resources, and often have difficulty figuring out how to fully utilize everything the library has to offer. Academic libraries need to become better acquainted with these students and partner appropriately with other agencies to ensure their academic success.

Vikki C. Terrile writes about people experiencing homelessness and housing and basic needs insecurity, which are discussed often in the context of public libraries but have not received much attention from academic libraries. Academic libraries have begun paying more attention as campus anti-hunger efforts are more prevalent. Students who experience varying levels of insecurity may spend long hours in the library, sleep in the library, use the library restrooms for bathing, or hide their belongings in the library. Consequently, these students may suffer academically because of low concentration levels and anxiety. Terrile recommends treating these students as whole people and investigates increased services to meet their needs (e.g., opening additional spaces for longer hours, providing open access materials, and loaning more forms of technology).

The final chapters of the collection highlight services to patrons with communication disorders, anxiety and depression, and mental illness. Like patrons suffering from personal violence, it can be challenging to work with patrons who have physical and mental challenges because of privacy issues and not wanting to be overbearing with people who may or may not self-disclose. Brady D. Lund discusses the need to create supportive environments for those who deal with autism spectrum disorders, disfluency/stuttering, deaf/hard-of-hearing, social anxiety/mutism, and aphasia. This includes maintaining eye contact and repeating instructions in slow, calm, and measured speech. Angel Sloss suggests that library staff engage in continuing education to dispel the myths about those with anxiety and depression, and learn how to establish the right campus and community partnerships. Sloss also mentions the stress and anxiety that racism causes for campus students. This is a salient conversation that all academic libraries need to have. Abigail L. Phillips urges academic libraries to think outside the proverbial box when working with students who deal with mental illness. Passive programming and complementary activities and therapies such as yoga classes, meditation and/or mindfulness sessions, book clubs, and coloring book sessions can go a long way in assuaging students' anxiety and stress. Phillips also stresses that university staff lack the proper mental health literacy or the training to appropriately support mentally ill students. This needs to change.

Synergies

There are several strong threads that run throughout the thirteen chapters. Not only are they spotlighting a variety of diverse populations, but they are embodying the tenets of cultural competence, empathy, intellectual humility, persistence, and a genuine need to serve others, not because they have to but because they want to celebrate the differences and cultural and social capital of others (Cooke 2016, Chapter 2). The authors detail their efforts to get to know their populations, which entails more than just saying hello or asking people for their names. Getting to know diverse communities requires relationship development over time and the willingness to be vulnerable with the people we are trying to serve. This allows these academic librarians to cocreate knowledge and services with patrons who really bring so much to the table. The aforementioned vulnerability also requires the willingness to fail and the ability to try, try again. Services to diverse populations are nuanced, complicated, and change over time.

These chapters also detail the challenges and rewards of managing diversity (Chapter 5). Diversity work is ongoing and requires consistent and ongoing efforts. As mentioned in many of the chapters, continuing education for all library staff is necessary as is commitment from academic library leadership. Creativity and an ability to take risks are also required.

Kudos to these academic libraries and librarians for having the hard conversations and empathy necessary to want to go above and beyond in their service to diverse populations. This collection is necessary and will hopefully inspire many more academic libraries to embark on this crucial work.

Note

1. Ahmed (2012, 10) writes about the importance of language as it pertains to diversity. Often the language of diversity used in policies and mission statements does not match the actual diversity being implemented in daily operations. She says, "to work for institutions, as practitioners do, can require that you develop a habit of talking in mission talk, what we can call 'happy talk,' a way of telling a happy story of the institution that is at once a story of the institution as happy.

Over the temporal course of the interview, the happier languages seemed to wear out, and a very different account of the institution was generated."

References

Ahmed, Sara. 2012. *On Being Included: Racism and Diversity in Institutional Life.* Durham, NC: Duke University Press.

Cooke, Nicole A. 2016. *Information Services to Diverse Populations: Developing Culturally Competent Library Professionals.* Santa Barbara, CA: ABC-CLIO.

Introduction

Julia C. Skinner and Melissa Gross

In response to a growing awareness of the prevalence of sexual assault on college and university campuses across the United States and around the world, we became concerned about the role of academic librarians in assisting survivors of sexual assault. We realized that this was a complex issue as these users, unless they self-identify, can be invisible, and their information seeking can be misread as an assignment related topic, rather than a very personal inquiry. Survivors of sexual assault are also difficult to study, both because they may not wish to self-identify and because of the difficulty of engaging with survivors about this topic without retraumatizing them in the process. Our solution was to develop the ISIS model (Skinner and Gross 2017) to help academic librarians understand the relationship between the healing process and information needs and potential information seeking related to healing. As we worked on that project, we realized that survivors of sexual assault are not the only sub-population that academic and other librarians work with who may be invisible unless they choose to self-identify. It was this recognition and the desire to assist librarians in improving their professional practice that was the genesis of this project.

In this book, you'll find guidance for a range of ways to engage with and support various campus communities that have often been overlooked in campus libraries, and society as a whole. Whether or not you identify as a member of any of these communities, we hope that you will learn more about each one's unique experiences within the campus space so you can best help them navigate their learning journey.

The work we do in academic libraries takes many forms, from cataloging to reference to programming, and crosses many spaces, including trade and community colleges, continuing education, and traditional four-year schools. We have attempted to bring in voices that speak to each of these, so that everyone across academic librarianship can find something within this work to inspire, educate, and improve.

To facilitate this, we have gathered a range of chapters together that represent boots on the ground programming and services alongside thoughtful research and ideas for where to go in the future. We have made a point of including the voices of researchers and practitioners, to lessen the artificial divide we often create between the two, and to begin a new dialogue where the wealth of our entire field's experience is brought to bear to best serve each patron we encounter.

Some of these communities are not ones you might think of as being overlooked, such as older students, but as Joseph Winberry and Bharat Mehra remind us, even these communities have their own challenges and experiences that must be considered. Amanda Roper, Andrea Kincaid and Andrew Foskey discuss how to best serve the needs of returning adult students at community colleges. Importantly, both of these chapters use a social justice lens in considering information work.

In some cases, we see the stories of those who may not wish to be identified but still require services, such as Jinxuan Ma and Lynne Stahl's chapter on supporting sexual assault survivors. Racine L. Amos considers how we support survivors of violence more broadly, looking at survivors of sexual assault as part of a study of interpersonal violence that also includes stalking and dating violence. And we see the stories of those who may not have had the same opportunities as other students, or who face additional barriers in school and beyond, such as Bobbie Bushman and Dale Monobe's chapter on serving formerly incarcerated students. Monte-Angel Richardson, Stephanie Rosen, Marna M. Clowney-Robinson, and Danica San Juan share how trauma-informed librarianship has been adopted at the University of Michigan.

We have included several chapters that focus on mental health, including those by Abigail L. Phillips and Angel Sloss. Increasingly, research shows us that students often face mental health challenges such as anxiety and depression, either as acute episodes or as part of a lifelong mental health journey. We also see increasing evidence that not only do campuses hold a sizeable neurodiverse population, but those individuals are often not provided with the services that best speak to the ways in which we engage with the world.

Vikki C. Terrile considers how academic libraries can assist students who are homeless or experiencing housing insecurity. Michelle Shea discusses a wide variety of ways academic librarians can strengthen outreach to Veterans and Military-Affiliated Families. Brady D. Lund discusses library services for individuals with communication differences.

When we put out the initial call for chapters, we kept our call intentionally broad, recognizing that there are many identities and experiences that fall outside of the *typical* student experience, and we were eager to represent as many as possible (though of course, *typical* is put in italics here as the range of student experiences mean there really is no one size fits all). We are incredibly proud of the breadth of work represented in these pages, speaking to a vast range of identities and experiences.

However, there were some subjects we hoped to cover that we were unable to find authors for, including the LGBTQ+ community, DREAMers, and people facing severe and/or chronic illnesses. Though the book is not exhaustive in its scope (and indeed, no book covering so much ground could ever hope to be), we still hope that some of the learning shared in these pages will inform work with many student and staff communities and will inspire future research that builds upon what is presented here to create a more truly inclusive professional literature.

Throughout the book, you'll find exciting new ideas for services and programming, such as Lorin K. Jackson's chapter on the benefits of embedded librarianship on college campuses, and Phillip Fitzsimmons and April K. Miller's ideas for making campus life more inclusive for English language learners.

In all cases, there is a hopeful message that we can indeed provide meaningful services by simply considering who we serve and by standing in their shoes in an attempt to understand their lived experience. But there is also an important reminder to continue critically examining our offerings and whether or not they serve as many patrons as possible, worth reiterating here and one you'll see echoed throughout the book.

Oftentimes when we discuss underserved communities, particularly those whose identities and experiences are stigma-laden (such as sexual assault survivors or formerly incarcerated individuals), there can be a tendency to see our work as one of remediation or a perception that these individuals may be somehow damaged or unable to navigate the world in a way that feels meaningful to those outside that population. However, as our chapter authors continuously remind us, each person and each population we encounter bring with them a wealth of unique experiences, some born from hardship and circumstance, and some born from hope and connection. As is always the case, when we connect with and serve others, we have the opportunity to learn ourselves, whether it be a new way to ingest information, a new perspective, or simply to be reminded of the power that exists in information work done mindfully and meaningfully.

Our hope with this volume is not to offer a comprehensive overview of all the populations we work with, or all the ways in which we can serve them, but instead see this as the beginning of a conversation. Because our campus communities are so inherently diverse, there are populations not represented here, and because our work is so varied there are ways of serving those populations that we and the chapter authors may not have included. We hope that this volume will inspire you to look closely at the students, faculty, and staff you encounter in your library and think of how you can serve them. And, we hope that you'll use what you learn not only to serve your own patrons but also to inspire conversations with your peers throughout the field, so that we can all continue to learn and grow together.

Reference

Skinner, Julia, and Melissa Gross. 2017. "The ISSAS Model: Understanding the Information Needs of Sexual Assault Survivors on College Campuses." *College & Research Libraries* 78(1): 23–34.

CHAPTER ONE

"Have the Library Brought to You"

Embedded Librarianship as Intentional Strategy to Support Underserved Patrons

Lorin K. Jackson

Introduction

Although much has been written about embedded librarianship as an extension of library services and as a way to meet patrons' needs beyond the confines of the traditional academic library space, these strategies have not been explicitly discussed as a way of intentionally strengthening diversity, equity, and inclusion (DEI) efforts. As an embedded librarian for a religion course at Swarthmore College in fall 2018, I found that embedded librarianship was a strategy that proved particularly helpful to underrepresented students, staff, and faculty.

This chapter reflects on my experience as an embedded librarian, situating it within the library and information science (LIS) literature. I begin by defining underrepresented populations and embedded librarianship. Then I draw on the concepts of library anxiety and vocational awe to explore the potential for embedded librarianship to promote DEI in libraries. Next, I discuss my experience with embedded librarianship in a religion course and what roles I filled, as a case study into embedded librarianship and supporting underserved populations. Finally, I present the altar project as a culminating installation for the class, along with recommendations for librarians who would like to implement similar programs at their institutions.

Underrepresented and Underserved

Who is underrepresented and underserved? What could their underrepresentation mean about the way they may or may not choose to interact with an academic library? The American Library Association (ALA) provides a clear statement on their website regarding the importance of providing "Programming to Promote Diversity" in libraries (American Library Association n.d.). The ALA describes how libraries can be instrumental in addressing larger societal injustices, despite their history of exclusion of underrepresented groups. In this statement, the ALA offers how we can define underrepresented community members and begin to understand their reticence to feel a sense of ownership or belonging to the library as an entity:

> The American Library Association recognizes the critical need for access to library and information resources, services, and technologies by all people, especially those who may experience language or literacy-related barriers; economic distress; cultural or social isolation; physical or attitudinal barriers; racism; discrimination on the basis of appearance, ethnicity, immigrant status, religious background, sexual orientation, gender identity, gender expression; or barriers to equal education, employment and housing. . . . Underrepresented patrons may experience several issues which limit their full, beneficial use of the library. Many of these issues may stem from a lack of representation in the services, staff, and collections of libraries. For many people, having never seen their perspectives represented in library staff and services, the library may be an unknown element in their day-to-day lives. (American Library Association n.d.)

Here, the ALA defines several factors that contribute to identifying a particular patron as underrepresented. The ALA highlights that there is quite a bit of diversity in defining how someone may be underrepresented, ranging from ethnic background, class status, gender identity, educational access, and ability. These factors may contribute to the underrepresented patron feeling further disconnected from the library and substantiate their unwillingness to view the library as a place that is for them to meet their information needs. Since these groups are defined as being underrepresented, for the purposes of this chapter, I will also characterize them as being underserved. The barriers that limit their access to the library create a dynamic where they are often or regularly denied the opportunity to have access to library services compared to those from represented, or privileged, communities in libraries.

Defining and Locating Embedded Librarianship

The concept of embedded librarianship originally grew from embedded journalism, which was formed during wartime journalistic coverage: "In this situation, [the] journalist becomes part of the military unit giving war coverage; and using a similar concept, [embedded librarianship] places a reference librarian right in the midst of where the user is to teach research skill[s] whenever and where ever instruction is needed (Abrizah, Inuwa, and Afiqah-Izzati 2016, 637). Like an embedded journalist, the embedded librarian's proximity to the information point of need allows for increased engagement. These methods of embedded librarianship, which place librarians outside of the library, or whenever and wherever they are needed, are helpful for all patrons. For traditionally underserved community members, in particular, embedded librarianship offers a way to help them understand that the library can serve their individualized, specialized needs and bring the academic library to them in a different way.

According to Abrizah, Inuwa, and Afiqah-Izzati (2016, 638), the role of an embedded librarian usually involves some common tasks, even though the role will be adapted to the specific context according to available resources at individual institutions:

> The reviews do suggest that EL in information literacy instruction sees librarians conducting the following specific tasks: help students to identify research problem (Hoffman, 2011); highlight key search concepts for students on their research (Soules et al., 2013); co-teach, insert information fluency and research instruction into course projects, ensure that students have a wide access to library materials and librarian expertise, teach how to use print resources, teach rudimentary internet searching, help teachers plan, implement, and evaluate online instruction, learning objects, digital resources and course design (Bezet, 2013).

Embedded librarianship can look like a composite of different roles depending on the context, so there is no one way to define embedded librarianship. However, there are commonalities to the myriad ways one could serve as an embedded librarian. Additionally, the role an embedded librarian takes will depend on the access and support given to librarians to fulfill this role at their institution (Abrizah, Inuwa, and Afiqah-Izzati 2016, 640). Embedded librarianship can present some challenges, as it does require increased outreach and a substantial time commitment from staff. Fleming-May, Mays, and Radom write about the importance of assessment of programming, as well, as a way to show accountability to institutional missions and goals (Fleming-May, Mays, and Radom 2015, 433). Planning to demonstrate the positive outcomes of embedded librarianship with data can help establish embedded librarianship and sustain its presence on campus.

Recent contributions to the LIS field about diversity, equity, and inclusivity reflect the timeliness of increasing support in libraries for underserved patrons. Fobazi Ettarh's concept of vocational awe, which "describes the set of ideas, values, and assumptions librarians have about themselves and the profession that result in notions that libraries as institutions are inherently good, sacred notions, and therefore beyond critique" (Ettarh 2018, In Brief) serves as a useful way to understand the structures in place that render libraries unwelcoming, inaccessible, or untouchable, particularly to an underrepresented population. In her piece, Ettarh breaks down how this vocational awe is reified by the role libraries play in society as an institution—as part of larger oppressive and systemic structures: "Librarianship, like the criminal justice system and the government, is an institution. And like other institutions, librarianship plays a role in creating and sustaining hegemonic values, as well as contributing to white supremacy culture" (Ettarh 2018, Part Two). Librarianship is an institution and libraries themselves are institutions, replete with the same oppressive structures that exist in the larger society. Worth considering here is the unique positioning of academic libraries as elitist repositories of knowledge in a higher education context, as well as how academic libraries are cultural sites of production that can be profoundly unforgiving for underrepresented populations.

Work has been done in the *#critlib*, or critical librarianship movement, as well, to address social justice issues in LIS fields. For example, Emily Drabinski writes about the possibilities of queering the catalog (Drabinski 2013). Violet Fox contributes to strengthening opportunities to connect *#critlib* to our work in libraries and communities (Nicholson and Seale 2017).

The library is often categorized as a static, immovable entity, existing in suspended animation. Things do not change—they stay, locked in on the shelves. Libraries seem to thereby wield an authority that is unquestionable. Embedded librarianship, for students alongside the professor, moves the librarian out of the seemingly impenetrable fortress of the lofty, academic library to the more dynamic, interactive level of the classroom environment, for example. In real time with embedded librarianship, the librarian is able to connect with the professor and students in an immediate way.

The Role of the Embedded Librarian and Library Anxiety

There are several roles an embedded librarian can play that support meeting their users at their point of need. Embedded librarians support instruction and information literacy efforts, providing access to various information resources and scholarly communication for different community stakeholders (such as students and faculty) (Abrizah, Inuwa, and Afiqah-Izzati 2016, 637). The line between the library and the classroom disappears as the students, as well as the professors, no longer have the responsibility to cross this line by themselves in order to create connections with the library. Instead, library services are brought to them without the need to reach out and find them independently.

For many students (and even faculty), academic library culture and the services provided therein may be unfamiliar until librarians present this information to them. Using Ettarh's (2018) ideology of vocational awe, once again, it is all too possible that the library could be viewed as more of an intimidating, disconnected space than a warm, welcoming one, particularly for underrepresented patrons. Referring to some early work from medical and social welfare contexts regarding the educational psychology of general help-seeking behaviors, Black notes that the "primary reasons for avoiding seeking help were found to be feelings of personal inadequacy, embarrassment, and loss of self-esteem" (Black 2016, 36). In addition to the social barriers that could limit one's access to the library, the way these patrons are underserved can impact them internally. They may begin to develop and believe they are unworthy or undeserving of help or support. Creating these narratives of unworthiness is an antithesis to the ultimate goal of education and libraries, which is to encourage and equip students with what they need to be successful.

Low self-esteem is a significant by-product to recognize as part of why someone from an underrepresented group may feel like the library is not a place for them. As Black further explains, research shows that the students who often struggle with seeking help are those "with low self-esteem, low perceptions of cognitive competence, and whose academic performance is poor" (Black 2016, 38). Avoiding support becomes a strategy for vulnerable students to protect their self-esteem, and there are psychological risks of further deepening wounds of social stigma through the admission of requesting support (Black 2016, 38).

For underrepresented students, seeking help and learning about available resources can be emotional. Requiring assistance can be seen as a detriment and a weakness. A librarian who reaches out to students and is warm can lessen stigma, build relationships, and increase opportunities for student success. Muszkiewicz draws this conclusion in her research about lessening student library anxiety: "The library as building and resource collection could almost be taken out of the equation altogether in terms of addressing students' library anxiety; showing that librarians are accessible, approachable people first will help alleviate student stress" (Muszkiewicz 2017, 224).

With embedded librarianship, the librarian can be in the classroom introducing resources available in the library and demystifying what library myths may exist for patrons. In my experience, embedded librarianship melts the facade that librarians are difficult to reach, intimidating, or even wizards of knowledge who will judge what students know. By showing up authentically and connecting student experiences with our own, we build rapport to demonstrate that the library can be the beating heart of a campus community.

Muszkiewicz notes that students having issues with using the library is not a recent idea (Muszkiewicz 2017, 224):

> Even before Mellon named library anxiety, librarians had been observing the phenomenon. In Swope and Katzer's (1972) survey it showed not only that students felt a level of anxiety in the library, but also that the reasons behind the anxiety were that they did not want to bother the librarian, and/or they felt foolish over the level of their knowledge. This reasoning is echoed in today's students, as well. Numerous studies show that students are reluctant to approach librarians due to fear of looking ignorant or a worry that they will disturb a busy working librarian . . .

Library anxiety can occur for any number of reasons for students and can be related to any number of experiences they have had with libraries. Understanding why underrepresented students may be cautious about using library services or asking for support can help librarians, especially embedded librarians, better serve them. Much like the reference interview, gaining insight into the information needs and the behavior that accompany those needs for underserved students can help us strategize how to better support them.

Building Significant Relationships

Embedded librarianship can and should be codeveloped. Partnership arrangements between the library and the involved classes allow for librarians to be humanized—to be seen holistically as people. This partnership and an increased frequency of interactions between the librarian and patrons lessen library anxiety (Muszkiewicz 2017). Even more so, when embedded librarians are able to be seen as people who want to help, they can make the class and the research therein all the more accessible. From this, the learning experience strengthens for students and connects to the goals of the larger institution.

For underrepresented students, whether in elementary school or in college, relationship building is foundational for learning. Ayalon discusses this need in his book *Teachers as Mentors: Models for Promoting Achievement with Disadvantaged and Underrepresented Students by Creating Community* (2011, 11):

> Generally, children perform better in nurturing environments. In discussing the factors that reduce youth violence, Prothrow-Stith and Spivak (2004) indicate that society needs to "create a protective and nurturing context in which all young people can grow and develop" (p. 65). They further specify that the way children are treated at home, at school, and within the

community has a significant impact on their success in life. Recent research found that schools that establish a climate where students feel connected to adults, teachers, and peers may lead to a higher retention rate and better academic achievement (Anderman, 2002; Nelson & Debacker, 2008; Oserman, 2000). Furthermore, when students feel that their school is a caring environment they tend to perceive their relationships with teachers more positively (Fredriksen & Rhodes, 2004). Supportive adults can enhance a youth's social capital. Social capital is defined as "a product of the social environment that when present or available increases the probability that individuals will achieve desirable outcomes" (Woolley & Bowen, 2007, 93).

Although Ayalon's work centers on K–12 education, underrepresented students in higher education contexts are impacted by their previous educational experiences. Many of the themes may be the same for underrepresented students regardless of the context. Social capital is important in college contexts, too, and are similarly established through a student's relationships to adults on campus.

As a Black, queer, gender nonconforming, disabled, femme-presenting librarian, the idea of relating to my teachers throughout my experience resonates with me. Factually, most librarians do not look like me, nor identify the way I identify: "A great number of studies document the lack of diversity among practicing librarians and library administrators, masters students and doctoral students in library and information science (LIS) programs, and faculty teaching in LIS programs [2–6]. The lack of diversity is most dramatic in terms of African Americans and Latinos" (Jaeger, Bertot, and Franklin 2010, 175–176). Statistically, only 3 percent of librarians are Latinx and 6 percent are African American (Jaeger, Bertot, and Franklin 2010, 175–176). Underrepresentation impacts the way the institution of the library works. By increasing the diversity of different identities in a library context, we encourage the opportunity for the potential of libraries to become more accessible to multiple members of the community, not just those who already exist in positions of power.

I would be remiss if I did not remain aware of the reality of my identity regarding my positionality in the academy and as an academic librarian. We do ourselves a great service by acknowledging who we are as foundational to the way we approach our work. We can ask ourselves: How might our identity(ies) relate to the environment in which we work? How may it impact the role we play in the classroom with students and/or with the professor as an embedded librarian? Gonzalez-Smith, Swanson, and Tanaka discuss the impact of ethnic identity on our workplace and the roles we play (Gonzalez-Smith, Swanson, and Tanaka 2014, 163):

Ethnic identity theory can also be applied in our understanding of librarian-student interactions. In 2012, a study on academic librarian approachability tested variables such as race/ethnicity, age, and gender and revealed that race does indeed play a role in the patron's perception of the librarian. Subjects identified with librarians who most resembled their own racial/ethnic characteristics and rated those librarians as the most approachable. The researchers further connected librarian approachability to student retention and academic success, especially for students of color, who use the library more often than their white peers.

In this cited study, a patron's perception of librarian approachability depended on their conceptualization of identity in relation to the librarian. In other words, seeing themselves in the librarian made for the capacity to build stronger relationships and thereby have more positive student outcomes, such as higher retention rates and academic success. Gonzalez-Smith et al. also observe that the impact of connecting with a librarian and the opportunity for building strong relationships supports students of color, specifically.

Embedded Librarianship in Practice

The course I embedded during fall 2018 was Decolonizing Afro-Latinx Religion, a religion class with Professor James Padilioni, PhD. I reached out to him initially via email, with the support of other librarians in my Research and Instruction department, to see if he would be willing to partner with me on the course. I described my relevant professional, educational background to him (in religion and philosophy, specializing in indigenous and African women's experiences). To my satisfaction, he agreed to let me work with the class, and we outlined the logistical elements of including me as an embedded librarian in the course.

In my role as an embedded librarian for the Decolonizing Afro-Latinx Religion course, Dr. Padilioni and I discussed in advance that I would support students in their religion research, help frame how to complete research in religion as a subject area, and would share library resources such as research guides and print resources that could supplement their work. I made myself available to the professor to provide additional resources for the material discussed in class. I created a specific online research guide with resources for the students' major final project in the class, which was to contribute to a class altar. Additionally, I would attend the class as often as I could (scheduled three times a week for an hour) and participate by raising my hand when I felt I had something to contribute to the conversation. The professor and I discussed that my engagement with the class community in this way would meet our mutually established goals of having students see me as both credible and congenial. Fellow embedded librarians may not typically function as students in a classroom context, but in our collaboration, we decided to take that approach in order to strengthen classroom community and students' relationships with me as a librarian.

In one of the first weeks of classes, Dr. Padilioni provided me with an opportunity to introduce myself to the class. I spoke about my academic background, my credentials, and some of the work I do in the library as a research and instruction resident librarian. During this presentation, I also spoke about and introduced resources that I could connect students to in the library.

As a result of this partnership, students were able to see collaboration between a professor of color and a staff member of color within the academic institution of the college. As members of underrepresented groups ourselves, we could mirror their identities and help them see themselves in positions of power to impart knowledge. The class was designed in a seminar format and had about twelve students. Almost all of the students in the class were students of color, so seeing us in these roles helped disrupt the narrative that college classrooms and academic libraries are not inclusive, as outlined at the beginning of this chapter.

Dr. Padilioni and I intended that the myriad ways I brought the library to underrepresented students would form a conscious (or unconscious) moment of empowerment for them regarding their abilities to do the same. We wanted them to know they could be authoritative resources for information about their culture, their experience, as well as their religious background due to the subject matter of the course.

Altar Project

From the beginning of the course, one component of the culminating projects for students was to contribute to the creation of an altar as a way to explore in real time one of the concepts taught in the course. I met with Dr. Padilioni, as well as a smaller group of student leaders from the course in a committee, to design the altar installation for the main library on campus. We also partnered with another course taught by the chair of the religion department (Religion and Food) to create several altars across campus: in the Interfaith Cultural Center, students created a pan-Caribbean altar influenced by the African and Latinx religious practices they were studying in each class. The Black Cultural Center created an altar that celebrated Black culture—past, present, and future. If anyone had questions about their project regarding religious figures or routines, I referred them to my altar creation research guide (https://guides.tricolib.brynmawr.edu/altar-creation) or offered one-on-one support through a research consult appointment in the library. Contributions to the altars from students included bringing materials, arranging them on the altars, photographing progress, and supporting students who were practitioners of the faiths or experiences being represented on the altars. Although I was available to support everyone in their endeavors for this project, my primary responsibility was to support the Día de Los Muertos altar housed in the main library.

When I met with the student committee from the class to design the main library's Día de Los Muertos altar, we decided together that it should celebrate the genius of underrepresented groups in predominately White institutions, such as academic libraries and other establishments of higher education. Our goal was to elevate the materials we had available in the library about and by people of color and noncisgender people by displaying materials and pictures of historical figures whose visibility on the altar would help underrepresented identities on campus see themselves included in the library space. These included such luminaries as Maya Angelou, Celia Cruz, Marielle Franco, W. E. B. Du Bois, and Sylvia Rivera.

The altar installation in the main library took the form of a pop-up exhibit that lived in the library for three weeks by the popular reading room on the first floor. There were some decorations, such as traditional Día de Los Muertos paper cutouts (*papel picado*) and a tablecloth. We also added some small electronic candle tea lights to decorate the boxes stacked with books and DVDs from the underrepresented folks alongside their pictures. We had numbers corresponding to each picture on the altar and a legend so visitors to the exhibit could match names with the portraits on the altar, especially in case they were new historical figures in their experience. The altar installations were symbolic in terms of their representations of shedding light onto significant figures in history from underrepresented groups. The altars themselves also served a similar purpose to the embedded librarianship collaboration—to demonstrate inclusivity, awareness, and appreciation on campus for the intellectual gifts provided by people from underrepresented groups. By seeing the altars, it was our hope that the campus community would feel support, gain a sense of belonging, and consequently, see recognition of their own innate talents and necessary presence in traditionally oppressive academic institutions, such as the library.

Reflections and Strategies

Although collaboration with professors as an embedded librarian is important, if given the opportunity or space, it is equally/more advantageous to collaborate with students and get to know them through class projects. I developed relationships with several students of color from the course because of my work with them. They shared with me that I changed their perception of the library and the library's services, and helped them feel like they had additional resources on this campus beyond what they originally thought possible. By working with them as an embedded librarian in their course, our relationships strengthened, but they also became more connected to the library and often sought out additional library services after the course ended.

Seeing a librarian more than once supports building stronger rapport and relationships to increase students' comfortability with the librarian, and thereby, the library, as a whole. Repeated class visits form a crucial foundation for implementing successful embedded librarianship. Fleming-May et al. (2015, 436) explain the advantage of working with students more than in one-shot information sessions, as studies show that over time repeated sessions with librarians quell information overload, whereby librarians oversaturate students with information in a limited time frame without opportunities to revisit key concepts or knowledge foundations. Building on previous presentations and allowing for recall helps solidify the information we share with students.

Once your library offers displays, exhibits, or events highlighting DEI efforts such as our joint collaboration for the altar project and the Día de Los Muertos pop-up, you open the door to establishing monthly, semiannual, or annual events elevating the experiences of underserved communities. Even if your library program lacks experience, beginning somewhere, preferably with the grounding of a faculty-embedded librarian partnership in a course, can be a starting point. Similar to using the backing of an established course and relationship with a faculty member to begin creating programming around DEI, partnering with other departments on campus is also an excellent way to develop relationships and bolster the campus community.

There were several key decisions that Dr. Padilioni and I made that contributed to the success of this embedded librarianship partnership. Early on in the process, I shared my educational and professional background with him, as well as potential ways we could collaborate. Dr. Padilioni graciously made space in his course for me to establish my authority and credibility as a librarian with his students over time, beginning with my initial class presentation. Communication was also necessary and incredibly generative between us. By speaking about the course and what was happening—whether over a lunch meeting or through email correspondence—we were able to adapt my role within the course together. Lastly, logistically, regular meetings and check-ins about the installation should be scheduled to support the implementation. There are several moving parts when working with different members of the campus community. Having consistent check-in points helps assure everyone is on the same page and working toward a shared goal.

Conclusion

Embedded librarianship is a concept and strategy that supports bringing librarians out of the traditional brick-and-mortar library to the wider campus community in an academic library context. In this chapter, I advocated that embedded librarianship presents a unique opportunity to connect with underrepresented students. Although there is no one universal definition of what embedded librarianship looks like, there are commonalities in the different roles librarians undertake. By being a part of a class as an embedded librarian and also being a member of underrepresented communities, students of color in the class had the opportunity to connect with me in a deeper way. I fortified relationships with them that helped them to see the library in a new way and exposed them to resources that would have been unknown without the opportunity. Through collaboration, communication, and innovation, we were able to bring the library to underrepresented community members successfully.

References

Abrizah, A., Samaila Inuwa, and N. Afiqah-Izzati. 2016. "Systematic Literature Review Informing LIS Professionals on Embedding Librarianship Roles." *The Journal of Academic Librarianship* 42, no. 6 (November): 636–643.

American Library Association. n.d. "Programming to Promote Diversity." Retrieved February 13, 2020, from http://www.ala.org/advocacy/diversity/cultural programmingtopromotediversity.

Ayalon, Aram. 2011. *Teachers as Mentors: Models for Promoting Achievement with Disadvantaged and Underrepresented Students by Creating Community.* Sterling, VA: Stylus Publishing.

Black, Steve. 2016. "Psychosocial Reasons Why Patrons Avoid Seeking Help from Librarians: A Literature Review." *The Reference Librarian* 57, no. 1 (January): 35–56. http://www.tandfonline.com/doi/abs/10.1080/02763877.2015.1096227.

Drabinski, Emily. 2013. "Queering the Catalog: Queer Theory and the Politics of Correction." *The Library Quarterly* 83, no. 2 (April): 94–111. https://doi.org/10.1086/669547.

Ettarh, Fobazi. 2018. "Vocational Awe and Librarianship: The Lies We Tell Ourselves." *In the Library with the Lead Pipe.* January 10. http://www.inthe librarywiththeleadpipe.org/2018/vocational-awe.

Fleming-May, Rachel Anne, Regina N. Mays, and Rachel Radom. 2015. "'I Never Had to Use the Library in High School': A Library Instruction Program for At-Risk Students." *portal: Libraries and the Academy* 15, no. 3: 433–456.

Gonzalez-Smith, Isabel, Juleah Swanson, and Azusa Tanaka. 2014. "Unpacking Identity: Racial, Ethnic, and Professional Identity and Academic Librarians of Color." In *The Librarian Stereotype: Deconstructing Perceptions and Presentations of Information Work*, edited by Nicole Pagowsky and Miriam Rigby, 149–173. Chicago: Association of College and Research Libraries.

Jaeger, Paul T., John Carlo Bertot, and Renee E. Franklin. 2010. "Diversity, Inclusion, and Underrepresented Populations in LIS Research." *The Library Quarterly* 80, no. 2 (April): 175–181. https://doi.org/10.1086/651053.

Muszkiewicz, Rachael. 2017. "Get to Know Your Librarian: How a Simple Orientation Program Helped Alleviate Library Anxiety." *Public Services Quarterly* 13, no. 4 (September): 223–240. http://www.tandfonline.com/doi/abs/10.1080/15228959.2017.1319780.

Nicholson, Karen P., and Maura Seale, eds. 2017. *The Politics of Theory and the Practice of Critical Librarianship.* Sacramento, California: Library Juice Press.

CHAPTER TWO

ESL Club Newsletter Contributes to Inclusiveness on Campus

Phillip Fitzsimmons and April K. Miller

Introduction

The *SWOSU ESL Club Newsletter* (https://dc.swosu.edu/esl) is one of the many activities that contribute to inclusiveness at Southwestern Oklahoma State University, in Weatherford. The newsletter has evolved since its first fall 2016 issue. The newsletter is a full-color, multipage, student-made production containing photographs and text and serving as the final assignment for the English as a Second Language (ESL) class taught by Ms. Tee Kesnan. The newsletter has been posted on the SWOSU Digital Commons, the university institutional repository (IR), since January 2017 (https://dc.swosu.edu). The four issues currently posted in the repository have been downloaded 176 times in fifteen countries as of June 5, 2020.[1]

The newsletter describes and shows photographs of the activities of the ESL Club throughout the semester. It is an opportunity for the students to celebrate their achievements and to share their activities with others on campus and internationally through the platform of the SWOSU Digital Commons (https://dc.swosu.edu). Librarians have worked with the students to format the newsletters for upload and continue to consult with both the students and instructor in preparation for future issues.

The newsletter has changed from an eleven-page newsletter called *SWOSU ESL Club Quartz Mountain ESL Camp* that showed activities at a Quartz Mountain Resort Arts & Conference Center into the *SWOSU ESL Club Newsletter: Spring 2017* to the *ESL Club & Women Speak: Our Home Away from Home* that emphasized two aspects of the group. The group has transformed again during the 2017–2018 academic year to become the International Conversation Club that includes all SWOSU students who want to participate in their activities.

The newsletters are an example of active learning and relationship building among librarians and students and the ESL instructor. The project requires students to interact with each other and to practice conversational, writing, and photography skills while creating the newsletters. The newsletter assignment is an example of the kind of instruction that has been recommended in the ESL instruction and library literature since the 1980s (Spack 1988). This paper will provide both a practical description of the project for students, the instructor, and librarians, as well as frame the context of the instructional method within the larger discourse of ESL instruction and inclusiveness within academic librarianship and instruction on a university campus. The SWOSU newsletter collaboration is especially significant because some research has indicated international students are likely an underserved group for college libraries, according to one study discussed later in this article (Allen 1993, 332).

Southwestern Oklahoma State University (SWOSU) consists of two campuses, with the main location in Weatherford, and a branch campus in Sayre. The regional university, with an FTE of 4,526 ("Fall 2009–Fall 2018" n.d.), lies between Oklahoma City and Amarillo, thus serving the educational needs of Western Oklahoma and the Texas Panhandle. Undergraduate degree offerings include nursing, allied health, technology, computer science, education, business, and others. The university also has a nationally ranked College of Pharmacy.

International Student Enrollment Trends

Enrollment by international students in American higher education has continued to grow steadily over the last forty years. According to the most recent data available, international students make up about 5 percent of college students in the United States (Institute of Education Sciences, National Center for Education Statistics 2018). This group will remain a significant portion of American higher education enrollment as the percentage of college-age Americans is shrinking. One estimate predicts a decrease in American birthrates will mean almost a 15 percent drop in college enrollment by the year 2030 (Grawe 2017, 45).

The choice by many international students to attend an American college is important to colleges and the communities in which they are located. The United States remains the top host of international students globally, and international students contributed $42.4 billion to the U.S. economy in 2017 through tuition, room and board, and other expenses, according to the 2018 Open Doors Report, an annual statistical survey on international students in the United States and produced by the International Institute of Education, Inc. (2018).

Higher Education Responses to International Students

With this incentive, the competition to recruit international students is strong among colleges not just in the United States, but in other countries with good higher education systems (Özturgut 2013, 3). Many colleges are already including a focus on international students in their recruitment and retention programs and are incorporating many types of strategies in order to attract and keep this type of student (3–4). Özturgut asserts that all such successful programs have one common factor: a personal approach that involves all stakeholders both on campus and off campus and that also addresses effective communication and relations across cultural and language barriers (11). More specifically, Özturgut's research indicates that best practices in recruitment of international students include providing academic support and utilizing campus resources; attending and participating in international education fairs and recruitment events; partnering with other organizations; marketing such as online advertising and brochures; utilizing staff and faculty, alumni, and agents; and word-of-mouth (6–7). Additionally, the same study cites these characteristics of effective retention efforts: student services staff specifically assigned to work with international students; academic programming and support; social and cultural engagement and support; and financial aid, health services, religious support, and immigration support. Özturgut concludes: "With the diversity of the stakeholders involved in such cultural exchanges individual cultural and or national groups have to be treated differently. Strategic planning has to be done accordingly. Faculty and staff have to be hired and trained accordingly with a specific emphasis on cross-cultural competency" (12).

Strategies in English as a Second Language Courses

In order to ensure academic success in American colleges for students whose native language is not English, many colleges have introduced ESL writing courses (Spack 1988, 29). One goal of such courses is to introduce international students to academic writing in English. According to the literature, because ESL instructors rarely have the background to teach in another content area, ESL writing teachers must instead focus on what makes good basic writing, such as general inquiry strategies, rhetorical principles, and tasks that can transfer to other course work (30). They often do this by assigning students to write on self-generated topics, although this strategy may not prepare students for academic writing in other courses (34).

Teaching Writing Skills

Writing about data is an exception. Writing teachers often work successfully with students on writing about data because they can gather data through observation, report significant details, formulate and test generalizations, and generate criteria for contrasting similar phenomena (41). Nonetheless, Spack warns that "students need consistent teacher input in the observation and interviewing processes, . . . [and] regular in-class collaborative workshops so that they can comment on and raise questions about each other's writing" (41).

In the same article, "perhaps the most important skill English teachers can engage students in is the complex ability to write from other texts, a major part of their academic writing experiences" (41–42). Furthermore, Spack quotes Bazerman as saying "we must cultivate various techniques of absorbing, reformulating, commenting on, and using reading [if students are to be prepared] to enter the written exchanges of their chosen disciplines and the various discussions of personal and public interest" (Spack 1988, 42).

Evolving as Academic Writers

Spack also suggests that writing tasks should allow ESL students to use knowledge they already have but also should develop new learning. She urges sequencing assignments that move students from a personal approach to a more critical approach, with the goal being to develop an independent perspective rather than to restate another's idea (44). Previous research has shown, Spack states, that international students in particular need to learn how to recognize yet still critique other points of view because many such students come from educational cultures where challenging authority figures is forbidden (44). The article provides a sample sequence:

> Students can initially write about their own experiences or views, then read, discuss, and respond informally in writing to the assigned readings. They can next be assigned the task of evaluating, testing the truth of, or otherwise illuminating the texts. Students can be directed to compare the ideas discussed in one or more of the readings with their own experiences, or they can be asked to agree or disagree or take a mixed position toward one of the readings. Making specific references to the readings, they can develop ideas by giving examples, citing references, and/or providing evidence from other texts on the subject. (44)

Research assignments in ESL classes can also require library use and other forms of information gathering so that a student learns to use multiple sources to inform a point of view (44).

Such an assignment builds on skills students have already practiced: reading, note taking, summarizing, paraphrasing, quoting, evaluating, comparing, agreeing/disagreeing, and so on. Students should have a fairly good sense of how to focus on a subject, provide evidence to support a point or discovery, and examine the implications of the material discussed (44).

Students' skills also develop as they move through the writing process, from planning to submission, with their "papers becoming the teaching tools for the course" (45). The ESL writing instructor is heavily involved in the beginning. Gradually, the students use their new skills and knowledge more naturally, and they gain a sense of agency in the writing process (45).

Learning Other Writing Genres

In "Re-Creating Literature in the ESL Classroom," Brice Heath also notes that ESL teachers commonly assign beginning students to write in a variety of genres as a way to learn the language, what the author describes as "learners creating literature" (1996, 776). Each genre gives practice in a different aspect of writing, such as description in poetry and comparative analysis in a set of directions. In particular, "genres that insist on moving listeners and readers to action or giving information they can verify . . . count as valued currency in institutions, such as schools . . ." (777). This type of writing may be less familiar to ESL, Brice Heath says, because not all cultures "value argument, explicit explanation, the giving of directions, or comparative analysis—especially if these come from the young, women, or those of lower caste or class" (777). Such assignments should include the chance to read or perform a work before classmates, as well as many redrafts after the critiques by the other students.

Best Practices in ESL Services

ESL classes with extensive writing will have these best practices, according to Brice Heath:

- The writing will "be read aloud" to an audience of classmates, who will "push" the writer to improve on intent and actuality in word choice.
- The writing will serve as a catalyst for class members to "explore common themes and experiences, differences in interpretations," and commonalities in "multiple understandings."
- Repeated practice is required to prepare for the creation of performances, exhibits or portfolios exhibition, performance, or portfolio to showcase the student's writing. Students typically prefer the practice routine if it leads to an exhibition, performance, or portfolio rather than the drudgery of preparing for "a test or task controlled by others."

- Students doing their own literary writing move through a range of emotions, memories, hopes, and expectations, which research on the brain and behavior says give(s) learning a boost. (777–778)

Other colleges are trying to improve diversity and inclusion with "cultural responsivness" in teaching that incorporates students' cultures and experiences into their education. This improves their classroom engagement, content relevancy, and the diversity of experiences (Pendell and Schroeder 2017).

Besides attracting international students through excellent academic programs, colleges are also turning to the improvement of support services, both in academics and in college life, as a key part of the retention of international students (Özturgut 2013, 9–10). Library services can be a partner in both areas, as international students use the college library for both schoolwork and socializing (Bordonaro 2006, 520). University librarians have tried and are trying several strategies to service the unique challenges facing international students (Ishimura and Bartlett 2014, 317).

Serving International Students

International students are likely an underserved group for college libraries, according to a University of Illinois study (Allen 1993, 332). Researchers administered a survey to a "random sample" of 750 of the school's 3,401 international students. A total of 395 students completed the survey (325). Of the students surveyed, 57.4 percent said they "used the library at least once a week" but less than once a day, while another 24.3 percent said "they used the library at least once a day" (326). The majority also stated "that the library occupies an important part of the educational environment." Seventy-two percent also said they felt only somewhat prepared or not at all prepared to use the library (327). The survey asked the respondents to identify library services that were new to them and those that they had used. Students could choose more than one answer and identified these library aspects that were new to them: computer database literature search, interlibrary loan, online catalog, online catalog workshops, term paper research consultation, large library collections, microfiche/microfilm, classroom instruction in the library, self-service copy machines, and open stacks.

Results of International Students Survey

Researchers (Allen 1993) could not verify conclusively if the issue was that students were unaware of the services or if they believed the services were not available for them. As for services used, students identified those at the following percentages: no services used, 44.6 percent; librarian-led library tour, 38.7 percent; librarian-led presentation, 19.6 percent; research methods course, 12.9 percent; term paper research counseling, 9 percent; research skills instruction in the library, 8.8 percent; self-guided tour, 3.4 percent; and other, 3.6 percent.

In describing the research, the author concluded "a basic, but crucial factor to be considered when planning for information literacy activities is the status of international students" (Allen 1993, 332). Such activities are typically aimed at undergraduates, but librarians must be aware that a significant cohort of the international student population are graduate students, who likely are unfamiliar with American academic libraries and may also not realize that information literacy instruction is available for them. Researchers specifically recommended that library instruction programs be developed to serve graduate students' needs and interests. In addition, one solution at the University of Illinois was to include a session on the library as part of the orientation for new international students on campus (332–333).

Newsletter Satisfies Best Practices

The newsletter collaboration at SWOSU has attempted to address some of the issues discussed above in the library and information science literature. The publication and circulation of the student-produced newsletter was an offshoot of ESL courses. An extracurricular ESL Club was formed to help international students adjust to and learn about the many cultures of Oklahoma, as well as those of the club members. Students took tours, traveled to famous Oklahoma sites, invited guest speakers, and gave presentations at meetings. Next, club members decided to chronicle their ESL Club activities in a newsletter format in 2016. Students wrote the content, shot photographs, and designed the publication.

ESL Newsletter Is Born

The newsletter provided an opportunity for SWOSU librarians to offer digital services to ESL instructor Tee Kesnan and SWOSU ESL students. The project is a good example of what Gina Macdonald and Elisabeth Sarkodie-Mensah recommend in "ESL Students and American Libraries," in which they write, "Hands-on experience helps break down barriers. It also gives the librarian/teacher a better sense of what students are and are not understanding than does simple lecture or lecture with student response" (1988, 430).

This example of an extended session is an integrated approach between the library and the English class, with the latter incorporating hands-on experiences for the students. As the newsletter project progressed, Kesnan suggested students seek assistance in troubleshooting the newsletter from Phillip Fitzsimmons, Reference and Digitization Services librarian at SWOSU.

Librarians Partner with Students

A new opportunity arose when the students discovered they could not distribute the newsletter as an email attachment, as they originally planned, because the file size was more than 100 megabytes. Fitzsimmons immediately diagnosed the problem, as the students did not know how to recrop and resize photographs. Fitzsimmons and Digitization Technician David Reed helped the students learn how to reduce the digital size without compromising the colorful, photo-rich publication. Besides enabling the newsletter to be emailed, Fitzsimmons received permission to upload the newsletter to the SWOSU Digital Commons, to be permanently available on the World Wide Web (https://dc.swosu.edu). Not only could the ESL students' families in their home countries view the newsletter, but also prospective international students could read in the words of their peers about attending SWOSU. The first issue appeared in fall 2016 (https://dc.swosu.edu/esl/1). The newsletter files have been downloaded more than 160 times as of November 1, 2019.

During the spring 2017 semester, under Kesnan's guidance, ESL Club members continued to produce the newsletter, which helped them expand their skills in writing, editing, and conversing in English. Fitzsimmons scheduled and taught a special instructional session with the newsletter staff on best practices in creating a digital file so that it could be converted to a smaller size that could be attached to an email, downloaded quickly, and to the SWOSU Digital Commons (https://dc.swosu.edu). He also discussed other benefits of adding publications to the repository, including students obtaining author reports showing international usage of the newsletter. Fitzsimmons asked SWOSU librarian April K. Miller, Sayre Campus librarian and promotion team leader to join in on the project. The Promotion Team handles campus and community outreach for the library, which made this partnership a perfect match. Miller, who has an undergraduate degree in graphic design, provided a second instruction session during the spring of 2018 for newsletter staff on principles and best practices of graphic design for the newsletter. In preparation, she reviewed the previous issues of the newsletters to give concrete examples of ways to improve the design of the newsletter.

Evolution of ESL Newsletter

As student staff members graduated and were replaced with new students, the newsletter continued to evolve over four issues and four academic years. However, as personnel changed, so did club priorities. During the fall of the 2019 academic year, the library team reached out to offer help with the newsletter to club members, but the students regretfully chose instead to discontinue the work-intensive publication for the time being. The librarians emphasize that this is not a student failure, but rather the falling off of a project that has had a good run and that can be continued later. Regardless of these difficulties, the project mirrors some of the research by Miriam Conteh-Morgan for improving library literacy for ESL students (2001). In the article "Empowering ESL Students: A New Model for Information Literacy Instruction," Conteh-Morgan proposes that information literacy classes be taught by instructors of ESL, with help from librarians, because international students are familiar and more comfortable interacting with their ESL instructors. Also, Conteh-Morgan asserts, international students are more relaxed in and prefer the hands-on, relaxed atmosphere of the typical ESL classrooms, as opposed to the usual, more formal, traditional library instruction. Under Conteh-Morgan's model, librarians and ESL instructors would collaborate on information literacy lesson plans, and information literacy instruction would be integrated into regular instruction over a series of classes (Conteh-Morgan 2001, 30–31). In the newsletter project, Kesnan served as the main sponsor in assisting students to produce the newsletters but called on library staff support when needed for technical support and to upload issues of their publication to the institutional repository. The collaboration also built a collegial relationship between the ESL instructor and librarians; such partnerships encourage international students to feel comfortable in accessing all of the library's services (Martin et al. 2012, 364).

Maintaining Relationships with International Students

In the same article, Martin et al. suggest that librarians can increase their awareness of ESL students' needs in ways similar to those of ESL instructors: by building relationships and being active in international student activities. Martin et al. paraphrases Hofstede's 1986 article saying,

> different value systems that Western instructors and non-Western students have can create problematic learning and teaching situations. He identifies four areas in which problems can occur:
>
> 1. differences in social positions of teachers and students;
> 2. differences in relevance of the curriculum;
> 3. differences in profiles of cognitive abilities; and
> 4. differences in expected patterns of teacher/student and student/teacher interaction. (354)

Furthermore, the same article identifies international students' preference for in-person communication as possibly interfering with the effective use of library services such as online reference. Additional time working one on one is usually the best response (Martin et al. 2012, 360).

Encouraging Agency in International Students

Even the current discontinuation of the newsletter reflects self-directed language learning as discussed by Karen Bordonaro in "Language Learning in the Library: An Exploratory Study of ESL Students" (2006). Bordonaro defines self-directed language learning as "a learner trying to progress independently of a language classroom in which the teacher directs the learning" (521). The first newsletter acted to improve their language learning by producing the newsletter outside the classroom as an extracurricular activity. However, they were succeeded by other students who, for a number of reasons, chose to direct their language learning with different methods. For example, all of the ESL students did research and created posters to participate in the 27th Annual SWOSU Research & Scholarly Activity Fair on November 21, 2019. Creating the posters was a great writing project and opportunity to participate in an annual campus event (https://www.swosu .edu/administration/osp/fair/index.aspx).

Collaborations Lead to Alliance

The newsletter project also formalized a relationship between the ESL instructor and the librarians. A one-time collaboration builds strong alliances, which in turn broadens librarians' understanding of working with ESL students (Bordonaro 2018, 59). Author Karen Bordonaro describes her own collaboration at Brock University, Ontario, Canada, with an ESL instructor. Mutual benefits cited by Bordonaro include stronger joint support of ESL student learning, affirming the importance of ESL instruction at colleges, emphasizing the role of libraries in academic life, and raising the professional profiles of both ESL instructors and librarians (68).

When Projects Stall

Collaborative projects ending, or going defunct, are nothing new, although few want to discuss a "failed" project. Dylan Burns discusses failure in their blog article stating, "Failures, or the perceptions of failure or disappointment, are difficult to talk about" (2017). In the business world, however, the many benefits of a failure at work are often discussed (Pasquariello 2017). Failure may be a setback, but it allows growth. By sharing our setbacks with other librarians, everyone can learn from the experience (Burns 2017). Pasquariello states five strategies when dealing with failure:

1. Let Go of the Idea that Failure is Always Bad . . .
2. Embrace Unpredictability . . .

3.   Consider Blame Carefully . . .
4.   Recognize the Complexity of Failure . . .
5.   Sometimes the Only Way to Learn is to Try and Fail. (2017, para. 13)

Things happen beyond our control, and librarians must always be ready with a plan B, plan C, and plan D just in case.

Not Meeting Expectations

Failure is not just one thing, for there are many levels and varieties of failure, and we must be flexible and analyze what went wrong. We cannot let ourselves be so focused on what went wrong that we miss what might have gone right or what we can learn from that wrong step (Pasquariello 2017). Price (2019) suggests keeping track of your programs and projects to help you analyze what worked and what did not. Use these to help decide how to proceed in the future. Brown and Ramsey (2015) discuss the constructive learning theory; this theory is built around the idea of using personal experiences to dynamically create new knowledge. They go on to say that "any amount of time and energy isn't wasted if something can be learned from failures" (16). By demonstrating our failures, we can serve as an example to others of how to move past the failures and still attain our goals (17).

Adjusting Programs and Services

Chase, McPherson, and Perry examine learning from failures to recreate services students will use (2018). In their example, they repurposed a space to create an Info-Café. They did everything "right" by offering incentives and launching a marketing campaign, but still the students did not come. Out of sixty-two sessions, only nine had attendees, and with a capacity for 320 students, only 26 attended with only 18 unique students. So, why did they not show up? Chase, McPherson, and Perry concluded some of the times interfered with other events on campus, the offerings of the Info-Café were not what the students wanted when they needed it, and repurposing furniture is good, but only if it is comfortable and fits the setting. These realizations led their project forward, expanding what was offered, getting better furniture, and surveying the students for their wants. The student surveys showed a request for workshops. The requested workshops were held with only one student attending. Now the workshops are online in video format with 469 views. The key takeaway is to learn from disaster and grow.

Deb Baker (2018), with her program series *Learn Life Hacks at the Library*, is another example of a low attendance program that eventually failed. In the fall of 2016 at sixteen different events, she had an attendance of only seventy-seven people. Whereas in the same fall, ten therapy dog visits saw an attendance of 416 people. Lessons learned show dogs are always people attractors. In the spring she tried again with different life hacks based on student feedback, to still more poor attendance. In the 2017–2018 school year, she tried more interactive displays and activities. One interactive display, the feedback wall where questions were posed to students and they answered by post-it notes, was always a big success. She found interactive and seasonal displays or activities work well together. Baker recommends doing more of whatever engages students, share photos of students participating in the interactive displays and events, capitalize on-campus connections, have more dogs, and most importantly let go of good ideas that do not work.

Finding New Opportunities

This is not the first time Fitzsimmons and Miller have experienced a failed joint project. In October 2018, the two collaborated to host a screening of the documentary *Paywall: The Business of Scholarship* during Open Access Week. The documentary explains what open access publishing is and discusses why it is necessary for researchers to be aware of the business model of publishers seeking to capitalize on one's research with little to no compensation for their hard work. The event was held at noon with an invitation for faculty, students, and researchers to bring their lunch and watch the movie together. Not one person attended the event. Analyzing what went wrong, the librarians found several issues that could have resulted in poor attendance. While bookmarks, postcards, and posters to market the event were produced, there were issues with the printer and materials arrived much later than anticipated. Due to printing issues, the librarians relied heavily on email to market the event to the faculty, which they believe factored into the low turnout. The event was scheduled on a Friday, which also could have affected turnout. The main takeaway of the failed event is that faculty buy-in is necessary for the success of an event such as this. Fitzsimmons and Miller plan to try again to plan future Open Access Week events, taking the knowledge gained from the first failure to create a better program in the future. Beginning earlier to plan and promote the next event will help.

Partnerships Aid in Success

With every failure, there is an opportunity for success. One successful event held in the library was a series of Native American art workshops titled *Make Your Own Moccasins with George Levi and Creg Lee Hart, Southern Cheyenne Artists*. This event was a partnership with the SWOSU Art Department and the Washita Battlefield National Historic Site in Cheyenne, Oklahoma. The workshop was a four-part series held from between November 2017 and

April 2018. Each session dealt with a different step in the moccasin-making progress and was held in three locations: SWOSU Weatherford Campus, SWOSU Sayre Campus, and the Washita Battlefield National Historic Site. Participants were required to register to attend, and class sizes were capped at twenty-five people. SWOSU Weatherford had an average of twenty-three participants attend; SWOSU Sayre had an average of twenty participants, and due to the high demand, the Washita Battlefield National Historic Site hosted two sessions with an average of twenty-five attendees a session. By the end of the four sessions, if attendees did their homework, each participant had a complete pair of moccasins. Pictures can be seen on the SWOSU Digital Commons (https://dc.swosu.edu/moccasin).

Diverse Activities Build Appeal

Another successful event held by SWOSU Libraries is the *De-Stress Fest* held the week of finals in the fall and spring semesters. Like many other libraries our event includes therapy dog visits and several passive program opportunities like adult coloring sheets, crafting projects, hula hoops, jump ropes, crossword puzzles, and jigsaw puzzles. During finals, the library stays open until 2:00 a.m. and provides light refreshments to students in the library after 8:00 p.m. This event is one that reaches a large number of students with little cost to the library. Seventy-five to one hundred students enjoy some feature of the event every night of the weeklong event. Students appreciate the snacks, the later hours, and the different activities available to help break the stress of studying.

Failure is a fact of life. Owens states, "If things don't work out quite as planned, there is no blaming or shaming. We look at what went wrong, codify our lessons learned, and have another great story that is part of our shared history as a creative and innovative library" (2018, 78–79). When it comes to nurturing environments that support innovation, creativity, and failure, we can all act as leaders (Brown and Ramsey 2015, 18). To move past failure, we must evaluate the true value of ourselves and our efforts (17).

Conclusion

Do, in part, to the evolutions of the newsletter, the *SWOSU ESL Club Newsletter* is one of the many activities that contribute to the inclusiveness at the university. It is an example of active learning and relationship building between students, the ESL instructor, and librarians. The newsletter creates an environment in which students can practice conversation, writing, and photography skills, which are types of instruction that have been recommended in instruction and library literature since the 1980s (Spack 1988). Research also shows that international students are frequently an underserved group in academic libraries, and with the enrollment of international students growing every year, it makes this partnership especially significant. Fitzsimmons and Miller do not see the ESL project as a failure; they view it as a project on hiatus and hope to continue to assist the ESL students in the production of future issues of the newsletter and to upload them or other projects to the institutional repository. They maintain regular, informal interactions with group members and the instructor on campus. No pressure is placed on students, but they have expressed the hopes to renew the partnership in the future in whatever capacity that may be. Failure at work is going to happen. It is how you handle that failure and grow from it that is important.

Acknowledgments

Fitzsimmons and Miller would like to thank the ESL students for sharing their work, and especially Ms. Tee Kesnan for her work and partnership on the newsletter project. We also want to thank Dr. Denise Landrum-Geyer for reading this chapter and making comments for its improvement.

Note

1. The "Downloads Dashboard Report" is not available to the public. It is a platform report generated by the administrator. Accessed November 1, 2019.

References

Allen, Mary Beth. 1993. "International Students in Academic Libraries: A User Survey." *College and Research Libraries* 54, no. 4 (July): 323–331. https://crl.acrl.org/index.php/crl/article/view/14823/16269.

Baker, Deb. 2018. "No Attendees? No Problem: Redefining Programs at Your Library." PowerPoint slides presented at the *ACRL NEC Conference*, May. https://scholarworks.umass.edu/do/search/?q=baker&start=0&context=10403826&facet=.

Bordonaro, Karen. 2006. "Language Learning in the Library: An Exploratory Study of ESL Students." *The Journal of Academic Librarianship* 32, no. 5 (August): 518–526.

Bordonaro, Karen. 2018. "Librarians and ESL Instructors as Campus Partners in Collaboration and Alliance Building." *Collaborative Librarianship* 10, no. 1 (June 5): 58–69. https://digitalcommons.du.edu/collaborativelibrarianship/vol10/iss1/8.

Brown, Deana, and Elizabeth Ramsey. 2015. "Translating Failure into Success." *PNLA Quarterly* 80, no. 1: 16–19.

Burns, Dylan. 2017. "Failure Is an Option or When Things Go Wrong." *ACRLog* (blog), June 15. https://acrlog.org/2017/06/15/failure-is-an-option-or-when -things-go-wrong.

Chase, Elizabeth, Patricia McPherson, and Heather Perry. 2018. "When Your InfoCafe Fails, Think of Your LMS as Take-Out: Learning from the Ser- vices Students Won't Use to Create the Services They Will." Paper pre- sented at the *ACRL NEC Conference*, May. https://scholarworks.umass.edu /acrl_nec_conf/2018/presentations/3.

Conteh-Morgan, Miriam. 2001. "Empowering ESL Students: A New Model for Information Literacy Instruction." *Research Strategies* 18, no. 1 (Decem- ber): 29–38.

"Fall 2009–Fall 2018 Headcount and Full-Time Equivalent." n.d. Southwestern Oklahoma State University. Retrieved November 1, 2019, from https:// www.swosu.edu/administration/research/2018/headcount-fulltime -equivalent-a.pdf.

Grawe, Nathan D. 2017. *Demographics and the Demand for Higher Education*. Balti- more, MD: Johns Hopkins University Press. Ebook.

Heath, Shirley Brice. 1996. "Re-Creating Literature in the ESL Classroom." *TESOL Quarterly* 30, no. 4: 776–779.

Institute of Education Sciences, National Center for Education Statistics. 2018. *Digest of Educational Statistics*. October. https://nces.ed.gov/programs /digest/d18/tables/dt18_306.20.asp.

Institute of International Education, Inc. 2018. "Number of International Stu- dents in the United States Reaches New High of 1.09 Million." Novem- ber 13. https://www.iie.org/en/Why-IIE/Announcements/2018/11/2018 -11-13-Number-of-International-Students-Reaches-New-High.

Ishimura, Yusuke, and Joan C. Bartlett. 2014. "Are Librarians Equipped to Teach International Students? A Survey of Current Practices and Recommenda- tions for Training." *The Journal of Academic Librarianship* 40, no. 3–4 (May 9): 313–321.

Kesnan, Tee, ed. 2016. *SWOSU ESL Club Newsletter: Fall 2016* 1 (Fall). https://dc .swosu.edu/esl/1.

Macdonald, Gina, and Elizabeth Sarkodie-Mensah. 1988. "ESL Students and American Libraries." *College and Research Libraries* 49, no. 5 (September): 425–431.

Martin, Julia A., Kathleen M. Reaume, Elaine M. Reeves, Ryan D. Wright, and Bill McKibben. 2012. "Relationship Building with Students and Instruc- tors of ESL: Bridging the Gap for Library Instruction and Services." *Refer- ence Services Review* 40, no. 3: 352–367.

Owens, Tammi M. 2018. "'Let's Try It!': Library Outreach in a Culture of Yes." *Public Services Quarterly* 14, no. 1 (February): 75–82.

Özturgut, Osman. 2013. "Best Practices in Recruiting and Retaining International Students in the U.S." *Current Issues in Education* 16, no. 2 (August 15). https://cie.asu.edu/ojs/index.php/cieatasu/article/view/1213.

Pasquariello, Kristy. 2017. "Facing Failure." *Public Libraries Online* 3 (May). http://
    publiclibrariesonline.org/2017/03/facing-failure.
Pendell, Kimberly, and Robert Schroeder. 2017. "Librarians as Campus Partners:
    Supporting Culturally Responsive and Inclusive Curriculum." *College &
    Research Libraries News* 78, no. 8. https://crln.acrl.org/index.php/crlnews
    /article/view/16748/18272.
Price, Chelsea. 2019. "Learning from Programming Flops (or Sometimes Pro-
    grams Fail . . . and That's OK!)." *Programming Librarian* (blog), February 7.
    http://programminglibrarian.org/blog.
Spack, Ruth. 1988. "Initiating ESL Students into the Academic Discourse Com-
    munity: How Far Should We Go?" *TESOL Quarterly* 22, no. 1: 29–51.

CHAPTER THREE

(Re)Connecting Adult Students to the Community College Library

Developing a Social Justice and Equity-Oriented Liaising Program to Support Returning Adult Students

*Amanda Roper, Andrea Kincaid,
and Andrew Foskey*

Introduction

Adult students face a unique set of challenges when coming back to school. Similarly, the library also faces challenges in developing services and information literacy instruction that adequately address adult learners' needs. In this chapter, we outline adult learning concepts and discuss how library staff at Kolwyck Library and Information Commons at Chattanooga State Community College created specific services and tailored information literacy instruction for adult learners. The library staff was confronted with this task when new state legislation enabled adult learners without a completed degree to return to school for free.

TN Reconnect

As a public institution, Chattanooga State Community College must respond to state legislation concerning higher education funding in Tennessee. One such initiative, TN Reconnect, has changed the way that both the college and the library support adult learners. The TN Reconnect program is an outgrowth of the Drive to 55, which is a state-sponsored initiative with the goal of helping 55 percent of Tennessee residents attain a college degree or certificate; in 2014, when Drive to 55 was launched, only 32 percent of Tennessee residents had reached that benchmark (TN Achieves 2019). Prior to launching TN Reconnect, the state offered traditional college students a last-dollar scholarship called TN Promise. This scholarship was only offered to graduating high school students and came with requirements such as participation in a mentoring program and completion of eight volunteer service hours per semester (Tennessee Board of Regents n.d.). This program was quite popular, and in order to meet the financial needs of nontraditional students (defined as those age twenty-five and older), the TN Reconnect program was launched. The core of the program is the same: students will be offered a last-dollar scholarship that pays for tuition and fees not covered by other sources, such as Pell grants ("Costs Covered by TN Reconnect" n.d.). TN Reconnect does not require mentoring or volunteering, but the student cannot already have completed a college degree ("Guidelines to Qualify for TN Reconnect" n.d.). Library leadership predicted that the TN Reconnect program would have a significant impact on our student population, which led to discussions about redesigning our liaison program to include a specific position that would reach out to the adult students at Chattanooga State.

Kolwyck Library Responds to TN Reconnect

In November 2018, Kolwyck Library hired Amanda Roper as the assistant librarian I: evenings and weekends supervisor/TN Reconnect liaison. This newly reworked position was intended to support the adult students returning to school as a result of the TN Reconnect program. The librarian's schedule was designed to coincide with the times when their liaison group would be most likely to use the library. Previously, there was certainly an effort to address the needs of adult students. The library was open evenings and weekends, and Refresh workshops offered at the beginning of the school year covered topics such as Microsoft Office basics and practical tips for academic success. However, there was not a holistic plan specifically geared toward adult students. The implementation of the TN Reconnect liaison provided the opportunity to develop consistent services for adult students in the library.

To find out more about the needs of these TN Reconnect students, the library participated in a campus-wide outreach effort called Adult Student

Recognition Day, providing these students the opportunity to learn about services and resources available to them on campus. We offered a survey (see Appendix) to ask adult learners what they value in their libraries, and they pointed to our research and computer skills workshops, having a variety of spaces to meet their needs, access to computers and printing, and one-on-one research help. They reported facing a variety of personal barriers to using the library, such as work, family, scheduling issues, and transportation. They also voiced an interest in basic computer skills and research workshops, indicating their desire to not only acquaint themselves with current technology but also to become information literate and savvy researchers.

Theory and Framework of Service for Adult Students

To develop a holistic model of library service and instruction for our returning adult students, we looked at several theoretical frames. We knew that addressing library instruction, library services, and the systemic barriers our students face could easily become overwhelming and, as a result, cause us to lose focus. Allowing a theoretical frame to guide our programmatic and instruction development would provide clarity and allow us to be reflective and purposeful in designing and assessing the library's ability to serve our returning adult student population. Paulo Freire's critical pedagogy, Malcolm Knowles's andragogical theory, and Constance Mellon's concept of library anxiety informed our understanding of how best to serve our students and provided a framework for developing library services and models of instruction.

Freire (1970) and Knowles (1973) eschewed the banking method of education and advocated for instruction that considers the lived experiences of students and empowers them to share their own knowledge during instruction. Mellon's (1986) study regarding library anxiety indicated that many students feel lost due to library size, unfamiliarity with where things are located, feeling overwhelmed about where to begin, and confusion about what one does in a library and how to ask for help. In addition to using Freire, Knowles, and Mellon to inform creating equitable and empowering library services, we also looked at how our lived experiences could inform our approach to serving adult students. Although she attended college at a traditional age, Amanda left high school to obtain her GED and had her oldest daughter during her freshman year at Brenau University. As a single mother living in poverty while in college, Amanda felt an affinity for our returning adult students who are juggling work, school, parenting, and transportation issues, and she can remember the anxiety of studying among so many competing demands. Amanda said she used the library quite a bit in college, but only while her daughter was in day care or with a babysitter. She worried about her daughter making noise and possibly being asked to leave. Amanda also never asked a librarian for research help; she was worried that she did not belong in college and by asking questions she would appear stupid or confirm that she did not belong. Amanda's experiences echo the anecdotal evidence we have all observed at the service desk. Returning adult students seem hesitant to ask for help, often apologize when they do have a question, and seem harried while completing tasks and concerned about their children being in the library with them. Combining Freire, Knowles, and Mellon with our own lived experiences helped us frame our approach to helping adult learners and encouraged us to serve our students with compassion.

Literature Review

We knew that we wanted to create a two-pronged liaison model that addressed the multifaceted needs of adult students. Examining how other libraries have modified and enhanced information literacy instruction and looking at deconstructing barriers and creating equitable library services for adult students were key in informing our own praxis.

Library Services for Adult Learners

Through one-on-one interviews, librarians at the Unitec Institute of Technology learned that having a child-free library policy does adversely impact student-parents (Barnes 2016). Student-parents at Unitec Institute of Technology have lower library use, are unable to fully participate in group studying or projects, and are less likely to ask for library assistance. Parents of preschool children with difficulties obtaining consistent child care were the most affected by Unitec's child-free policy. One of the most needed resources for Unitec single-parent students was access to books and wi-fi to complete assignments. The child-free policy inhibited students from using the library's space, resources, and expertise. Eliminating the child-free policy and creating family-friendly study rooms were key steps to offering equitable library services to student-parents.

Portland State University's library created a family study room with computers, scanners, and study desks for adults; in addition, there are toys, child-sized furniture, and engaging wall art for the children of adult students (Petit 2014). Student-parents are only permitted to use the study room when they are accompanied by their children. Finding effective methods of advertising the family study room has been challenging. To eliminate potential barriers, the University of Toronto's Family Study Space in the Robarts Library does not require student-parents to reserve the study space, and they have plans to offer research consultations with librarians in the family study space (Carliner and Everall 2019).

To assist with eliminating barriers to using the library for returning adult students, librarians should be mindful of the physical comfort of the library and offer library services with compassion and respect for returning adult students (Cooke 2010). Flexible schedules for librarians who work with returning adult students, the availability of a credentialed librarian during night and weekend hours, and online availability through chat and email can meet the needs of adult students (Cannaday 2012).

Information Literacy Instruction for Adult Learners

Librarians at Duquesne University conducted an empirical study to assess annotated bibliographies from information literacy courses geared toward adult learners (Rapchak et al. 2015). Duquesne's findings indicated that adult learners struggled the most with evaluating the sources they used. The librarians understood that source evaluation would be a key skill for adult learners when they graduate; students will no longer have access to library databases and will need to evaluate free or limited sources available on the web. After this study, the assignment was changed and focused on evaluating sources; in addition, students shared and discussed the sources they found and the evaluation methods they used.

Embracing a critical information literacy model, Lau-Bond (2016) had students share and critically reflect on search terms and topics. She also explained why she chose certain research tools instead of other options to clarify the research process for students. This met the adult learners' desire for learning rooted in their lived experiences.

Sharing and valuing the lived experiences of adult learners, eschewing library jargon, and asking students about perceived problems and potential wins in their research process is rooted in nonoppressive, social justice–oriented instruction praxis (Keer 2010). The result of valuing adult learners as equals in the research process is increased engagement and persistence during the research process; learners are more likely to feel they have a voice and are contributing to the larger body of scholarship.

Mississippi State learned that collaborative contact between faculty members and librarians was key in giving librarians access to class instruction and in encouraging faculty members to share and promote library contact information and services (Cannady et al. 2012). Adult learners are frequently daunted by technology and experience technostress; returning adult students may tell the librarian that they are nervous about technology, but many adult students may exhibit unease and frustration or neglect to ask questions due to embarrassment (Quinn 2000). Quinn recommends a relaxed approach to instruction with technology, avoiding jargon, being mindful of pacing and behavioral cues that indicate students are ready to move to the next step, and allowing adult learners to practice searching while the librarian is present. A learner-centered classroom that values demonstrating the immediacy of new information and encourages students to participate as cocreators of knowledge by sharing their lived experiences yields engaged students and decreases library anxiety (Cooke 2010).

Implementation of Library Services for Adult Learners

With the implementation of TN Reconnect, Kolwyck Library is refining, revising, and marketing services relevant to adult learners. A major priority was extended hours during evenings and weekends, allowing adult students to access computers and quiet study space away from the distractions of home or to meet with fellow students in our collaborative group spaces. Often, space is what students think they need the most, but what differentiates the library from another popular study space like a park or a coffeehouse is the help of a professional librarian. The availability of a credentialed librarian during what some would term "off-hours" or evenings and weekends is invaluable to nontraditional students because their needs often do not fall into traditional service hours. In fact, our library schedules not one but two credentialed librarians during these off-hours in case one is involved with instruction, allowing adult students to receive one-on-one research help at the times more convenient to them. In-house technology support provides another valuable layer of service not found elsewhere. We also allow food and drink so these students might think of the library as their academic home away from home.

The survey administered at the Adult Student Recognition Day event shed light on the specific needs of adult students (see Appendix). Seventy of the 580 students who attended the event completed the survey. Library staff and student assistants were on hand to help students take the survey on iPads. They, like traditional students, want a variety of spaces to meet their needs at the time, including individual quiet study space and group study space. They need access to computers and printing, materials, and one-on-one research help. We have found anecdotally that adult students would prefer to study in the library to take advantage of time away from family, but sometimes must bring their children with them. Given this evidence, and after consulting with campus police to ensure our open-door policy for supervised children aligned with campus policy, Kolwyck Library will add a "family study room" for student-parents to study while keeping their children independently entertained and confined to a safe space. This special study room will be enclosed and equipped with a table, chairs, and a laptop. The evening and weekend librarian collaborated with an early childhood education class to get recommendations for developmentally appropriate materials for children. Two of the students in the class submitted ideas for "literacy buckets" for toddlers and preschoolers. A few of the toys from the literacy buckets will be integrated into the family study space. A children's play rug, Leap pads, children's books, and toys will keep the children occupied while their parents do schoolwork. Adult students also reported their interest in basic computer skills and research workshops, indicating their desire to not only acquaint themselves with current technology but also to become information literate and savvy researchers.

The survey confirmed the value of extended hours. Students were asked what days and times they were most likely to use the library. A third of students reported that Monday–Thursday evenings, 6:00 p.m.–9:00 p.m., was the best time for them, and one out of five students reported that weekends worked best for them. Though the traditional weekday hours are still the most preferred, a significant number of students are also coming in during evenings and weekends. According to hourly head counts for the academic year 2018–2019, eighty to one hundred students visit the library on Saturdays and Sundays. The study rooms for collaborative work were booked 28–33 percent of operating hours on weekends, compared to 29–37 percent of operating hours during the week.

Students were also asked what one thing they would wish for in the library. Students mostly responded that they would like coffee and tea, food, more books, and more quiet study space. This indicates students feel more comfortable when they have their basic needs met, such as food, drink, and shelter.

Implementation of Library Instruction for Adult Learners

Another way the library supports adult learners is through our course-integrated information literacy instruction. Upon the implementation of TN Reconnect, new opportunities arose for collaborating with faculty to offer tailored library instruction for adult learners. These classes were in two different departments, English and Education.

English Composition for Adult Learners

Toward the end of the fall semester of 2018, an English professor sent a campus-wide email asking for help spreading the word about a new section of ENGL 1020 that was geared specifically for adult learners. This course would meet once a week in the evening, in order to accommodate the schedules of full-time workers. Around this same time, the Kolwyck Library at Chattanooga State hired Amanda Roper, the new TN Reconnect librarian. As the library's coordinator of instruction, Andy immediately saw an opportunity for collaboration and contacted the professor to introduce the new TN Reconnect librarian and ask if they could visit her class. The professor was receptive, and they ended up crafting a library instruction session that was catered to the unique needs of adult learners.

The first step was to sit down with the professor to discuss her needs for the class. Because this class was designed for students who were returning to school, she felt the need to make the research assignments more practical than in the typical ENGL 1020 classes, where the emphasis was on classical literature. For this course, she assigned literary essays that had themes that related to the students' lived experiences. They discussed different ways that they could help the students identify credible sources that related to these essays. She also wanted them to feel comfortable using the library, so she asked if she could have the class meet in the library each week. Since the class only met once a week, and in the evening, the librarians were able to accommodate this request. She also scheduled two librarian visits: one to introduce the class to the TN Reconnect librarian and one research skills–based session.

After meeting with the professor, Andy sat down with the TN Reconnect librarian to discuss their plan for these sessions. The plan for the first visit was simply for Amanda to introduce herself and let the students know that she was there to help them specifically in the evenings and on weekends. The hope was that this would help alleviate some of the library anxiety that they may have been experiencing, which according to Constance Mellon, can leave students "unable to approach [their] problem logically or effectively" (1986, 163). For the second session, they wanted students to feel at ease, so they held the research session in the same library classroom where the class had been regularly meeting. This room contains some technology but is not dominated by technology like the regular library instruction classroom. Having the class here eliminated the possibility for students to be distracted or frustrated by too much technology, since some adult learners may "not have the metacognitive skills, motivation, or confidence to engage in" technology-based learning (Knowles et al. 2005, 237).

At a librarians' meeting that semester, there was a discussion about frustrations with the ACRL *Framework for Information Literacy for Higher Education*. One common theme was simply not having enough time for implementation. The group consensus was to take inspiration from one piece of the *Framework*, so for this class, Amanda and Andy decided to explore frame one: "authority is constructed and contextual" (ACRL 2016). They developed an activity where the students were invited to workshop their topics and asked them to think about what would make someone an authority on that topic. They used the example of parenthood, which they felt would be relatable to a class with student-parents. In the example, the parent is the authority on how best to parent their children, since it is their lived experience that informs their decisions. During the class, they used Ray Bradbury's story "The Veldt" (Bradbury 2017) as an example, since it is relatively modern and covers the themes of parenting and technology. They demonstrated how to create a concept map based on the sample topic and asked the students to think of related topics. Then the students were led through a discussion about the concept of authority and how it can differ based on their individual research needs.

Since one of the goals of the professor was to have the students feel comfortable using the library, they decided to assess the students' comfort level with research, both before and after the instruction session. Andy's initial thought was to use an app like Kahoot (Kahoot! 2020) to collect the assessment data, which uses students' own mobile devices. But in keeping with the low-tech nature of the class, they decided to use Plickers (https://get.plickers .com), a paper alternative that allows students to answer questions by holding up a card with a QR code on it. The professor, or in this case the librarian, scans the room with a mobile device and the students' answers are collected automatically. At the start of the session, they passed out the Plicker cards and asked the students the following question: "How comfortable do you feel with academic research?" Fifty percent of the class answered "not very comfortable," and 50 percent answered "somewhat comfortable." At the end of the session, the students were asked, "Now how do you feel about academic research?" Fifty percent reported that they were "somewhat comfortable" with research, and 50 percent said they were "very comfortable."

Early Childhood Education Final Practicum

In January 2019, several librarians attended a presentation held in the library on Chattanooga State Community College's Student Research Symposium. The librarians were there with a "menu" of information literacy instruction offerings that are available to assist students in preparing their research projects and analysis for the Student Research Symposium. One of the early childhood education professors approached Amanda after the session and said she wanted her, as the TN Reconnect librarian, to work with her students in her Final Practicum course (ECED 2365). The Final Practicum class was composed of eight returning adult students who all had full-time jobs in addition to their practicum hours. The professor said her students were overwhelmed by the research process and found assembling a literature review daunting. Many of the students were nondegree seeking and simply completing education courses required by their employer. She was concerned that her students may not understand how research and the symposium could bring value to their professional lives.

The professor and Amanda scheduled a time for instruction; she asked Amanda to teach her class about the components of a literature review, how to read a research article, evaluating sources, clarifying and strengthening research problems, and exploring library databases. Amanda embraced a critical pedagogical model to the classroom; she wanted students to bring their lived experiences and knowledge to the classroom and wanted students to understand that their research can impact their career and the lives of the children they teach. One way this critical pedagogical model manifested is that Amanda did not do canned searches; instead, she worked with students to create research problems and used their examples during class. Students were able to see that research is not a clear-cut process, but rather one with dead ends, new inspirations, and a constantly refining topic of interest. Her hope was that this would help the students realize that getting a few or unhelpful results did not mean that they were doing research incorrectly. Throughout the class period, she emphasized the library's evening and weekend hours and encouraged them to book research appointments for more help.

All eight students booked late afternoon or weekend research appointments with Amanda to work on their literature review. Most of the appointments lasted up to an hour, and the students' stress in finding and analyzing articles was palpable. One challenge was conveying to students that a literature review is a broad survey of the literature and not two or three topical articles one would use in a research paper. After meeting with students, Amanda talked to the professor and they agreed that it would be useful to the students for them to have more access to her throughout the research project.

In summer 2019, Amanda had the opportunity to attend a high-impact practices (HIPs) symposium and join a small group of faculty members working on curriculum redesign that would implement HIPs into course work. She decided to use this opportunity to increase her availability to students online, in person, and in the classroom. This curricular enhancement will allow Amanda to work closely with students throughout the research process. In addition to an on-ground information literacy session, students will be able to communicate directly with her through their online course module. Although students can schedule research appointments at the library, an online, embedded model of instruction makes phone and online chat research appointments more feasible. By meeting busy, returning adult students where they are, Amanda hoped to alleviate the stress of having to secure transportation, time away from work, and/or child care issues. The newly redesigned Final Practicum course with an embedded librarian will be piloted in the spring of 2020.

Challenges and Future Recommendations

One of the challenges of working at a state institution is responding to initiatives that come down from the state legislature, such as TN Reconnect. A sudden influx of returning adult students changes the nature of our service population, and in order to accommodate the shift in our student body, the library must be innovative in our approach to ensure that these students have the unique resources that they require to succeed.

When considering services for adult students, our initial focus was student-parents, but in the future, we hope to expand our focus to other adult student populations such as veterans, homeless, first-generation students, LGBTQIA+, and students of color. The Adult Student Recognition Day survey gave us our starting point for determining the needs of adult students. As we continue to expand services for adult students, we will also continue to assess their needs with tailored surveys and focus groups.

While reflecting on information literacy instruction for adult students, we were able to determine that they felt more at ease with the research process. However, we did not assess their success in their courses. For future semesters, it would be helpful to collaborate with the Office of Institutional Research in order to track adult students who received library instruction to determine if they persisted in earning their degrees.

Conclusion

Kolwyck Library responded swiftly to the implementation of TN Reconnect. As academic librarians, we are responsible for meeting a variety of student needs, but this new program allowed us to focus on a specific population, adult learners. By investigating the published research pertaining to andragogy and library anxiety, in addition to our own lived experiences, we were able to craft a set of services and instructional sessions appropriate for adult learners and their unique circumstances. Moreover, understanding their needs enabled us to serve our adult students with compassion, respect, and flexibility.

References

ACRL (Association of College and Research Libraries). 2016. "Framework for Information Literacy for Higher Education." Last modified January 11, 2016. http://www.ala.org/acrl/standards/ilframework.

Barnes, Joanne. 2016. "Student-Sole-Parents and the Academic Library." *New Zealand Library & Information Management Journal* 56, no. 1: 46–51.

Bradbury, Ray. 2017. "The Veldt." In *Reading on the River: A Literary Anthology*, edited by Chattanooga State Community College Humanities Department, 133–143. Southlake, TX: Fountainhead Press.

Cannady, Rachel, Stephanie King, and Jack Blendinger. 2012. "Proactive Outreach to Adult Students: A Department and Library Collaborative Effort." *The Reference Librarian* 53, no. 2: 156–169. doi:10.1080/02763877.2011.608603.

Carliner, Jesse, and Kyla Everall. 2019. "Playtime at Robarts Library: Opening a Family-Friendly Study Space at the University of Toronto." *College & Research Libraries News* 80, no. 2: 100–103, 111. doi:10.5860/crln.80.2.100.

Chattanooga State Community College. n.d. "Costs Covered by TN Reconnect." Retrieved October 25, 2019, from https://www.chattanoogastate.edu/costs-covered-tn-reconnect.

Chattanooga State Community College. n.d. "Guidelines to Qualify for TN Reconnect." Retrieved October 25, 2019, from https://www.chattanoogastate.edu/guidelines-qualify-tn-reconnect.

Cooke, Nicole. 2010. "Becoming an Andragogical Librarian: Using Library Instruc-
    tion as a Tool to Combat Library Anxiety and Empower Adult Learners."
    New Review of Academic Librarianship 16, no. 2: 208–227. doi:10.1080/13
    614533.2010.507388.

Freire, Paulo. 1970. *Pedagogy of the Oppressed.* New York: Bloomsbury Academic.

Kahoot! 2020. https://kahoot.com.

Keer, Gretchen. 2010. "Critical Pedagogy and Information Literacy in Commu-
    nity Colleges." In *Critical Library Instruction: Theories & Methods,* edited by
    Maria T. Accardi, Emily Drabinski, and Alana Kumbier, 149–159. Duluth,
    MN: Library Juice Press.

Knowles, Malcolm S., Richard A. Swanson, and Elwood F. Holton. 2005. *The
    Adult Learner.* 6th ed. Amsterdam: Routledge.

Lau-Bond, Jennifer. 2016. "Social Justice, Adult Learning Theory, and Critical
    Literacy." In *Critical Literacy for Information Professionals,* edited by Sarah
    McNicol, 79–88. London: Facet Publishing.

Mellon, Constance. 1986. "Library Anxiety: A Grounded Theory and Its Devel-
    opment." *College and Research Libraries* 47, no. 2: 160–165. https://crl.acrl
    .org/index.php/crl/article/view/14195/15641.

Petit, Joan. 2014. "A Family-Friendly Study Room for Student-Parents and Their
    Children at Portland State University Library." *OLA Quarterly* 20, no. 1:
    36–39.

Rapchak, Marcia E., Leslie A. Lewis, Julie K. Motyka, and Margaret Balmert.
    2015. "Information Literacy and Adult Learners: Using Authentic
    Assessment to Determine Skill Gaps." *Adult Learning* 26, no. 4: 135–142.
    doi:10.1177/1045159515594155.

Tennessee Board of Regents. n.d. "TN Promise." Retrieved October 25, 2019,
    from https://www.tbr.edu/initiatives/tn-promise.

TN Achieves. 2019. "Drive to 55." https://tnachieves.org/about-us/drive-to-55.

APPENDIX: ADULT STUDENT RECOGNITION DAY SURVEY

Created by Andrea Kincaid, Lead Public Services Librarian

The survey was administered on iPads using Surveys in LibWizard. There
were seventy responses.

Which library resources and services are you most likely to use? Check
all that apply. (required)

- ☐ Individual, quiet study space
- ☐ Group study space
- ☐ Place to socialize or relax
- ☐ Computers and printing
- ☐ One-on-one research help
- ☐ One-on-one technology help

☐ Accessing leisure books, magazines, and videos
☐ Accessing academic books, journals, and videos
☐ Checking out books for children and teens
☐ 24/7 access to electronic books, journals, and videos
☐ Other

What library workshops are you most likely to attend? Check all that apply. (required)

☐ Research workshop
☐ Basic Computer Skills workshop
☐ None
☐ Other

What times are you most likely to visit the library? Check all that apply. (required)

☐ M–F morning (7:30 a.m.–11:00 a.m.)
☐ M–F lunch (11:00 a.m.–1:00 p.m.)
☐ M–F afternoon (1:00 p.m.–4:00 p.m.)
☐ M–Th dinner (4:00 p.m.–6:00 p.m.)
☐ M–Th evening (6:00 p.m.–9:00 p.m.)
☐ Saturday afternoon (1:00 p.m.–6:00 p.m.)
☐ Sunday afternoon (1:00 p.m.–6:00 p.m.)

What days are you most likely to visit the library? Check all that apply. (required)

☐ Monday
☐ Tuesday
☐ Wednesday
☐ Thursday
☐ Friday
☐ Saturday
☐ Sunday

If you could have anything you wanted or needed at the library, what would that be? (required)

What is one thing that prevents you from using the library as much as you would like? (required)

CHAPTER FOUR

The Ivory Tower's Gray Library

Evaluating Services for Older Adult Students in Academic Libraries

Joseph Winberry and Bharat Mehra

Introduction

People in the United States—and around the world—are aging in a more educated and technologically savvy information society (Lenstra 2016; United Nations 2015). In 2014, according to the American Association of Retired Persons, there were 108.7 million people fifty years or older, including 76.4 million baby boomers (born 1946–1964), compared with 49 million Gen Xers (born from early-to-mid 1960s to early 1980s) and 82 million millennials (born early 1980s to mid-1990s/early 2000s) (Gillan 2014). Many large industries such as health care and transportation are already getting revolutionized thanks to this major demographic shift toward an aging population in their workforce and customer base as better health and/or economic necessity keep older people active and in the workplace longer (Coughlin and D'Ambrosio 2012; Nikolich-Žugich et al. 2016). This has also resulted in older adults seeking additional formal education at a university or other academic institution to further their training and competence and ensure that their knowledge, skill sets, and credentials remain up to date with the contemporaneous workforce demands (Caudill 2016; Kennedy 2013; Parks, Evans, and Getch 2013).

Yet, ageism and prejudice against older persons continue to be a pervading aspect of American life (Nelson 2005, 2017). As estimates of millennial numbers are projected to continue increasing (Fry 2018), we encounter societal trends and information services predominantly catering to young people, as a result of stigmas associated with growing older and discrimination toward elderly populations witnessed in the past few decades (Blackham 2019; Lachs 2010; Nerenberg 2019). Furthermore, older adults continue to find ineffective information support services to meet their needs and expectations, including at the library, particularly in areas related to health, social support, education, business, networking, legal information, and other domains (Bennett-Kapusniak 2018). Given that land-grant institutions were established with the intention of providing people with the practical education necessary for success in the contemporary workforce, it is important that these institutions, in particular, are seen as serving the needs of older adult students displaced by changing demographic and economic realities (U.S. Congress 1925, Section 304).

The National Center for Education Statistics–Integrated Postsecondary Education Data System (2017) has identified a total of 10,962 students fifty years old and older enrolled in the twenty-five degree-granting postsecondary, land-grant institutions with the highest enrollment of older adult students in the United States. This chapter explores how the academic libraries in these institutions are responding to contemporary realities and providing information support offerings and services for the older adult students in their midst. Research methods involved include content analysis of the websites of the top twenty-five universities with the highest number of older adult students enrolled in fall 2017. The framework of the strategic diversity manifesto (SDM) (Mehra and Davis 2015) is employed as an evaluation tool to document the existing types of information offerings these university libraries are providing to older adults in terms of seven subcategories in three broad themes as they relate to information sources, information policy and planning, and connections (both internal and external). This research provides empirical evidence regarding current information responses, gaps in these services and offerings, and possible future strategies to adopt. The chapter discusses significant themes based on best practices that will extend intersections of theory development and praxis to identify strategic actions that university libraries can develop to improve their programs and services to meet the needs of this underserved population.

Context of Study: Higher Education

Students of "higher education"—defined as "education beyond school, especially to degree level at a university or similar educational establishment"—is a major topic of academic research (Oxford English Dictionary 2019). Although the student body is segmented and studied in a variety of ways, one well-noted distinction going back several decades is between traditional and nontraditional students, who were thought to have more barriers in accessing and succeeding in higher education (Cross 1980). Who constitutes a "nontraditional student" in higher education has been widely debated, with numerous factors such as background (race and gender), enrollment patterns, financial and family status, and high school graduation being considered depending on the researcher (Gilardi and Guglielmetti 2011). Despite these variations, the single most cited distinction between "traditional students" and "nontraditional students" is age (Bean and Metzner 1985; Chao and Good 2004; Donaldson and Graham 1999).

But what age constitutes a traditional or nontraditional student is debated among scholars and practitioners alike. Traditional students are often considered to be between age eighteen to twenty-two, although increasingly the transition year has been seen as age twenty-five (Chung, Turnbull, and Chur-Hansen 2014). This presents challenges for discussing students of nontraditional age, as this transition year varies from study to study. Still, these differences seem minimal when considering that due to the increased understanding of "lifelong learning," the educational journey of people continues for many decades beyond even the most generous starting points of nontraditional student age (Schuetze and Slowey 2002). Thus, in order to foster meaningful observations about the most senior age group as well as to help demonstrate the social justice imperative of serving them, this study will use the term "older adult students" to describe nontraditional students age fifty years and older enrolled at postsecondary institutions (Aagard, Antunez, and Sand 2015, 1–2).

A Social Justice Imperative

What is the social justice imperative for serving older adult students? The answer is in part economic. Elizabeth White is a graduate of Harvard Business School who had a long career in public service and as an entrepreneur when the great recession transformed her life in a way she had never expected: for the first time in her adult life and despite her many talents, degrees, and accomplishments, she could not find full-time work. Her story exemplifies the paradoxical situation of older adults who found themselves unemployed or underemployed despite their stellar credentials. White writes and lectures about her experience as well as the experience of others like her in numerous settings and venues. Her book—which was originally self-published in 2016—was recently adapted and released by a major publisher, indicating that her story has struck a nerve with a larger audience (White 2019).

Perhaps White's experience struck a nerve because she is not an anomaly. Instead, her experience—and the experience of many other older adults—are direct results of an ageist hiring process, which in the era of automation and rapidly evolving technology favors a younger talent pool (Malul 2009).

Sometimes age bias can appear benign, such as job descriptions that require advanced computer skills; such descriptions dissuade older people from applying (Turek and Henkens 2018). But sometimes the prejudice against older workers—particularly low-skilled older workers—is more pronounced. Neumark, Burn, and Button (2017) sent out 40,000 résumés where the only differences between résumés were age; they found "compelling evidence" to suggest that older workers face age discrimination when applying for the low-skilled positions the study was geared toward (4). Education has long been seen as a way to move up in society. But even as governments are raising retirement ages and financial gurus are telling people to work to seventy and beyond, ageism in hiring for low- and high-skilled positions persists (Akhtar 2019).

Clearly, this is not just an economic justice issue, as a human being does not lose their value because they are no longer producing in a market economy; personal enrichment and satisfaction have also long been identified as important motivators for older adult students going back to school (Scala 1996). But whether an older adult has returned to the classroom to embark on a new career or for personal enrichment, the academic library can and should be an ally of theirs as a force for social change (Mehra and Srinivasan 2007). Academic libraries alone cannot ensure older adult students overcome bias in the job market; that is a systemic issue that requires a larger, societal response (Abrams et al. 2015). But academic libraries can help older adult students develop the skills and confidence necessary to compete in the job market and fight back against stereotypes and prejudice both in the workplace and in the larger society. Researchers can also assist in the struggle.

Despite the social justice imperative, research on older adults has been seen as a gap in the library and information sciences research. Asla, Williamson, and Mills (2006) found numerous gaps in information behavior research for older adults, especially as it relates to research on people age eighty-five and older. The literature on serving older adult students in academic libraries is particularly limited. Aagard, Antunez, and Sand (2015) provided the first major study of this topic, suggesting that there are several opportunities for researchers interested in exploring how older adult students utilize academic library resources. The realization that "the information society is an aging society" should promote future library and information sciences literature focused on older adults, including how older adult students utilize academic libraries (Lenstra 2016, 2).

Research Methods

Although literature searches suggest gaps in research, the decision was made to use website content analysis methods to see where gaps exist in practice. Since research suggests that students often seek out resources on their own rather than engage a librarian, the decision was made to focus this study on what online resources can be identified (Silipigni Connaway and Randall 2013). As such, this study will help representatives of the studied university libraries understand what older adult students may find when searching online for resources specific to their own needs and characteristics. It is understood, however, that search strategies different than the ones laid out in the data analysis subsection may lead to different results.

The purpose of this study is to focus on what is available, not on what is missing. The researchers appreciate the various responsibilities that academic library faculty and staff must prioritize throughout their workdays. Although one expected outcome of this chapter is a showcase of best practices in academic library services for older adult students, another expectation is that the findings will demonstrate to academic librarians the importance of and illuminate their own passion for increasing specific services for older adult students in academic libraries of all sizes and capacities. SDM provides a framework for the content analysis.

SDM Framework of Application

SDM was created to evaluate how certain diverse populations (Who terms such as racial minorities, people with disabilities, LGBT people, etc.) were represented in the information resources of specific public libraries (Mehra and Davis 2015). These information resources What categories, outlined in Table 4.1, allow for the evaluation of diverse representation across numerous aspects of the library. The How processes for identifying whether or not these Who terms were represented in the What categories are discussed more in the data analysis subsection.

The researchers' decision to utilize the SDM framework for this study builds on past research; the SDM has previously been applied to public libraries, an archive, and an aging services organization, but this study is the first published study to apply the SDM to an academic library (Forehand 2018; Movius 2018; Smith 2018; Winberry 2018). Given the setting of an academic library as well as the focus on the Who term, "older adult," some adaptations to the SDM were necessary:

1. It was considered a given that the academic libraries would have some books about older adults, even some about older adult students specifically. The researchers decided that since providing educational information is a foundational tenet of academic libraries, the institution would only receive recognition for A.1 Collections if a specific title related to older adults was spotlighted somewhere on the website. Research guides and databases focused on older adults would be credited as these would likely be more purposely curated than books on the subject.

Table 4.1   "What" Categories of the Strategic Diversity Manifesto

Category	Subcategory
A. Information Sources	A.1 Collections (e.g., print and electronic monographs and periodicals, web portals, and online and physical exhibits)
	A.2 Resources (e.g., databases and print indexes, research guides, funding opportunities and paid work opportunities)
B. Information Policy and Planning	B.1 Diversity committee (e.g., identification of committee member's contact information)
	B.2 Diversity representation (e.g., diversity statement, inclusion in strategic plan)
C. Connections (Internal and External)	C.1 Centers and organizations, departments and offices (e.g., physical and/or intellectual access to internal agencies and units in the library)
	C.2 Community engagement (e.g., connections to external community-based diversity agencies)
	C.3 News and events (e.g., information on internal/external activities and events)

2. The decision was made to increase the C.3 section to news and events in order to increase the likelihood of capturing relevant events, including those that have occurred more than one year ago.

Data Collection

A list of 109 land-grant, degree-conferring institutions were compiled from data available through the National Center for Educational Statistics–Integrated Postsecondary Education Data System. Specific statistics on undergraduate and graduate students age fifty and older were extrapolated for the most recent year available, 2017. The decision was made to focus on the statistics of the twenty-five institutions with the highest enrollment of students age fifty years and older as this was seen as a manageable data set capable of producing useful findings for other researchers and practitioners. These institutions are listed in Table 4.2.

Data Analysis

After identifying the list of twenty-five institutions, a list consisting of websites for the institutional libraries was compiled. The websites were then divided up randomly among the researchers and evaluated using two

Table 4.2   Top 25 Land Grant Institutions by Older Adult Student Enrollment

Number	Institution Name	Library URL	No. of OAS
1	University of Minnesota–Twin Cities	https://www.lib.umn.edu	871
2	University of Massachusetts–Amherst	https://www.library.umass .edu	644
3	Rutgers University–New Brunswick	https://www.libraries .rutgers.edu	636
4	University of Alaska Fairbanks	http://library.uaf.edu	583
5	University of Florida	http://cms.uflib.ufl.edu	553
6	Colorado State University–Fort Collins	https://lib.colostate.edu	533
7	University of Arizona	http://new.library.arizona .edu	531
8	Ohio State University–Main Campus	https://library.osu.edu	472
9	New Mexico State University–Main Campus	http://library.nmsu.edu	449
10	University of Maryland–College Park	https://www.lib.umd.edu	417
11	University of Hawaii at Manoa	http://manoa.hawaii.edu /library	406
12	Oregon State University	https://osulibrary .oregonstate.edu	404
13	West Virginia University	https://lib.wvu.edu	387
14	North Carolina State University at Raleigh	https://www.lib.ncsu.edu	377
15	Washington State University	https://libraries.wsu.edu	368
16	Utah State University	https://library.usu.edu	348
17	University of Arkansas	https://libraries.uark.edu	344
18	Texas A&M University–College Station	https://library.tamu.edu	342

(continued)

Table 4.2   (*continued*)

Number	Institution Name	Library URL	No. of OAS
19	University of the District of Columbia	http://udc.libguides.com	342
20	Oklahoma State University–Main Campus	https://library.okstate.edu	337
21	Purdue University–Main Campus	https://www.lib.purdue.edu	337
22	Tennessee State University	http://www.tnstate.edu /library	323
23	University of Nevada–Reno	https://library.unr.edu	323
24	University of Rhode Island	https://web.uri.edu/library	319
25	University of Missouri–Columbia	http://library.missouri.edu	316

search strategies associated with the SDM How process (Mehra and Davis 2015, 22):

1. Search string command in Google: [diversity Who term (older adult)] site: [library URL]. Other variant terms were used with results reviewed for relation to the topic such as older adult student or diversity committee.
2. If an academic library website has a site search box, older adult and other terms were searched for in order to identify whether or not related topics were discussed on the website.

Once the researchers completed evaluations for their assigned websites, select evaluations were checked by the other researcher. Intercoder reliability was above 90 percent.

Quantitative Overview

The numeric findings are summarized in Table 4.3, while more detailed results are available in the appendices (located at https://tinyurl.com/Ivory TowerGrayLibrary). The detailed results may include generic examples of diversity and inclusion that are not specific to older adults and therefore are not recognized in Table 4.3 but are still worth noting in recognition of the libraries' efforts.

Table 4.3   Results of Website Content Analysis

Number	Institution	A.1	A.2	B.1	B.2	C.1	C.2	C.3	Total
1	University of Minnesota–Twin Cities	0	1	0	0	1	1	1	4/7
2	University of Massachusetts–Amherst	0	1	0	0	1	0	0	2/7
3	Rutgers University–New Brunswick	1	1	0	0	0	0	0	2/7
4	University of Alaska Fairbanks	0	1	0	0	0	0	0	1/7
5	University of Florida	1	1	0	1	0	1	1	5/7
6	Colorado State University–Fort Collins	0	1	0	0	0	0	0	1/7
7	University of Arizona	0	1	0	0	1	1	0	3/7
8	Ohio State University–Main Campus	1	0	0	0	0	0	1	2/7
9	New Mexico State University–Main Campus	1	1	0	0	0	1	0	3/7
10	University of Maryland–College Park	1	1	0	1	0	1	0	4/7
11	University of Hawaii at Manoa	1	1	0	0	0	0	0	2/7
12	Oregon State University	1	1	0	0	0	1	0	3/7
13	West Virginia University	0	1	0	0	0	0	0	1/7
14	North Carolina State University at Raleigh	1	0	0	0	0	0	0	1/7
15	Washington State University	0	0	0	0	0	0	0	0/7
16	Utah State University	0	0	0	0	0	0	0	0/7
17	University of Arkansas	0	0	0	0	0	0	0	0/7
18	Texas A&M University–College Station	0	1	0	1	0	0	1	3/7

(continued)

Table 4.3 (*continued*)

Number	Institution	A.1	A.2	B.1	B.2	C.1	C.2	C.3	Total
19	University of the District of Columbia	0	0	0	0	0	0	0	0/7
20	Oklahoma State University–Main Campus	0	0	0	1	0	0	0	1/7
21	Purdue University–Main Campus	0	1	0	0	0	0	0	1/7
22	Tennessee State University	0	1	0	0	0	0	0	1/7
23	University of Nevada–Reno	0	1	0	1	1	1	0	4/7
24	University of Rhode Island	0	1	0	0	1	1	0	3/7
25	University of Missouri–Columbia	1	1	0	1	1	1	1	6/7

Thematic Analysis

Upon reviewing the results of the data analysis, several themes were evident. The first theme is broad inclusion. As expected, all of the institutions had some collections related to older adults; several of them even had resources for older adult students specifically. But very few institutions spotlighted collections on older adults, meaning that patrons already looking for these resources could find them in the catalog but patrons who may unknowingly benefit from the information were less likely to stumble on any examples on the website. In the same way, many of the institutions did have a diversity committee or participated in a university-wide diversity committee. Some, such as the University of Missouri, mention age in their diversity statement (http://library.missouri.edu/staff/committees/diversity-committee). However, there was no identification of purposeful representation of older adults in diversity committees. Together these findings suggest that topics of older adults in academic libraries are mentioned in general terms, but only mentioned specifically in rare instances.

The second theme is community engagement. There were several examples of engagement with internal and external audiences on aging issues. This includes examples like the University of Minnesota's Bio-Medical Library,

which provided a health literacy program for Minnesota seniors (https://hsl
.lib.umn.edu/biomed/services/outreach/partnerships) and the University of
Rhode Island Libraries, which hosted a panel on health and libraries that
included at least one representative who provides health information services to older adults (https://harrington.uri.edu/news/2017/04/02/2017-gslis
-annual-gathering). These examples reinforce the role that land-grant institutional libraries can and do play as centers of civic engagement and discussion,
a trait essential for public libraries but important for publicly funded academic
libraries as well (Yates 2014).

A third theme is older adult representation. The researchers agreed that
certain resources such as LibGuides or databases are more specifically curated
as they require more human and financial capital to produce or obtain than
individual books. A search of internal resources suggested that materials on
older adults are available in the library. However, these are often related to the
health of older adults and the role of students in caring for them. The University of Florida had a few examples of these (http://guides.uflib.ufl.edu/Geriatrics
/other-resources and https://guides.uflib.ufl.edu/consumerhealth/seniors).
These are important tools for students of all ages. There were also resources in
which older adults were represented as students rather than patients, such as
Texas A&M's LibGuide on education for older adults (http://tamu.libguides
.com/c.php?g=652964) or as part of a larger social justice effort in the Lib-
Guides of institutions like Purdue University (http://guides.lib.purdue.edu
/agriculture201/Ageism). The representation of older adults as patients as well
as students and as members of marginalized populations provides a more
diverse and complex representation of the role of older adults in society.

The themes of broad inclusion, community engagement, and older adult
representation help conceptualize a strategic plan of action for academic
libraries to increase the representation of older adult students.

Strategic Plan of Action

The themes that emerged from the content analysis suggest a strategic plan
of action that can direct further research in this area as well as provide practitioners with ways to evaluate their existing services against the best practices
of the land-grant institutions with the largest older adult student populations.
This multilayered strategic plan of action focuses on the representation of
older adult students, as the statistics and literature review suggest that older
adult students are a growing population on campus that deserve more focused
attention. Figure 4.1 illustrates the components of the strategic plan of action.

This strategic plan of action includes three components and two approaches.
One component of the strategic plan of action is the inclusion of a diversity
statement. Six of the twenty-five land-grant institutions had some form of
older adult representation, usually by including age in their library's diversity

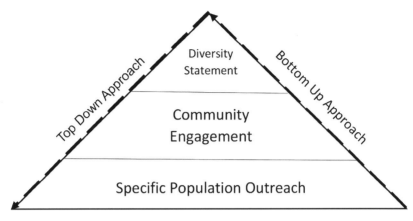

Figure 4.1   Strategic Plan of Action for Older Adult Student Inclusion in Academic Libraries

statement. A diversity statement is an easy way to indicate to stakeholders—either in general or specific population terms—that the diversity of patrons is recognized and appreciated. All academic libraries would be well served by having a diversity statement independent from their parent organization, one that includes age among the varied forms of diversity represented in the statement. The policy implications of the diversity statement can then be expounded on further in strategic planning documents as diversity is a term that can be convoluted; a diversity statement, which includes age, should be one component of a larger, meaningful effort by academic libraries to be more representative of older adult students (Peterson 1999).

A second component is community engagement. This requires creating or building on existing internal and external connections where discussing the needs of older adults and older adult students creates a variety of opportunities for academic libraries to demonstrate their commitment to supporting this population. This can include the types of events going on in the library that showcase community or university efforts. The Ohio State University hosted a number of related events, including a workshop on caring for both older adults and young children (https://library.osu.edu/blogs/osulstaff/2018/05/page/2) and a blog post on a new Elder Care Certificate Program being offered on campus for those who care for or interact with older adults (https://library.osu.edu/blogs/osulstaff/2019/02/01/university-news-10). Although events particular to older adult students are rare, these institutions are working creatively to show connections between university library resources and older adults in the community. One example is Texas A&M's Our Stories, Our Voices: The Old Lesbian Oral Herstory Project (https://cushing.library.tamu

.edu/news/2017/09/The%20Old%20Lesbian%20Oral%20Herstory%20Project
.html). This project was a community and university archive collaboration
that provides a way of understanding and interacting with the stories of older
adults in a way that is separate from the stereotypical discussions of older
adults as frail clients that nursing students or other medical professionals
could expect to see throughout their career. It also illustrates the important
reality of intersectionality as older adults have complex identities developed
throughout their lives, which have resulted in experiences that if shared would
be educational and enjoyable for students of any age (Cooke 2016).

A third component is direct outreach to older adult students. There are
several actions that can be taken to improve recognition of older adult students, but outreach has long been seen as important to providing services to
a diverse patron base in academic libraries (Walter 2005). Such outreach has
resulted in important insights for academic libraries. Aagard, Antunez, and
Sand (2015) found that the older adult students surveyed in their study were
overall very pleased with the services and resources available to them at their
university; other academic libraries would benefit from similar efforts or
designating a particular librarian to coordinate this work. The University of
Massachusetts–Amherst's undergraduate outreach librarian—who takes part
in diversity and inclusion efforts on campus—is an example of someone in
such a role (https://www.library.umass.edu/about-the-libraries/strategic-plan).
Together, these components provide a flexible framework for reviewing services for older adult students.

There are two approaches for completing this strategic plan of action: a
bottom-up or top-down approach. The bottom-up approach involves starting
the process of increasing the representation of older adult students by beginning with direct outreach to them. The top-down approach begins with
changes at the administrative level, such as creating an inclusive diversity
statement. Different institutions will have their own reasons for choosing one
approach over the other. Both approaches will lead to an increase in older
adult student representation in the academic library. Additional research
could expand this framework while also applying it to other specific diverse
population groups that continue to be underserved.

Conclusion

Many of the land-grant institutions studied are doing important work
related to the topics of social justice, diversity, and inclusion in general. Academic libraries are already reaching out to various, diverse student cohorts
such as transfer students and international students among others; some of
these institutions are making direct appeals to older adult students in
particular—but more work can be done. Based on the findings of the SDM

content analysis, this study suggests that academic libraries build on what they are already doing in order to increase services for and representation of older adult students through a strategic plan of action. As the world's population ages, the need to provide specific services to older adult students will become more and more apparent. Academic libraries that begin working to meet these needs now will not only be ahead of demographic trends but will also reaffirm their commitment to being an inclusive institution attentive to the many forms that diversity can manifest.

References

Aagard, Mary C., Marilia Y. Antunez, and Jaime N. Sand. 2015. "Learning from Degree-Seeking Older Adult Students in a University Library." *Reference Services Review* 43, no. 2: 215–230.

Abrams, Dominic, Hannah J. Swift, Ruth A. Lamont, and Lisbeth Drury. 2015. *The Barriers to and Enablers of Positive Attitudes to Ageing and Older People, at the Societal and Individual Level.* Technical report. Kent, UK: Government Office for Science.

Akhtar, Allana. 2019. "3 Million Older Americans Can't Find High-Paying Jobs, and It Has Nothing to Do with Skills. Here's the One Barrier They Face That No One's Addressing." May 7. https://www.businessinsider.com /retraining-doesnt-help-older-workers-find-jobs-because-of-ageism-2019-5.

Asla, Terryl, Kirsty Williamson, and John Mills. 2006. "The Role of Information in Successful Aging: The Case for a Research Focus on the Oldest Old." *Library & Information Science Research* 28, no. 1: 49–63.

Bean, John P., and Barbara S. Metzner. 1985. "A Conceptual Model of Nontraditional Undergraduate Student Attrition." *Review of Educational Research* 55, no. 4: 485–540.

Bennett-Kapusniak, Reneé K. 2018. *Public Library Programs and Services for Midlife and Beyond: Expanding Opportunities for a Growing Population.* Santa Barbara, CA: ABC-CLIO.

Blackham, Alysia. 2016. *Extending Working Life for Older Workers: Age Discrimination Law, Policy and Practice.* Oxford, UK: Bloomsbury Publishing.

Caudill, Jason. 2016. "The Changing Role of Post-Secondary Instruction for Non-Traditional Students: Partnering with Employers for Workplace Development." In *Proceedings of EdMedia 2016—World Conference on Educational Media and Technology*, 1153–1157. Vancouver, BC, Canada: Association for the Advancement of Computing in Education (AACE).

Chao, Ruth, and Glenn E. Good. 2004. "Nontraditional Students' Perspectives on College Education: A Qualitative Study." *Journal of College Counseling* 7, no. 1: 5–12.

Chung, Ethel, Deborah Turnbull, and Anna Chur-Hansen. 2014. "Who Are Non-Traditional Students? A Systematic Review of Published Definitions in

Research on Mental Health of Tertiary Students." *Educational Research and Reviews* 9, no. 22: 1224–1238.

Cooke, Nicole A. 2016. *Information Services to Diverse Populations: Developing Culturally Competent Library Professionals.* Santa Barbara, CA: ABC-CLIO.

Coughlin, Joseph, and Lisa D'Ambrosio, eds. 2012. *Aging America and Transportation: Personal Choices and Public Policy.* New York: Springer Publishing.

Cross, K. Patricia. 1980. "Our Changing Students and Their Impact on Colleges: Prospects for a True Learning Society." *The Phi Delta Kappan* 61, no. 9: 627–630.

Donaldson, Joe F., and Steve Graham. 1999. "A Model of College Outcomes for Adults." *Adult Education Quarterly* 50, no. 1: 24–40.

Forehand, Olivia G. 2018. "Efforts to Overcome Homelessness in the Pruitt Branch of the Nashville Public Library." *The International Journal of Information, Diversity, & Inclusion (IJIDI)* 2, no. 4: 72–83.

Fry, Richard. 2018. "Millennials Projected to Overtake Baby Boomers as America's Largest Generation." *Pew Research Center.* https://www.pewresearch .org/fact-tank/2018/03/01/millennials-overtake-baby-boomers.

Gilardi, Silvia, and Chiara Guglielmetti. 2011. "University Life of Non-Traditional Students: Engagement Styles and Impact on Attrition." *The Journal of Higher Education* 82, no. 1: 33–53.

Gillan, Becky. 2014. "Top 10 Demographics & Interests Facts about Americans Age 50+." May 14. https://blog.aarp.org/2014/05/14/top-10-demographics -interests-facts-about-americans-age-50.

Institute of Education Sciences, National Center for Education Statistics. 2018. *Digest of Education Statistics.* April. https://nces.ed.gov/programs/digest /d17/tables/dt17_303.40.asp.

Kennedy, Sharon A. 2013. *Classroom at the End of the 'Line': Assembly Line Workers at Midwest Community and Technical Colleges.* Scotts Valley, CA: CreateSpace Independent Publishing Platform.

Lachs, Mark. 2010. *Treat Me, Not My Age: A Doctor's Guide to Getting the Best Care as You or a Loved One Gets Older.* New York: Penguin.

Lenstra, Noah J. 2016. "The Community Informatics of an Aging Society: A Comparative Case Study of Senior Centers and Public Libraries." PhD diss., University of Illinois at Urbana-Champaign.

Malul, Miki. 2009. "Older Workers' Employment in Dynamic Technology Changes." *The Journal of Socio-Economics* 38, no. 5: 809–813.

Mehra, Bharat, and Ramesh Srinivasan. 2007. "The Library-Community Convergence Framework for Community Action: Libraries as Catalysts of Social Change." *Libri* 57, no. 3: 123–139.

Mehra, Bharat, and Rebecca Davis. 2015. "A Strategic Diversity Manifesto for Public Libraries in the 21st Century." *New Library World* 116, no. 1/2: 15–36.

Movius, Liz. 2018. "An Exploratory Case Study of Transgender and Gender Nonconforming Inclusion at a Metropolitan Library in the Southeastern U.S."

The International Journal of Information, Diversity, & Inclusion (IJIDI) 2, no. 4: 37–51.

Nelson, Todd D. 2005. "Ageism: Prejudice against Our Feared Future Self." *Journal of Social Issues* 61, no. 2: 207–221.

Nelson, Todd D. 2017. *Ageism: Stereotyping and Prejudice against Older Persons.* 2nd ed. Cambridge: The MIT Press.

Nerenberg, Lisa. 2019. *Elder Justice, Ageism, and Elder Abuse.* New York: Springer Publishing.

Neumark, David, Ian Burn, and Patrick Button. 2017. "Age Discrimination and Hiring of Older Workers." *Age* 6, no. 1: 1–5.

Nikolich-Žugich, Janko, Dana P. Goldman, Paul R. Cohen, Denis Cortese, Luigi Fontana, Brian K. Kennedy, M. Jane Mohler et al. 2015. "Preparing for an Aging World: Engaging Biogerontologists, Geriatricians, and the Society." *Journals of Gerontology Series A: Biomedical Sciences and Medical Sciences* 71, no. 4: 435–444.

Oxford English Dictionary. 2019. "Higher Education." http://www.oed.com.

Parks, Rodney, Brett Evans, and Yvette Getch. 2013. "Motivations and Enculturation of Older Students Returning to a Traditional University." *New Horizons in Adult Education and Human Resource Development* 25, no. 3: 62–75.

Peterson, Lorna. 1999. "The Definition of Diversity: Two Views. A More Specific Definition." *Journal of Library Administration* 27, no. 1–2: 17–26.

Scala, Marisa A. 1996. "Going Back to School: Participation Motives and Experiences of Older Adults in an Undergraduate Classroom." *Educational Gerontology: An International Quarterly* 22, no. 8: 747–773.

Schuetze, Hans G., and Maria Slowey. 2002. "Participation and Exclusion: A Comparative Analysis of Non-Traditional Students and Lifelong Learners in Higher Education." *Higher Education* 44, no. 3–4: 309–327.

Silipigni Connaway, Lynn, and Kevin M. Randall. 2013. "Why the Internet Is More Attractive Than the Library." *The Serials Librarian* 64, no. 1–4: 41–56.

Smith, Laura E. 2018. "Diversity and Inclusion at East Tennessee State University's Archives of Appalachia." *The International Journal of Information, Diversity, & Inclusion (IJIDI)* 2, no. 4.

Turek, Konrad, and Kène Henkens. 2019. "How Skill Requirements Affect the Likelihood of Recruitment of Older Workers in Poland: The Indirect Role of Age Stereotypes." *Work, Employment and Society* (May 29): 1–21. https://doi.org/10.1177/0950017019847943.

United Nations, Department of Economic and Social Affairs, Population Division. 2015. *World Population Ageing 2015.* https://www.un.org/en/development/desa/population/publications/pdf/ageing/WPA2015_Report.pdf.

Walter, Scott. 2005. "Moving beyond Collections: Academic Library Outreach to Multicultural Student Centers." *Reference Services Review* 33, no. 4: 438–458.

White, Elizabeth. 2019. *55, Underemployed, and Faking Normal.* New York: Simon & Schuster.

Winberry, Joseph. 2018. "Shades of Silver: Applying the Strategic Diversity Man-
    ifesto to Tennessee's Knox County Office on Aging." *The International
    Journal of Information, Diversity, & Inclusion (IJIDI)* 2, no. 4. https://doi.org
    /10.33137/ijidi.v2i4.32203.

Yates, Frances. 2014. "Beyond Library Space and Place: Creating a Culture of
    Community Engagement through Library Partnerships." *Indiana Libraries*
    33, no. 2: 53–57.

CHAPTER FIVE

Supporting Veterans and Military-Affiliated Families in an Academic Library

Michelle Shea

Military veterans are unique patrons in the academic space, as they enter libraries with considerable real-world experience. Research projects have personal meaning, and scholarly pursuits need more justification to be worthwhile. As noted by Vacchi (2012), many people "draw improper inferences about student veterans based upon . . . stereotypes," even though veterans often "adjust well to campus" and "equal or best their nonveteran peers in the classroom" (16). For military-affiliated students, a college degree can represent a lifelong dream, a path to sustained career success, or a method for keeping the mind sharp. Since veterans who attend our institution include recently discharged locals and retirees from other states, we must offer a range of services that account for these differences. As evidence of our university's priorities, the campus mission statement promotes "partnerships with regional community colleges, the military presence in [this] region, and the community at large," which includes current and potential students (Texas A&M University–Central Texas 2018). To align with this goal, the library has positioned itself as an essential resource for veterans. We have created displays, compiled information, taught research strategies, and offered outreach opportunities based on our military ties. By providing strong academic assistance and qualified personnel, the library acts as a public commons for veterans to gather as learners in a supportive space.

Honoring Veterans with Displays

In November 2018, our library created an extensive display for Veterans Day, using printed materials, banners, memorabilia, and models near the main library entrance. It was a collaboration between the library, college staff, and veteran students. Planning and coordinating duties were shared between two reference librarians and our business coordinator, who had existing contacts who were willing to participate. After some discussion, we narrowed our list to the director of academic technology, the risk and safety manager, a library specialist, and a senior undergraduate student. All of these individuals expressed interest in lending objects related to their past service, in order to share military memories and mementos with the campus.

Through email correspondence and face-to-face conversations, the librarians arranged times for items to be analyzed. On one occasion, we visited a navy veteran's office to view a few compiled materials. Primarily, he showed us his old military yearbooks, which included key missions from individual years of service. The veteran also had other memorabilia, including a mug, a hat, and certificates of appreciation. After identifying the articles most valuable for the display, we settled on a pickup date and followed up at that point. We prioritized primary materials; however, we also considered items that were created subsequently for events honoring veterans. Other keepsakes included military gear, such as helmets or medical kits, as well as spent artillery shells, dog tags, and other items of personal and professional significance.

The librarians wanted to make the process smoother for the individuals lending materials, so we decided to box up and carefully transport the items both to and from the library. This involved repurposing mail carts to move heavier articles, while also using the elevators to transition between floors. To keep items safe, our staff utilized a glass display case, near the entrance of the library, for organizing objects. As a sign of respect, we arranged everything based on the founding dates of each military branch. According to the Brookhaven Veterans Association (2013), the order is as follows: Army, Marine Corps, Navy, Air Force, and Coast Guard. We also kept a record of items as they were received so that we could return everything to the original owners at the conclusion of the project.

To the side of the display case, the library installed a temporary physical model of an army barracks that was built by a veteran (see Figure 5.1). It had facsimiles of bunker walls, protective internal barriers, and an armored vehicle, which gave viewers a look at the basic structure of a base.

Students and professors who walked by were excited to examine the creation from all angles, showing that there was a high interest in military-related artifacts. We also acquired mannequins to exhibit an army fatigue uniform

Figure 5.1   A Model Barracks, Created by an Army Veteran Who Works at the University

and a formal navy suit, which were both stationed against beams for support. These outfits were lent to us by individuals linked to the university, under the condition that we return the items in the same condition as given.

The next matter of business was to pick books for display, which needed to be comprehensive for historical and personal aspects of the military. The librarians were selective, as we have 32,000 physical and electronic items for the search term "military" or "war" in our collection. When we decided to focus only on skirmishes linked to the United States, the additional keyword "America dropped that total to about 15,400 materials. Finally, after limiting for print items only, we had more than 5,700 possible options for display. This is still quite a large number for an institution of our size, so further narrowing was done through date limiters, identification of key wars, and an emphasis on personal accounts. The goal was to represent U.S. wars from varying time periods, including World War II, Vietnam, and more recent conflicts. Memoirs and biographies by prisoners of war and other soldiers were integrated chronologically, while supplemental books on modern, applicable advice for veterans helped bring the display to the present (see Figure 5.2).

As a final touch, our head reference librarian located banners for each military group, as well as a U.S. flag. We draped these pennants below the book display and ensured they were adjacent, not overlapping. To avoid

Figure 5.2   A Section of the Veterans Day Book Display

desecration, each ensign was also raised high enough to avoid touching the floor. Finally, we clipped the flags securely to the ends of the display counters by using clothespins, tape, and needles, while also tucking in edges respectfully. When the display period ended, we called the ROTC department about proper flag folding methods. Serendipitously, a veteran student heard this request while in the library and offered to help fold the U.S. flag into a neat triangle, as guided by the official procedures. I held one end of the flag in the way he suggested, while he carefully layered lengthwise folds to create a three-cornered parcel. Although the United States Department of Veterans Affairs (n.d.) has digital documentation about this method, many soldiers learn flag folding as part of their training. Our librarians want to honor both our country and the men and women who serve, so we try to respect military conventions whenever possible.

Veterans Affairs Information on Campus

The library strives to provide all students with accurate information, which includes directory support for veterans. Sportsman and Thomas (2015) advocate for campuses to host veterans centers with "academic advising, resources for counseling, financial aid, tutoring, mentoring" and "a space for returning soldiers to meet, socialize, and study" (50). Our library partially serves as this center of activity, as evidenced by the many study room reservations and conversations that can be heard on our first floor. Beyond our space, however, the university also has a designated office for Veterans Affairs. Although librarians could simply connect students to these on-campus specialists, we should still strive to educate ourselves on the key issues of the department. Sometimes, students will describe their concerns using military terminology, particularly when looking for forms, so we need to be knowledgeable enough to interpret what is needed. University and government websites can provide a lot of this desired information.

On our campus's website, a keyword search for "military & veterans services" will retrieve the webpage for that internal department. This support office processes VA requests related to regulations at the state and federal level. To receive approval for funding, veteran students must abide by chosen degree plans, have their classes "certified" as necessary for graduation, and get "parent institution letters" approved when taking dual-campus classes (Texas A&M University–Central Texas 2019a). If students have questions about whether their military service would count for course credit, we direct them to campus experts who can do a degree audit. Much of the information is online, on at least a factual level; however, any interpretations based on individual situations would be beyond the scope of our duties. Although our institution is more likely to hear these types of questions, all university libraries should be aware of veteran students' potential information needs.

For financial benefits, veteran eligibility is based on the number of active-duty years and the specific dates of military service. Generally, individuals need an honorable discharge for at least some coverage of tuition, as described in the most recent Post-9/11 GI Bill (U.S. Department of Veteran Affairs 2019a). Housing can be considered as part of the training expense, up to a certain amount, while books and school materials can be partially covered with a stipend (U.S. Department of Veterans Affairs 2019b). Some states also have their own subsidies for former troops. For example, according to the Texas Education Code (2019), a veteran is eligible for tuition exemption if he or she "currently resides in this state," "entered the service" in Texas, and "declared this state as [his or her] home of record" (§ 54.341). Spouses or dependents may also be eligible, if a veteran was a casualty of war, including death or permanent disability. It is important to note that military tuition reduction plans may exclude the concurrent use of other types of veteran-related funding, so it is important for prospective students to be well informed before filing required documents.

If all of these resources are not sufficient to cover the total amount, veterans have additional options. The Yellow Ribbon Program, which involves tuition matching from both the campus and the federal VA department, can help make up a portion of the difference. Our university caps its allotment to two students per fiscal year, as a result of our smaller population and higher rate of qualified individuals (U.S. Department of Veterans Affairs 2019c). Some campuses have unlimited funding or student enrollment allowances, but those locations tend to have fewer military students in residence. Soldiers who paid a set fee while on active duty may also be entitled to extra monthly funds, as part of the Montgomery Bill (U.S. Department of Veteran Affairs 2019d). Academic librarians just need to know that there are many avenues to help veterans pay for education. Funding will likely be one of the most common concerns for these students, outside of the more conventional academic questions.

In partnership with our Career and Professional Development department, the library recruits federal work-study students for our tutoring program and public service desks. According to the U.S. Department of Veterans Affairs (2019e), GI bills can provide for work-study allotments. As our job posting only specifies that applicants attend classes and be eligible for financial assistance, it is feasible for many interested veteran students to apply. The Military & Veterans Affairs office on campus is another viable option for student workers with military experience, although participation in a VA funding source is also required (Texas A&M University–Central Texas 2019d). A final option that current military-affiliated students might consider is the "Academic Internship Placement Program" (Stamper 2019), which is a collaboration between our campus and Fort Hood, one of the largest army bases in the country. When students are looking for employment opportunities, we can confidently recommend this option, as it combines purposeful academic study with the benefits of real-world training on an active military base.

When questions are financial in nature, there are often monthly reporting requirements and specifications that go beyond our job descriptions. If available, local or campus offices for military service can help students navigate the forms and paperwork that must be submitted for program eligibility. Librarians can then direct active duty, veteran, and military family members to more informed points of contact, while still fulfilling the role of information provider.

Research Assistance for Veteran Learners and Military Topics

According to Sportsman and Thomas (2015), veterans may need "more detailed guidance" when starting college; however, this requirement may "decrease as time passes and the service members become more acclimated to procedures and campus life" (46). The librarians strive to be accessible, positive, and target driven with our veterans, who benefit from the same kinds of clear objectives as those outlined during their years of military service. For example, veterans want to learn how to research, so we recommend library subject guides specific to their degrees. These digital webpages have lists of curated databases, which we can model using practical searches. After one-on-one consultations at the reference desk, many veterans have mentioned how they regretted not asking for help sooner.

As a reference librarian, my process has been to clarify the assignment goals, to move through searching steps slowly, and to check for understanding at each major point. Afterward, I will often ask the veteran to do a similar search using the same resources, while providing reassurance that I am ready to support them when needed. If the student struggles to understand an explanation, good teaching practice dictates that we offer real-world examples that "present information . . . in an authentic context" (Dasgupta 2013, 79). This gradual release of responsibility particularly benefits older, military-affiliated learners, who may need extra support to feel comfortable and capable with electronic sources. When veteran students feel secure in our advice, they are likely to become repeat visitors or offer positive comments about our services. Peers who hear good word-of-mouth feedback may then give the library a chance, even if they might not have visited otherwise.

Every semester, our library assists with a social work policy class, in which all the reference librarians schedule one-on-one consultations with students. The laws deal with societal issues that veterans often face, including mental health concerns, homelessness, disabilities, and welfare. As noted by Daley, Carlson, and Evans (2015), the "vast majority of students" in social work careers "will be working with military or veteran clients" for those same types of reasons (77). In Central Texas, this need is made evident by the homeless assistance programs, counseling centers, and trauma wings that are located across the area. The research process for this policy project helps students, branch-affiliated or otherwise, become more socially aware.

For this course, one specific topic linked to the military is the Patriot Act, since it is concerned with homeland security. Although many of the law's provisions have expired, social discussions on the matter have continued. Often veterans end up selecting this act because it addresses issues, such as terrorism surveillance and intelligence gathering, which may connect to their past experiences. Like most students, ex-military learners research topics that are of personal interest. With these sessions, it is not in our job description to make judgment calls; rather, we help direct faculty, staff, and students to resources that encourage inquiry and discovery about the world. We want to offer our veterans a chance to interact with University-Central material in an authentic way, while also acknowledging that the searching process is iterative and builds on itself as new information is learned.

Other reasons for veterans to visit us include our military studies databases. These include EBSCO's *Military & Government Collection* and the *Military Database* by ProQuest. Although many search functions will overlap between sources, the indexing for these databases allows for subject headings such as "armed forces," "international relations," and "military aircraft." As an example, if a student from our online aviation program used the chatbox to ask about the history of military flight, we might use EBSCO's thesaurus option to narrow down their focus. Are they interested in "navy air bases," "air defense," or some other aspect of the topic? Do they have personal experiences in the military or civilian life that might provide additional keywords or synonyms for their research? Questions like these, framed in accessible language, can help both military- and nonmilitary-affiliated students make the most of our online resources.

For military research, the government provides a lot of useful leads. These sources include articles directly from the Department of Defense, U.S. intelligence agencies, or military branches. Typically, we think of using .gov sites for statistics or general information, but some .org databases linked to the military can also be considered. One such option is the *Homeland Security Digital Library* (HSDL), which was created in partnership with the Naval Postgraduate School. On this site, students can get information about featured topics, such as "border security" or "domestic terrorism" in the form of published and PDF-formatted, open-access reports. Thematically linked websites and postgraduate theses on military topics are also provided if students want to gather numerical data or alternative perspectives. Other searching options include time lines for stateside attacks, special collections from multiple government agencies, and a weekly blog. Since our campus offers a master's degree in homeland security, which includes topics such as "advanced criminology" and "foundations of information security," it is imperative that our librarians be familiar with both common and niche digital sources related to military research (Texas A&M University–Central Texas 2019b).

Library Services for Military-Connected Patrons

The library is the hub of the school community. As a result, we tend to get questions for wide-ranging reasons. As noted by Grallo, Chalmers, and Baker (2012), the library as an "information commons" can serve as a "support system for students with information needs not directly related to their coursework" (186). In practice, this includes queries on technology, directions, and student service offices, such as recreation or student affairs. We also can refer military students to our counseling center, if they are in need of personal advice. Occasionally, we ask staff members from these departments to stop by or answer a question by phone, since we have a small, collegial campus. In most cases, however, the librarians need to problem solve using research skills, quick thinking, or printed reference materials we keep on hand for common inquiries. In academic libraries, we must be prepared for questions that are both simple and highly complex, which requires a well-rounded understanding of many subject areas and sources.

At the beginning of the semester, students want to know about course scheduling, class locations, and financial aid. Although we do not directly manage these areas, our librarians strive to find answers after the first instance of a question type, so that later requests can be solved with certainty. For example, a veteran visiting from out of town had received a graduate degree from our institution and needed help printing transcripts. Added security measures dictate that all official degree records be retrieved through the online Banner system. Recent students should have little trouble navigating, as they use this digital tool regularly while in attendance; however, the veteran, in this case, had finished his schooling before the new restrictions were in place. As the librarian on duty, I contacted the registrar's office on the student's behalf and also sought assistance from one of the academic technology aides. With this multipronged approach, we helped the veteran retrieve his unofficial transcript, save it to an external drive, and ensure he felt respected and heard. Although the former student was understandably frustrated with the complicated prospect of using an online portal, he left with positive feelings about the assistance he received. In another case, I helped a female veteran scan and upload a required health services letter to her VA account. Although I was technically off-duty, I knew that a little technical assistance would not take much time. Good librarianship means going the extra mile, particularly when it is not expected.

Whenever there are veteran-oriented events, we need to be aware of key information, such as the topic, location, and date. For example, in October 2018, our campus sponsored the Annual Central Texas Military History Symposium on the fiftieth anniversary of the Tet Offensive. In September 2019, the conference presentation focused on the Pacific War. Experts from the academic, archival, and military world were invited to speak on the focus theme while sharing their own experiences and research (Texas A&M University–Central Texas 2019c). Although there are flyers posted in certain locations, many students will come to ask about these talks. Additionally, our campus may hear about open house or reenactment events from historical institutions in the Central Texas area, such as the Calvary Museums at Fort Hood or the Texas Military Forces Museum in Austin. The archives librarian coordinates her work with the history department, so she would be our first point of contact in those particular instances. As each librarian is a subject liaison for different areas, we pool information to help our military-affiliated students get answers. Often this knowledge sharing is achieved through phone calls or the passing on of business cards for the librarian who will be most able to assist. The goal is for patrons to leave with answers or enough information to proceed in their search, which may rely on resources housed at nearby universities, libraries, museums, or federal repositories.

Visitors who have never been on campus are pleasantly surprised at the range of library services available to them. We have a microfiche reader that is used by community members occasionally to view dated military service records. Recently, our collection development librarian showed a veteran's spouse how to load the photographic sheets onto the machine for this very purpose. There is a computer designated exclusively for this use, as well as government microfiche that can be viewed for more general historical inquiries. For example, the microfiche in our collection include topics such as the U.S. Army in World War I, wartime cablegrams, Germany in World War II, FBI guidelines, and state memos for Texas departments.

Any recruit records older than sixty-two years are archived and made available to the public (National Personnel Records Center 2019), but newer ones, such as those from the Vietnam, Gulf, and Afghanistan Wars, will be restricted by privacy laws. Each military branch also has its own contact office that can provide directions on how to acquire individual records, either digitally through a portal or with a formal written request. Librarians can locate this initial directory information or suggest webpages and forms that can help patrons continue their search.

Other patrons have requested papers from our archives, including documents from army officials. Our archivist and her team have digitized many letters, pamphlets, newspaper articles, and images linked to local military history. These items help show the historical partnerships that have sprouted in our community, including events connected to school districts and local colleges. For example, General Robert Shoemaker wrote a Fort Hood graduation speech that "thanks . . . the staff and faculty of the participating Colleges and Universities and the Fort Hood Education Services Division" (Shoemaker 2001). Although this speech was written over fifteen years ago, our university is still listed as one of the collaborating institutions for the same educational branch. Another letter from Shoemaker (2005) mentions that "Tarleton–Central Texas," our previous designation, hosted evening classes on the Shoemaker High School campus. The university may have started off small, but we have gradually grown alongside our educational partners. These connections brought extended higher education to the area as the closest alternative institutional options were at least two cities away. Students could take classes at a nearby community college, both then and now, before transferring their credit hours toward a four-year degree. For individuals researching history or curious veteran students, sources like these could be invaluable. Local military troops have been consistently linked to this city's K–12 and higher education efforts, even before our university's inception, so we are honored to preserve a small piece of this tradition with our archives.

Work with Military-Affiliated Children

As the education librarian, I have gotten requests related to tutoring for resident military children. We run an on-campus first- to fifth-grade instructional program during the fall and spring semesters, based on reading and math assignments. This weekly offering seemed like a good way to correspond with the community as all of the local campuses serve active-duty families. For the 2018–2019 school year, Killeen ISD, the closest district, had over 16,000 students who were "military connected," as indicated by Public Education Information Management System (PEIMS) reports (Texas Education Agency 2019). According to a questionnaire, which was distributed at our most recent orientation meeting, about 30 percent of our current tutoring students are military affiliated. To target this key population, the outreach librarian and I present at meetings for school librarians to get the word out about our tutoring program. We repeat these visits every year or two, as a refresher on our services.

Other work with military-affiliated students has been within the districts. Our library collaborates for special community events, such as STEM and festival days at local campuses. We provide supplies and personnel, so the schools only need to offer an engaging audience. As a bonus, each location is adopted by a particular troop or battalion, meaning there are often military volunteers working at the same time. These external partnerships help the library do good work with military-affiliated families and soldiers, while also building awareness for our services. Over time, librarians focused on educational outreach can improve trust between organizations, which keeps lines of communication open for future collaborative endeavors.

Every year, our library allies with Fort Hood on initiatives related to military-connected children. The army base hosts annual talks to discuss partnerships between military families, school districts, higher education institutions, and subject matter experts. Our university's role is to share information on our cooperative efforts, which includes the aforementioned tutoring program. By discussing educational issues with area representatives, we can brainstorm how to handle gaps in service and determine what is working. For example, Fort Hood Child & Youth Services (2018) coordinates activities for homeschooler families. The schedule includes traveling events, like museum days, park stops, and library visits. Although our library hasn't worked with this group yet, we see potential in these types of partnerships after attending the meetings.

Annually, two of our university librarians visit the military base for an Earth Day event. Many educational organizations, across Central Texas, gather in a designated pavilion to host activities and presentations for children. These projects include models and crafts on water usage, gardening, recycling, animal conservation, and other sustainable practices. To ensure everything runs smoothly, the event organizer provides all presenters with a map, contacts list, and scheduled agenda. As a security measure, every person must be pre-approved in order to drive on base. For one-time access, participants could send identifying information to the coordinator, who would authorize check-ins at a specific gate. The process normally involves "security vetting" at a visitor center to acquire a ninety-day pass (Fort Hood Army Base 2019); however,

I had already requested a yearlong educator clearance to facilitate my occasional work with Fort Hood. Although events on the base require a bit more planning to attend, the valuable result is closer bonds between military families and educational institutions.

Fort Hood has supported our children's programming financially as well, in the form of small grants from an army spouses' club. The library applies for these funds annually, since we brainstorm new camp ideas and adjust existing programs every year. For example, in the spring of 2019, I requested capital for a Future City STEM camp that the library would be running in the summer. The grant paperwork asked how many military-affiliated families we serve so that the grantor could see how our library programming connects to their target demographic. Since about 48 percent of our college students are linked to the military, as indicated in emails to faculty, we made the case that many people on campus who would see our STEM flyers might be in this group. On our camp registration form, we asked parents to self-report their military status. Thirty-five percent of our girls-only session attendees were from military families and 32 percent of our coed session registrants were, showing a clear link between our programming and service to military families. That number does not even account for the additional diversity of our campers, as we had students from multiple schools districts, homeschoolers, and children with disabilities as part of our total count as well. Library outreach of this nature may encourage current troops and veteran-status individuals to view our university in a positive way, which can lead to later inquiries about college programs or even active enrollment. At least one parent asked about our campus and library services while waiting for their child during camp, so these community connections do work.

Conclusion

Academic librarians owe it to their patrons to be well informed about how to help veterans, military-affiliated families, and members of the public. Current and former military students are likely present on every college campus, even when services are not widely promoted. With even small changes, libraries can show their appreciation for these individuals and their personal and scholarly contributions. Displays can be created on a smaller scale, military database and webpage information can be organized for ease of use, and public events can be planned to promote or advocate library benefits for servicemen and women. If academic libraries are able to do these tasks in partnership with other departments, then the entire campus has reason to take notice.

Recognizing that a military background is an asset to the college environment is a good first step toward improved service to veterans. The goal of any university should be to encourage a nuanced campus population, including diverse student viewpoints and age groups. Specifically, the work experiences, military training, and life skills of veterans can enhance the campus culture in positive ways. These students may be more motivated and focused, which raises the bar for everyone. They can also share new perspectives and add unique social dimensions. Although military-affiliated individuals are often underrepresented and underserved, libraries have the materials, the personnel, and the space to make valuable contributions to this important student group.

References

Brookhaven Veterans Association. 2013. "The Complete Order of Precedence of Flags in the US." https://www.bnl.gov/bera/activities/va/pdf/2013-Flag Etiquette.pdf.

Daley, James G., Joan Carlson, and Pinkie Evans. 2015. "Military Social Work as an Exemplar in Teaching Social Work Competencies." *Journal of Social Work Education* 51 (January): S76–S88. doi:10.1080/10437797.2015.1001288.

Dasgupta, Anamika. 2013. "More Than Just a Reference Librarian." *Reference Librarian* 54, no. 1: 78–80. doi:10.1080/02763877.2013.738131.

Fort Hood Army Base. 2019. "Access Passes." https://home.army.mil/hood/index .php/my-fort/visitor-information/fort-hood-access-passes.

Fort Hood Child & Youth Services. 2018. "Homeschool Activities Calendar." Print flyer.

Grallo, Jacqui, Mardi Chalmers, and Pamela Baker. 2012. "How Do I Get a Campus ID? The Other Role of the Academic Library in Student Retention and Success." *Reference Librarian* 53, no. 2: 182–193. doi.org/10.1080/027 63877.2011.618787.

Homeland Security Digital Library. 2019. "Home Page." https://www.hsdl.org/c.

National Personnel Records Center. 2019. "NPRC Records Holdings." https:// www.archives.gov/personnel-records-center.

Shoemaker, Robert M. 2001. "Fort Hood Graduation Speech." https://vital.tamuct .edu:8443/vital/access/services/Download/vital:965/SOURCE1?view=true.

Shoemaker, Robert M. 2005. "Letter from General Shoemaker to the Judges for the HEB Excellence in Education Award." https://vital.tamuct.edu:8443 /vital/access/services/Download/vital:2969/SOURCE1?view=true.

Sportsman, Michel A., and Lisa Thomas. 2015. "Coming Home to School: Challenges and Strategies for Effective Teaching with Military Veterans." *InSight: A Journal of Scholarly Teaching* 10 (January): 43–55. https://files. eric.ed.gov/fulltext/EJ1074051.pdf.

Stamper, Peggy. 2019. "Academic Intern Program Making History." *Fort Hood Sentinel*. http://www.forthoodsentinel.com/living/academic-intern-program -making-history/article_2a18299e-5560-11e9-92fa-6b91abef0278.html.

Texas A&M University–Central Texas. 2018. "Academic Master Plan: 2018 to 2022." https://www.tamuct.edu/about/AMCT%20Strategic%20Plan%20 2018-2022.pdf.

Texas A&M University–Central Texas. 2019a. "Veterans Affairs Frequently Asked Questions." https://www.tamuct.edu/veterans-affairs/faq.html.

Texas A&M University–Central Texas. 2019b. "Course Catalog: M.S. Homeland Security." http://catalog.tamuct.edu/graduate_and_professional_catalog/graduate-programs/ms_homeland_security/#mastersciencehomelandsecuritywithoutthesistext.

Texas A&M University–Central Texas. 2019c. "Annual Central Texas Military History Symposium." https://www.tamuct.edu/coas/coas-special-topics/symposium.html.

Texas A&M University–Central Texas. 2019d. "VA Work Study Application." https://www.tamuct.edu/veterans-affairs/docs/ted-diane-connell-va-work-study-intial-application-cover-letter.pdf.

Texas Education Agency. 2019. "Student Program and Special Populations Reports." https://rptsvrl.tea.texas.gov/adhocrpt/adspr.html.

Texas Education Code. 2019. "Higher Education: Tuition and Fees." https://statutes.capitol.texas.gov/Docs/ED/htm/ED.54.htm.

United States Army Human Resource Command. 2019. "Accessing or Requesting Your Official Military Personnel File Documents." https://www.hrc.army.mil/TAGD/Accessing%20or%20Requesting%20Your%20Official%20Military%20Personnel%20File%20Documents.

U.S. Department of Veterans Affairs. n.d. "Correct Method of Folding the United States Flag." https://www.va.gov/opa/publications/celebrate/flagfold.pdf.

U.S. Department of Veterans Affairs. 2019a. "Post 9-11 Bill." https://www.benefits.va.gov/gibill/post911_gibill.asp.

U.S. Department of Veterans Affairs. 2019b. "Post 9-11 Bill Payment Rates." https://www.benefits.va.gov/gibill/post911_gibill.asp.

U.S. Department of Veterans Affairs. 2019c. "TX State Yellow Ribbon Program Information." https://www.benefits.va.gov/gibill/yellow_ribbon/2019/states/tx.asp.

U.S. Department of Veterans Affairs. 2019d. "Montgomery GI Bill Active Duty." https://www.benefits.va.gov/gibill/mgib_ad.asp.

U.S. Department of Veterans Affairs. 2019e. "Work Study." https://www.va.gov/education/about-gi-bill-benefits/how-to-use-benefits/work-study.

Vacchi, David T. 2012. "Considering Student Veterans on the Twenty-First Century College Campus." *About Campus* 17, no. 2: 15–21. doi.org/10.1002/abc.21075.

CHAPTER SIX

Academic Librarian Engagement against Campus Sexual Violence

Jinxuan Ma and Lynne Stahl

Introduction

Among the most pervasive and multifarious public health issues in the United States, sexual violence refers to "sexual activity when consent is not obtained or not given freely" (Centers for Disease Control and Prevention [CDC] 2019, para. 1). Terminology around sexual violence is anything but straightforward, and compelling cases exist for both the term "victim" and "survivor" to characterize someone who has been subjected to sexual violence (Campoamor 2018; Papendick and Bohner 2017; Schwark and Bohner 2019). This study follows guidance from the Rape, Abuse, and Incest National Network (RAINN) in its usage of "survivor" for "someone who has gone through the recovery process, or when discussing the short- or long-term effects of sexual violence" (RAINN n.d., para. 3), uses the phrase "sexual violence" as "an all-encompassing, non-legal term that refers to crimes like sexual assault, rape, and sexual abuse" (RAINN n.d., para. 2).

Campus Sexual Violence

Each year, millions of individuals experience adverse physical and psychological effects as direct or indirect results of sexual violence. Such trauma can lead to severe and chronic health issues over a lifetime for individual survivors, or even to death. As college campuses are pervasively afflicted by sexual violence and other forms of sexual misconduct, campus sexual violence has become an entrenched, often underaddressed epidemic.

The problem of sexual violence on college campuses is often exacerbated by a phenomenon that has come to be known as campus rape culture, which refers to "multiple pervasive issues that allow rape and sexual assault to be excused, legitimized and viewed as inevitable" (Giraldi and Monk-Turner 2017, 116; see also White and Smith 2004, 174). Jozkowski and Wiersma-Mosley (2017) have detailed the "patterns of power and control in university systems that contribute to the occurrence and facilitation of sexual assault" (89). Campus rape culture manifests in numerous forms and contexts, some more widely recognized than others. Fraternities, for example, often serve as social hubs on college campuses and are known for their party culture; existing studies have found that sexual assault and other misconduct of a sexual nature occurs at increased rates during and after fraternity-sponsored social events (Jozkowski and Wiersma-Mosley 2017).

Although campus rape culture is unfortunately ubiquitous and largely recognized as a component of systemic misogyny, discourses on the topic may not always adequately address its disproportionate effect on specific populations. Linder and Harris (2017) have advocated for what they call a "power conscious" approach to campus sexual violence, which entails the recognition that sexual violence is anchored not just in sexism but also in racism, transphobia, ableism, classism, homophobia, and more, and that the role of other demographic factors than gender must not be overlooked. To combat sexual violence, advocates must understand its history and the racial history of sexual violence laws in the United States. Following the Civil War, for instance, White men used false accusations of sexual violence by Black men against White women to maintain their dominance in post-Abolition culture; meanwhile, White men perpetrated sexual violence against Black women with relative impunity (Donat and D'Emilio 1992).

Further, the per-victim lifetime monetary cost of rape can reach $122,461, accumulating approximately $3.1 trillion (2014 U.S. dollars) for the estimated 25 million reported adult victims of rape over their lifetimes (CDC 2019, para. 3). The economic effects of sexual violence may be less frequently discussed than its physical and psychological effects, but they are likely to have a compounding effect on populations that already tend to face economic adversity—particularly when access to affordable health care may not be available.

Theoretical Frameworks

Library services for sexual violence survivors face both philosophical and practical limitations. Many survivors may not wish to identify as such, and asking them to do so poses serious psychological distress and ethical issues, so obtaining accurate statistics is not easy. Research has found that minority populations (e.g., LGBTQ+ students, students with disabilities, and students of color) are victimized at higher rates than nonminority populations—a discrepancy that signals the need for culturally specific resources and responses (Association of American Universities [AAU] 2019, 33; see also Cantor et al. 2017; Fedina, Homes, and Backes 2018, 90). Demographic factors affect the likelihood of reporting, and it follows that they also play a role in information-seeking behavior. Both historically and in the present day, for example, sexual violence survivors of color may refrain from reporting for fear of a potential confrontation between police and assailants of color, they may be reluctant to interact with police themselves, or they may be deterred from reporting by perceived expectations of cultural "loyalty" when the assailant is of the same race (Washington 2001).

The Information Seeking of Sexual Assault Survivors Model

As Harris and Dewdney (1994) have established, information-seeking behavior is largely contextual and varies in relation to the circumstances of a given instance of assault or instance of misconduct, not just according to the survivor's background. They further extrapolated six principles around domestic violence survivor information-seeking behavior, which they as well as Skinner and Gross (2017) contend are broadly generalizable: (1) information needs arise from the help-seeker's situation; (2) the decision to seek help or not seek help is affected by many factors; (3) people tend to seek information that is most accessible; (4) people tend to first seek help or information from interpersonal sources, especially from people like themselves; (5) information seekers expect emotional support; and (6) people follow habitual patterns in seeking information (as cited in Skinner and Gross 2017, 26).

With attention to these principles, Skinner and Gross (2017) developed the Information Seeking of Sexual Assault Survivors (ISSAS) model in hopes of illuminating the particular ways in which sexual violence survivors seek information, with the ultimate aim of enabling academic libraries to better serve this population. Informed by related work in psychology and sociology, the ISSAS model aligns its approach with the typical stages of the survivor healing process. It delineates the following series of decision points: (a) perception of the availability of help, (b) enablers and barriers, (c) selecting information sources, and (d) assessing answers. Most important, perhaps, is the assertion that at every stage, the information seeker must "perceive that help is available, [otherwise] she or he is not going to continue the process of seeking that help and may go back to reassess needs—or may decide that for now the need cannot be met" (Skinner and Gross 2017, 28).

Critical Librarianship

The notion of library as place has been addressed extensively in library and information science research (see Aabø and Audunson 2012; Aabø, Audunson, and Vårheim 2010; Mann 2001; Shoham and Klain-Gabbay 2019; Westbrook 2015), and both public and academic libraries are places survivors might go in a time of need. Librarians may seek to contribute to the prevention of sexual violence and the creation of resources for those who have survived it (Fedina, Holmes, and Backes 2018). Efforts by academic librarians in this area exemplify one form of recent pushes toward what has come to be known as "critical librarianship." Diverging from traditional (albeit widely contested) notions of libraries as neutral spaces, advocates of critical librarianship have argued that neutrality actively harms marginalized groups and that instead of pursuing it, librarians "should examine and fight attempts at social oppression" (Farkas 2017, para. 1).

Two recent developments have given critical librarianship a renewed sense of urgency: (a) the ongoing proliferation of fabricated or misleading online news alongside the rise of racist, homophobic, and misogynistic discourses, and (b) the *#MeToo* movement, which has unfolded in recent years alongside a slew of sexual assault allegations against prominent male figures such as Hollywood producer Harvey Weinstein as well as the former USA Gymnastics team doctor Larry Nassar's conviction for numerous counts of sexual violence in a high-profile trial. Given the extent to which sexual violence is intertwined with race, class, gender, ability, and sexual orientation (AAU 2019; Linder and Harri 2017), it follows that the resources librarians create to support information seeking related to sexual violence should take an intersectional approach that considers these demographic variations in frequency of incidence as well as reporting tendencies.

Method

The notion of critical librarianship informed the development of the research question that guided this study: In what capacities have academic librarians acted as agents against campus sexual violence and as advocates for survivors? The content analysis that follows was designed to identify and characterize the current practices and advocacy efforts of academic libraries—including both two- and four-year public (n=90) and private (n=50) institutions—in battling campus sexual violence and providing support to survivors via the Internet. A total of 156 academic libraries' relevant webpages were retrieved through structured Google searching and subsequent scrutiny of retrieved webpages on an individual basis. The search queries were built using Boolean operators between major keywords of "academic library" (such as college or university library services, information resources, LibGuide) and "campus sexual violence" (namely, acquaintance or date rape, college or campus rape, sexual or dating violence, campus or college sexual abuse, campus or college sexual assault, campus rape culture, campus rape prevention, #MeToo or "Me Too" activism, sexual harassment or misconduct, survivor groups). Many of those keywords were adopted from the retrieved library LibGuides.

The unit of analysis was each retrieved academic library webpage that presents announcements (e.g., news, press release, events, exhibits), blog posts, LibGuides (e.g., courses, research, resources, topics, subjects, collections, catalog search), videography, webinar, and more. Researchers created a codebook based on the notion of critical librarianship through iterative scrutiny, comparison, categorization, discussion, and reflection. Each retrieved webpage, including both textual and graphic information, was analyzed according to types of library services addressing campus sexual violence. To ensure reliability, the researchers repeatedly conferred to reach consensus on the codebook and achieve a high coder agreement (96 percent) on coding and consistency of analysis.

Findings

The findings show that some academic librarians have drawn on the energy of the #MeToo movement as a means to enact critical librarianship within the milieu of higher education, where sexual assault and harassment are established problems with specific contextual attributes. Five categories emerged as characteristic of academic librarians' endeavors in battling campus sexual violence, as shown in Table 6.1. Those categories include (a) announcement—publicizing library-sponsored or campus events or exhibits to encourage conversations on preventing and responding to campus sexual violence (e.g., the #MeToo movement); (b) information provision—providing research-based evidence regarding sexual violence or other relevant issues; (c) referrals—presenting links and/or contact information primarily for survivors rather than research purposes, such as the RAINN, local centers, crisis hotlines, and so forth; (d) social engagement on sexual violence—promoting content framed in relation to contemporaneous news/social media/activism against sexual violence, such as the #MeToo movement and the Women's March; and (e) supporting resources—linking to supporting library information sources, such as both physical and electronic collections, archives, and other curations.

In addition to characterizing the various institutions by type, the researchers noted whether or not they claimed a religious affiliation. Of the institutions

Table 6.1 Retrieved Library Services to Combat Campus Sexual Violence across Institutions

	Announcement n (%)	Information Provision n (%)	Referrals n (%)	Social Engagement on Sexual Violence n (%)	Social Engagement on Unrelated to Sexual Violence n (%)	Supporting Resources n (%)
Community College (N=19)	5 (26)	9 (47)	13 (68)	7 (37)	2 (11)	13 (68)
Military Academy (N=1)			1 (100)			1 (100)
Private College (N=18)	6 (33)	12 (67)	11 (61)	12 (67)		3 (17)
Private University (N=32)	8 (25)	12 (38)	10 (31)	11 (34)	13 (41)	21 (66)
Public College (N=5)	1 (20)	2 (40)	4 (80)	1 (20)		2 (40)
Public University (N=65)	13 (20)	15 (23)	31 (49)	12 (48)	6 (9)	56 (86)
Total Webpages (N=178)	33 (19)	50 (28)	70 (39)	43 (24)	21 (12)	96 (54)

(n=140), thirty-six claimed a religious affiliation. Institutions were designated as having strong affiliations if religion and/or religious values explicitly appeared in the institution's mission statement, while those whose religious affiliations were not included in the mission statement were designated as weak. Of the thirty-six institutions with religious affiliations, twenty-one were strong and fifteen were weak.

Table 6.1 breaks down the study's findings by resource type (column) and institution type (rows). For this study's purposes, institution type was defined as follows: (a) community college—public institution offering two-year degrees such as associate's degrees; (b) private college—private four-year institution offering almost exclusively undergraduate degrees, for example, liberal arts colleges; (c) private university—private four-year institution offering graduate as well as undergraduate degrees; (d) public college—public four-year institution offering almost exclusively undergraduate degrees; (e) public university—public four-year institution offering graduate as well as undergraduate degrees; and (f) military academy—four-year college or university that seeks to prepare students to serve in officer corps.

Proactive Measures against Campus Sexual Violence

Announcements of preventive educational events, exhibits, lectures/talks via the library homepage, blogs, or social media accounts emerged from the data as one common form of active library involvement (33 out of the retrieved 156 academic library webpages, or 21 percent) in battling campus sexual violence and supporting survivors. Examples of such displays and programs hosted or sponsored by libraries ranged widely: a library display in observance of Sexual Violence Awareness Month, a program on violence against women, a press release of library grant to support comprehensively documenting the *#MeToo* movement and its influence, an incentivized survey of campus sexual violence awareness using *#iSpeak* and *#WeSpeak* hashtags, and a display of the *#MeToo* movement in higher education showcasing books, newspapers, magazines, and multimedia artifacts.

These library initiatives took the form of information sources in a variety of mediums, including both traditional (e.g., library physical collections, archives, electronic resources, artifacts) and creative (e.g., multimedia displays or exhibitions, on-campus lectures, film screenings, series or conversations) formats. As one library art installation titled "I Want a Rape Free Campus" indicates, some of these resources gave explicit voice to student and faculty attitudes toward sexual violence on campus. In addition, many libraries also actively promoted new initiatives, legal issues, and multidisciplinary perspectives on the *#MeToo* movement, or other non-library-initiated events related to the awareness and prevention of sexual violence and creation of a culture of respect. However, the presence of substantial outdated information and broken links may raise concerns about the feasibility of sustainable educational interventions.

Information-Based Support Primarily for Campus Sexual Violence Survivors

The core professional competency of librarianship is to provide relevant and reliable information resources for users. Many library services are pursued at the point of need and have a sense of urgency. Compiling resources under headings such as "Where You Can Go for Help" or "If You Need Help Now" is one approach to serving point-of-need inquiry. These resources, provided by 45 percent of all retrieved webpages (n=70), commonly comprised well-organized online links and contact information for organizations and professionals that offer practical assistance and specialized services for those affected by sexual violence. Such informational support is particularly valuable for those who live in rural or isolated areas and have limited access to supporting resources. Examples of on-campus services include Title IX coordinators or committee members, counselors, emergent clinic services, student affairs offices, and victim support centers.

More comprehensive resources of both local and national scope often spanned nonprofit organizations, community support, professional and specialized services, such as crisis hotlines, community resource centers, shelters, free food/meals, emergency cash/clothing and household goods, housing assistance, medical care, mental health, legal aid, and job search materials. In addition, some libraries included resources for particular demographic groups ranging from veteran students to LGBTQ+ students to racial minorities. However, relatively few resources provided demographic-specific resources on sexual violence beyond a book or two. Individual liaison librarians or subject librarians were often listed as the contact for users to follow up or seek assistance.

Multidisciplinary Research-Based Information Resources as Instructional Intervention

As the 2019 AAU campus climate survey on sexual assault and misconduct reports, an alarming knowledge gap exists among college students regarding the definition of sexual violence or misconduct, where to get help, how to report, and what happens when an incident is reported (AAU 2019, 67). A variety of LibGuides (n=50), including research guides, subject/topic guides, course/study guides, and how-to guides were found that provide rich research-based information resources linking to library books, journals, databases, scholarly articles, archives, and other available information. An extensive bibliography of those guides with relevant concepts or search queries offers users the means to further explore ways to improve campus culture and prevent sexual violence and other misconduct. These guides also frequently addressed broader cultural issues such as social justice, civil rights, public policy, inclusion, discrimination, and activism.

Examples of LibGuides include an extensive research guide on sexual violence, bystander behaviors, and domestic violence, showcasing Title IX and campus policies, legal resources, and case law; a course/study guide about scholarly activism in the 1960s linking to library search tools, subject guides, repositories of primary source materials, databases, and other catalogs; a subject/topic guide on the *#MeToo* movement distinguishing between related issues such as *MeToo* and *Time's Up* based on library collections; and a how-to guide on improving LGBTQ+ awareness among students and instructors. These guides not only highlight library collections but also present a broad range of curated resources, such as faculty- or student-led research projects; digitized student-created zines about sexual violence, consent, and rape culture; and infographics titled "Stop Silencing Victims" and "Start Talking about the Issues."

Engaging Social Movements against Campus Sexual Violence

Social engagement on sexual violence included the invocation of social media hashtags such as *#MeToo* as well as nationally recognized movements and activities like Denim Day, an event to raise awareness around sexual violence, and Take Back the Night, an event and organization dedicated to combating sexual and intimate partner violence. Of all institutions (n=140), forty-three webpages featured resources including social engagement on sexual violence.

In general, these resources might be divided into two broad categories based on their temporality in relation to sexual violence: proactive and reactive. Those that support research and activism related to sexual violence work to address systemic cultural issues, while those that direct survivors to other support channels respond to manifestations of those issues in the form of sexual violence. On another level, all of these resources are in one way or another reacting to the epidemic of sexual violence, and their provision exceeds the traditional professional boundaries of academic librarianship.

Links to Existing Library Collections Related to Campus Sexual Violence

Supporting resources included links to relevant library information sources, such as physical and electronic collections, archives, and other curations. Supporting resources were typically directional rather than content based, taking the form of search tips, links to generic databases and websites, and suggested readings without additional commentary. Of all retrieved webpages,

46 of 156 (29 percent) included at least one resource geared toward a specific demographic group. Most often, these resources addressed sexual violence in the context of race, gender identity, or sexual orientation. Notable outliers included one resource related to sexual violence in the military as well as one resource focused on the rights of the accused.

Variation among Religious Institutions

Resources provided by librarians at institutions with strong religious affiliations varied widely. Some mentioned related social movements such as *#MeToo* but did not specifically address sexual violence. One private college with a strong Reformed Baptist affiliation used relatively neutral language to describe women's activism:

> The mobilization of women throughout the past century and around the world has many causes. From voting and civil rights to *#MeToo* and '*the right to choose* [sic],' many women are prepared to come together and take a stand in response to issues they are passionate about.

Existing research indicates that an institution's religious affiliation may adversely affect the reporting experience for survivors of sexual violence. At the Mormon institution Brigham Young University, for example, students who report sexual violence may face repercussions based on the way the report is interpreted by the institution's spiritual leader (Brown 2016).

Others, however, provided links to campus sexual violence response resources and directly addressed campus rape culture. A LibGuide from an institution with a strong Lutheran affiliation, for example, described sexual assault as "a problem that has been with us for far too long." Another private college with a strong Christian affiliation featured an online, full-text sampling of student-created zines about sexual violence, consent, and rape culture housed at the library, which indicates that librarians and students at the institution are engaging in hands-on ways with the topic of sexual violence. One private university with a strong Christian affiliation focused specifically on sexual violence in religious contexts, providing a LibGuide on sexual misconduct perpetrated by faculty and clergy.

Discussion

The findings of this content analysis indicate that critical librarianship associated with critical information engagement entails both thinking about systems of knowledge, including our own, and taking concrete steps to put thought into action. Often, these steps fall at the intersection between the American Library Association's Core Values and the oppressive structures that have created vast gaps in financial, social, and educational privilege throughout the United States. An important part of critical librarianship lies in dispensing with the notion that libraries are neutral spaces and librarians neutral figures; those positions that tend to be seen as "neutral" are in fact "indicative of the status quo" (Ettarh 2014). Activities such as collection development and information provision, for example, entail the valuation and prioritization of certain voices and require librarians to make subjective decisions. However well informed, these decisions are always political. All communities are different, so the most effective forms of action will vary according to the community's composition, needs, and circumstances. In the absence of any one-size-fits-all solutions, librarians must work with the tools and knowledge at their disposal—and in order to ensure that sexual violence-related information resources are appropriate to their communities, the librarians who create them would be well advised to consider the multiple factors at play.

Challenges, Benefits, and Opportunities

Beyond acknowledging that campus sexual violence is a widespread problem that affects marginalized populations disproportionately, how can academic librarians work proactively to combat it—while respecting the limits of their qualifications? As information professionals who are intimately familiar with the workings of higher education, academic librarians may be most well suited to help foster a deeper understanding among students of academia's infrastructure—what Title IX is, what the Clery Act entails, which populations are most vulnerable to sexual violence, and why. However, as employees of institutions subject to Title IX regulations, many academic librarians are designated as mandatory reporters of sexual misconduct. This means that librarians cannot be a confidential source of support for students who disclose instances of sexual violence. Weiss and Lasky (2017) have noted that while Title IX's mandatory reporting policies ostensibly aim to facilitate reporting and increase institutional accountability, critics contend that they may put survivors at greater risk in the form of negative attention and bureaucratic duress. Further, the dictates of mandatory reporting may compromise student-faculty relations and "open discourse" in and outside of class, as awareness of faculty/staff disclosure obligations may silence students who wish to discuss incidents with a trusted person—but not necessarily with university officials with whom the students have no relationship.

Ettarh (2018) considers the concept of "job creep," which entails a gradual, often informal, extension of job duties over time (Van Dyne and Ellis 2004). A noteworthy example of job creep in public libraries is the increasing expectation that librarians be trained to administer Narcan in the event of an opioid overdose; this expectation stems from the overflow of opioid addiction beyond what the pool of trained professionals such as social workers and addiction specialists can handle. By the same token, the fact that librarians have taken it upon themselves to provide resources to sexual violence survivors may be a symptom of the extent to which more official channels may be outmatched by demand or otherwise inadequate (Pérez-Peña 2013). This possibility does not mean that librarians are wrong to provide such information resources, but as with Narcan administration, it speaks to the position of libraries in providing stopgap measures to systemic problems. As Skinner and Gross (2017) have emphasized, academic librarians are not typically credentialed in psychological or social welfare nor in law enforcement. Under Title IX, they are required to report any incidences of sexual misconduct disclosed to them by members of their institution. They must be aware not only of their legal obligations but also of ethical and professional boundaries related to the topic of campus sexual violence.

The practice of creating LibGuides—which are among the most common forms of information academic librarians create as a means of meeting information needs (Hicks 2015)—has been called into question on several points, including LibGuides' tendency to isolate and decontextualize research tools and information (Sundin 2008) and to limit users' scope of research to sources listed on a given LibGuide, and to position librarians as the ultimate arbiters of what may or may not be useful in a given area (Hicks 2015). However, Drabinski (2019) writes that critical librarianship is largely about "surfacing" the many "structures that produce us as librarians, our spaces as libraries, our patrons as students, faculty, and the public" (49). These structures include both material structures that often remain unseen, such as the machines and networks that facilitate Internet connections, and ideological structures, such as the politics and assumptions that guide us unconsciously as we develop, evaluate, organize, seek, and use information.

Limitations notwithstanding, the existence of the dozens of LibGuides on sexual violence that this search retrieved at the very least suggests that many librarians acknowledge the pervasiveness of campus rape culture and recognize it as a barrier to student academic performance and success. Limited though they may be, they effectively "surface" a cultural epidemic and bring to it both visibility and information resources that may help in both preemptive and remediating ways—that is, they direct those conducting research on the issue to relevant resources, and they direct those affected by sexual violence to relevant resources. In doing so, they help to offset the many institutional and cultural silencing mechanisms that often keep survivors from reporting sexual violence, seeking help, or understanding that what has been done to them is violence in the first place (Manne 2018).

In addition to the retrieved results that incorporated social engagement related to sexual violence, this study's search queries turned up twenty-two results that incorporated social engagement on issues unrelated to sexual violence. These webpages promoted content framed in relation to contemporaneous news/social media/activism against other social injustice or violence than sexual assault, such as Black History Month, women's rights, an exhibition exploring LGBTQ+ history and scholarly activism based on library archives and collections, and resources for immigrants and undocumented students. The presence of resources related to race, sexuality, dis/ability, and immigration status indicates some sense among academic librarians that addressing such topics is among their job duties—and yet, only 26 percent of the resources on sexual violence provided information that accounted for demographic differentiation in sexual assault frequency and outcomes. This discrepancy suggests that however well intended these information resources are, they do not take an intersectional approach to the topic of sexual violence.

For critically invested academic librarians, the development of information resources such as LibGuides that are dedicated to the problem of sexual assault and campus rape might be considered "surfacing" cultural and institutional structures that too often enforce silence and provide inadequate support to survivors. However, critical librarianship entails intersectional approaches that understand race, class, sexuality, gender identity, and indigeneity as factors that manifest in and structure all social relations. Given the high rate of sexual violence incidence against racial and sexual minorities as well as individuals with disabilities (Fedina, Holmes, and Backes 2018)—and particularly individuals who fall under more than one of those categories, such as transgender people of color—the resources librarians create should provide targeted support in corresponding proportions. For instance, the organization End Rape on Campus (EROC) reports that 18.8 percent of Black women, 24.4 percent of mixed-race women, and 34.1 percent of American Indian/Alaska Native women experience rape in their lifetime, compared to 17.7 percent of White women (EROC n.d.).

In the context of academic libraries, many librarians have built-in opportunities to engage themselves and the populations they serve in this type of intersectional analysis when teaching. Some librarians have adopted critical approaches to information literacy instruction, which can take myriad forms. Such approaches might involve research instruction sessions that ask students to reflect on the political nature of Library of Congress Subject Headings, discussions of historic underrepresentation in the literary canon, examinations of the "invisible labor" in the digital humanities (Opel and Simeone 2019), or any number of activities that analyze structures of power and privilege in relation to knowledge and information. Digital literacy instruction is another potential venue for interventions, as librarians might use these opportunities to help students understand nonphysical forms of sexual violence such as doxxing, cyberstalking, and cyber harassment—particularly as campuses continue to increase online course offerings and degree programs.

Limitations

Devised on the basis of their feasibility, the research methods employed here may exclude alternative library efforts to combat campus sexual violence. One main limitation of this study is its necessarily narrow approach: only those efforts at combating sexual violence that take the form of documented, discoverable online resources. As the product of a prominent, well-established company with a wide reach and robust development team, Springshare's Lib-Guides may be better indexed and more discoverable to Google than blog posts on individual university webpages or other "homegrown" formats—to say nothing of events or materials with no digital component or online after-life. It is therefore difficult to identify and assess what other measures librarians may be taking, formally or informally, to combat campus sexual violence. Further, it is impossible to know the extent to which Google's algorithms and customized ranking functions affected the retrieval of results on the individual machines, browsers, or IP addresses used in the search process. The prevalence of Google as a first resort for information searches among students (Head and Eisenberg 2011), however, made it the most viable option in spite of the likely variability among individual users' results.

Future Study

Additional analysis might examine factors such as the prevalence of fraternities and sororities on campus, institutions' demographic makeup, stature or scope of athletic programs, rural versus urban setting, and the presence or absence of federal funding. For greater permanence and searchability, moreover, librarians who engage in efforts to develop relevant sexual violence–related resources might also consider archiving their materials in institutional repositories where possible, or other long-term storage channels. Further analysis of practices at institutions with religious affiliations might shed further light on the particular challenges of sexual violence prevention and response in those contexts; at the Mormon institution Brigham Young University, for example, students who report sexual assault may face repercussions based on the way the report is interpreted by the institution's spiritual leader (Brown 2016).

Conclusion

It is hoped that this study has made a generative contribution to the limited body of research on the distinctive and critical roles of librarians in combating campus rape culture; provided an analysis of the existing climate and resources that account for structural inequalities and demographic specificities related to campus sexual violence; and considered ways in which the notion of critical librarianship might be brought to bear in ongoing and future efforts to counter campus rape culture and support survivors of sexual violence. Beyond a discussion of the challenges and limitations of library information provision, informational support, and social engagement, it has sought to propose actionable tactics for working proactively to counter campus rape culture through everyday professional practice such as information literacy and evidence-based research instruction. This study's findings emphasize the fact, moreover, that campus sexual violence is not a monolith. Its effects may manifest differently according to variables such as religious affiliation, sexual orientation, gender identity, dis/ability, race, veteran status, and more. Whatever measures academic librarians ultimately take in combating campus sexual violence, therefore, accounting for demographic differentials is a crucial step in providing effective support.

Acknowledgments

We acknowledge with gratitude the assistance of Catherine Price, a graduate research assistant at Emporia State University, in gathering the initial data.

References

Aabø, Svanhild, and Ragnar Audunson. 2012. "Use of Library Space and the Library as Place." *Library & Information Science Research* 34, no. 2 (April): 138–149. https://doi.org/10.1016/j.lisr.2011.06.002.

Aabø, Svanhild, Ragnar Audunson, and Andreas Vårheim. 2010. "How Do Public Libraries Function as Meeting Places?" *Library & Information Science Research* 32, no. 1 (January): 16–26. https://doi.org/10.1016/j.lisr.2009.07.008.

AAU (Association of American Universities). 2019. "Report on the AAU Campus Climate Survey on Sexual Assault and Misconduct." https://www.aau.edu/sites/default/files/AAU-Files/Key-Issues/Campus-Safety/FULL_2019_Campus_Climate_Survey.pdf.

Brown, Sarah. 2016. "A Sex-Assault Case at Brigham Young Puts Honor Codes in the Spotlight." *The Chronicle of Higher Education,* April 18. https://www.chronicle.com/article/A-Sex-Assault-Case-at-Brigham/236145.

Campoamor, Danielle. 2018. "I'm Not a Sexual Assault 'Survivor'—I'm a Victim. It's Time to Reclaim the Term Victim." *Harper's BAZAAR,* May 21. https://www.harpersbazaar.com/culture/features/a20138398/stop-using-survivor-to-describe-sexual-assault-victims.

Cantor, David, Bonnie Fisher, Reanne Townsend, and Samuel Peterson. 2017. "Gender Identity and Sexual Victimization: What Does the AAU Survey on Sexual Assault and Misconduct Reveal about Gender Minorities?" Panel presentation at the 2017 annual meeting of the American Society of Criminology, Philadelphia, November 16.

CDC (Centers for Disease Control and Prevention). 2019. "Preventing Sexual Violence." Last modified March 12, 2019. https://www.cdc.gov/violence prevention/sexualviolence/fastfact.html.

Donat, Patricia L. N., and John D'Emilio. 1992. "A Feminist Redefinition of Rape and Sexual Assault: Historical Foundations and Change." *Journal of Social Issues* 48, no. 1 (Spring): 9–22. https://doi.org/10.1111/j.1540-4560.1992 .tb01154.x.

Drabinski, Emily. 2019. "What Is Critical about Critical Librarianship?" *Art Libraries Journal* 44, no. 2 (April): 49–57. https://doi.org/10.1017/alj.2019.3.

EROC (End Rape on Campus). n.d. "Survivor of Color Prevalence Rates." Retrieved October 1, 2019, from https://endrapeoncampus.org/new-page-3.

Ettarh, Fobazi. 2014. "Making a New Table: Intersectional Librarianship." *In the Library with the Lead Pipe,* July 2. http://www.inthelibrarywiththelead pipe.org/2014/making-a-new-table-intersectional-librarianship-3.

Ettarh, Fobazi. 2018. "Vocational Awe and Librarianship: The Lies We Tell Ourselves." *In the Library with the Lead Pipe,* January 10. http://www.inthe librarywiththeleadpipe.org/2018/vocational-awe.

Farkas, Meredith. 2017. "Never Neutral: Critical Librarianship and Technology." *American Libraries*, January 3. https://americanlibrariesmagazine.org/2017 /01/03/never-neutral-critlib-technology.

Fedina, Lisa, Jennifer L. Holmes, and Bethany L. Backes. 2018. "Campus Sexual Assault: A Systematic Review of Prevalence Research from 2000 to 2015." *Trauma, Violence, and Abuse* 19, no. 1 (January): 76–93. https://doi.org/10 .1177/1524838016631129.

Giraldi, Ashley, and Elizabeth Monk-Turner. 2017. "Perception of Rape Culture on a College Campus: A Look at Social Media Posts." *Women's Studies International Forum* 62 (May–June): 116–124. https://doi.org/10.1016/j .wsif.2017.05.001.

Harris, Roma, and Patricia Dewdney. 1994. *Barriers to Information: How Formal Help Systems Fail Battered Women.* Westport, CT: Greenwood.

Head, Alison J., and Michael B. Eisenberg. 2011. "How College Students Use the Web to Conduct Everyday Life Research." *First Monday* 16, no. 4 (April). https://doi.org/10.5210/fm.v16i4.3484.

Hicks, Alison. 2015. "LibGuides: Pedagogy to Oppress?" *Hybrid Pedagogy,* April 26. https://hybridpedagogy.org/libguides-pedagogy-to-oppress.

Jozkowski, Kristen N., and Jacquelyn D. Wiersma-Mosley. 2017. "The Greek System: How Gender Inequality and Class Privilege Perpetuate Rape Culture." *Family Relations* 66, no. 1 (April): 89–103. https://doi.org/10.1111 /fare.12229.

Linder, Chris, and Jessica C. Harris. 2017. "Power-Conscious Approaches to Campus Sexual Violence." *Inside Higher Education*, December 1. https:// www.insidehighered.com/advice/2017/12/01/understanding-role-power -plays-campus-sexual-assaults-essay.

Mann, Thomas. 2001. "The Importance of Books, Free Access, and Libraries as Places—and the Dangerous Inadequacy of the Information Science

Paradigm." *The Journal of Academic Librarianship* 27, no. 4 (July): 268–281. https://doi.org/10.1016/S0099-1333(01)00214-2.

Manne, Kate. 2018. *Down Girl: The Logic of Misogyny.* New York: Oxford University Press.

Opel, Dawn, and Michael Simeone. 2019. "The Invisible Work of the Digital Humanities Lab: Preparing Graduate Students for Emergent Intellectual and Professional Work." *Digital Humanities Quarterly* 13, no. 2.. http://www.digitalhumanities.org/dhq/vol/13/2/000421/000421.html.

Papendick, Michael, and Gerd Bohner. 2017. "'Passive Victim—Strong Survivor'? Perceived Meaning of Labels Applied to Women Who Were Raped." *PLoS ONE* 12, no. 5 (May): 1–21. https://doi.org/10.1371/journal.pone.0177550.

Pérez-Peña, Richard. 2013. "College Groups Connect to Fight Sexual Assault." *The New York Times*, March 19. https://www.nytimes.com/2013/03/20/education/activists-at-colleges-network-to-fight-sexual-assault.html.

RAINN (Rape, Abuse, and Incest National Network). n.d. "Key Terms and Phrases." Retrieved October 1, 2019, from https://www.rainn.org/articles/key-terms-and-phrases.

Schwark, Sandra, and Gerd Bohner. 2019. "Sexual Violence—'Victim' or 'Survivor': News Images Affect Explicit and Implicit Judgments of Blame." *Violence Against Women* 25, no. 12 (January): 1491–1509. https://doi.org/10.1177/1077801218820202.

Shoham, Snunith, and Liat Klain-Gabbay. 2019. "The Academic Library: Structure, Space, Physical and Virtual Use." *The Journal of Academic Librarianship* 45, no. 5 (September): 1–10. https://doi.org/10.1016/j.acalib.2019.102053.

Skinner, Julia, and Melissa Gross. 2017. "The ISSAS Model: Understanding the Information Needs of Sexual Assault Survivors on College Campuses." *College & Research Libraries* 78, no. 1 (January): 23–34. https://doi.org/10.5860/crl.78.1.23.

Sundin, Olof. 2008. "Negotiations on Information-Seeking Expertise: A Study of Web-Based Tutorials for Information Literacy." *Journal of Documentation* 64, no. 1 (January): 24–44. http://dx.doi.org/10.1108/00220410810844141.

Van Dyne, Linn, and Jennifer B. Ellis. 2004. "Job Creep: A Reactance Theory Perspective on Organizational Citizenship Behavior as Over-Fulfillment of Obligations." In *The Employment Relationship: Examining Psychological and Contextual Perspectives,* edited by Jacqueline A-M. Coyle-Shapiro, Lynn M. Shore, M. Susan Taylor, and Lois E. Tetrick, 181–205. Oxford: Oxford University Press.

Washington, Patricia A. 2001. "Disclosure Patterns of Black Female Sexual Assault Survivors." *Violence Against Women* 7, no. 11 (November): 1254–1283. https://doi.org/10.1177/10778010122183856.

Weiss, Karen G., and Nicole V. Lasky. 2017. "Mandatory Reporting of Sexual Misconduct at College: A Critical Perspective." *Journal of School Violence* 16, no. 3 (July): 259–270. https://doi.org/10.1080/15388220.2017.1318575.

Westbrook, Lynn. 2015. "'I'm Not a Social Worker': An Information Service Model for Working with Patrons in Crisis." *The Library Quarterly* 85, no. 1 (January): 6–25. https://doi.org/10.1086/679023.

White, Jacquelyn W., and Paige H. Smith. 2004. *A Longitudinal Perspective on Physical and Sexual Intimate Partner Violence Against Women.* Washington, DC: National Institute of Justice.

CHAPTER SEVEN

Bringing Trauma-Informed Practices to Underserved Patrons at University Libraries

Monte-Angel Richardson, Stephanie Rosen,
Marna M. Clowney-Robinson, and
Danica San Juan

Introduction

Historically, librarians have assisted underserved patrons with locating services to meet their informational needs (Westbrook 2015). Homeless patrons, first-generation students, faculty, staff, and members of marginalized communities benefit from librarians' ability to interface between their responsibilities and those of other professions, such as social work (Morris et al. 2016). Service professionals around the world are adopting trauma-informed (TI) approaches in hopes of improving the psychological and emotional well-being of people using their facilities. A TI approach is based on knowledge of the impact of trauma, aimed at ensuring environments and services are welcoming and engaging for service recipients and staff (Trauma Informed Oregon 2019). A TI approach is sensitive to the diverse experiences that may induce trauma responses in individuals based on race, ethnicity, socioeconomic status, sexual orientation, and gender.

University libraries serve a diverse demographic of patrons, including undergraduate, graduate, and doctoral students from a variety of backgrounds.

Aside from students, university libraries serve patrons who reside within the community. These libraries also serve faculty and staff, including research assistants, tenured faculty, lecturers, administrative staff, and graduate student instructors. Among patrons, there is great diversity regarding ethnicity, race, socioeconomic status, gender, sexual orientation, citizenship status, ability status, and mental health. At the University of Michigan (UM) in 2018, the number of people who walked through the doors of all libraries was 397,183,800 (UM Library 2018). Given the role librarians have historically taken to meet patrons' needs within and outside of the library, and the diversity of patrons served, TI approaches would be beneficial to implement in the university library setting. Although there exist diversity and equity courses to train staff on interacting with patrons, no training presently exists regarding TI practices within university libraries.

To this end, the UM Library has developed the first known TI training program to take place at a university library. During the 2018–2019 academic year, the Trauma Informed Librarianship (TIL) initiative conducted extensive research regarding the need for TI practices at university libraries, followed by the development of a training program piloted with library staff. Research on the needs of staff and training activities were developed for the purpose of building this TI training program. In this chapter, we will present this data and training materials, along with a general discussion of the need for TI approaches at university libraries. We will approach the topic by addressing library staff's identities, experiences, and backgrounds that influence their engagement with patrons. It is hoped that this chapter can help guide future TI initiatives taking place at university libraries.

The Movement toward Trauma-Informed Care

Individual trauma refers to an event, series of events, or set of circumstances perceived by an individual to be harmful or life threatening (SAMHSA 2019). Trauma can impact every area of human functioning, and an individual's experience of trauma has been shown to increase the risk of mental and physical illness, including depression, addiction, liver disease, diabetes and asthma, suicide attempts, and premature death (Morris et al. 2016). The increased understanding of trauma's impact on the individual is rooted in the experiences of U.S. veterans. The study of their trauma symptoms including flashbacks, intrusive thoughts, nightmares, excessive sweating, and racing heart rate led to the development of the post-traumatic stress disorder (PTSD) mental health diagnosis (Van der Kolk 2014).

Since then, trauma has been identified as impacting more than the veteran population and is listed as a public health concern by the Center for Disease Control (Dahlberg and Mercy 2009). Studies such as the Adverse Childhood Experiences Studies (ACES) expanded the definition of trauma to include experiences such as childhood abuse, neglect, historical trauma from political violence, and sexual abuse (SAMHSA 2018). The prevalence of these experiences was also uncovered in ACES findings, where of the 17,000 adults studied from 1995 to 1997, almost two-thirds reported at least one ACE (Felitti et al. 1998). Based on these findings and many others, addressing trauma is now viewed as the expectation rather than the exception not only in health care settings but in communities.

The TI approach was developed to recognize and increase awareness of trauma as it may manifest in clients accessing social services. The Substance Abuse and Mental Health Services Administration (SAMHSA) lists four assumptions of a trauma-informed program, organization, or system: (1) realizes the widespread impact of trauma and understands potential paths for recovery; (2) recognizes the signs and symptoms of trauma in clients, families, staff, and others involved with the system; (3) responds by fully integrating knowledge about trauma into policies, procedures, and practices; and (4) seeks to actively resist retraumatization (SAMHSA, 2014). Applied to university libraries, this approach aims to improve the psychological and emotional well-being of patrons and staff accessing library services and using these spaces.

Trauma-Informed Practices at Libraries

The interest in and need for TI libraries are growing (Doktor 2016; Johnson 2018; Nienow and Zettervall 2018). At least three libraries across the United States have offered training to educate staff on implementing a TI approach: the San Francisco (SAMHSA 2017), Denver (Vaccarelli 2015), and Folsom public libraries (Doktor 2018). Based on the four assumptions of a TI approach, these libraries trained staff in identifying the impact of trauma, recognizing the signs and symptoms in patrons and staff, responding by integrating knowledge about trauma into library policies and practices, and actively resisting retraumatization.

One reason why a TI approach is only present at a handful of libraries is due to concerns expressed by library staff of being too involved in patrons' lives (Doktor 2018). Libraries receiving pushback for incorporating TI approaches may benefit from connecting to Whole-Person Librarianship (WPL) and universal design methodologies. WPL is a movement to reveal how social work and librarianship values overlap and encourage both professions to work in tandem to meet the needs of patrons (Nienow and Zettervall 2018). Examples of what WPL has accomplished include providing case management and community resources to homeless patrons, providing training on how to intervene during mental health crises, advocating for TI library policies, and educating staff and community members about marginalized patrons (District of Columbia Public Library 2014; Evanston Public Library 2017; Vaccarelli 2015).

Universal design pertains to the design of buildings, programs, services, or environments to make them accessible to all people, regardless of age, ability status, gender identity, or other factors (Wilson 2017). The aim of universal design is to create accessibility to the maximum potential rather than meeting minimum standards. Examples of universal design approaches include maximizing accessibility to buildings by ensuring the presence of elevators for persons with disability, prayer rooms for individuals with varying faiths, and gender accessible restrooms for people with diverse gender identities.

Despite the embrace of WPL and even universal design methods in library spaces, there is presently a gap in the literature regarding the implementation of the TI approach at university libraries. To describe trauma and TI as it pertains to library settings, some basic definitions and library-specific examples are provided in Table 7.1.

The Role of Library Staff

The focus of present TI efforts at UM libraries is on equipping front-facing staff with skills and practice serving patrons in potentially retraumatizing scenarios. Library front-facing staff are defined as those who interact directly with patrons, either face to face or online (Robinson 2005). This includes those who work in circulation, reference, and operate online services such as the Ask a Librarian online interface, where patrons can communicate with library staff in real time over instant message, text message, or phone. Front-facing staff include both full- and part-time employees and may include university students. Staff represent diverse gender, sexual orientation, race, ethnicity, ability, mental health, and socioeconomic identities. As such, the needs of front-facing staff are intersectional and varied.

Needs and Experiences of Library Staff

Research has revealed that, by addressing staff needs and implicit biases, library patrons can be more effectively served (Burns and Green 2019; Hines 2017; Westbrook 2015). However, little research exists regarding the needs of front-facing university library staff. To address this gap, we conducted a needs assessment based on the responses, feedback, and evaluations provided by UM Library staff who participated in several events during the winter semester of 2019, including stress reduction workshops, focus groups, and evaluations and feedback provided by staff attendees of TI training sessions. These data sources were combined with results from a literature review conducted to identify sources regarding relevant topics such as disability accommodations in the library, staff-patron interactions, coworker interactions, supervisor and staff interactions, and university

Table 7.1   Trauma Terms and the Library

Term	Definition	Example
Burnout	The physical and emotional exhaustion that workers can experience when they have low job satisfaction and feel powerless and overwhelmed at work (Smullens 2015).	Nighttime library staff often feel that the differences in their schedules leave little time or ability to participate in wellness and self-care activities.
Gatekeeping	The activity of controlling, and usually limiting, general access to something (Matteson, Chittock, and Mease 2015).	In a 2019 needs assessment, UM front-facing library staff noted a difference between what they can do and what they want to do to help patrons, using licensing agreements and limited access to open source information as examples.
Imposter syndrome	A psychological pattern in which a person doubts their accomplishments and has a persistent internalized fear of being exposed as a "fraud" (Mullangi and Jagsi 2019).	Many individuals within the university setting report experiencing imposter syndrome. Scholars believe that imposter syndrome is but a symptom of institutional inequity, and that promoting equitable representation in leadership positions is an appropriate treatment.
Microaggressions	The everyday verbal, nonverbal, and environmental slights or insults, intentional or unintentional, which communicate derogatory or negative messages to target persons based on their marginalized group membership (Moore and Alabi 2018).	In a library-initiated study of social influences on patron's experiences, several interviewees reported witnessing or experiencing a microaggression at the University of Michigan.

(*continued*)

Table 7.1   *(continued)*

Term	Definition	Example
Vicarious trauma	The emotional residue of exposure that individuals have from working with people as they are hearing their trauma stories and become witnesses to their pain, fear, and terror that trauma survivors have endured (Trippany et al. 2004).	University libraries have offered refuge to individuals escaping or experiencing a crisis, which can result in vicarious trauma for library staff. At the University of Michigan, students took shelter during an active shooter threat lasting over three hours (Rahal 2019). Without proper addressal and aftercare, such an experience could result in vicarious trauma for on-duty library staff.

library climate. The combination of these sources helped determine the criticality of each identified need. Similar needs were combined into larger categories.

Table 7.2 outlines the needs articulated by staff. These needs fall into four main categories: (1) organizational restructuring to incorporate TI policies and procedures; (2) increased TI-related training and educational opportunities for staff; (3) recognition of differing TI needs of patrons and staff based on identities; and (4) greater availability of resources and library spaces for patrons and staff. These categories are reflected in the table, including specific examples of needs related to each. Staff largely expressed a desire for a library-specific TI pedagogy incorporating multiple spheres of library life, including interactions between patrons and staff, methods of addressing trauma-inducing safety concerns, emergency response and preparedness, and knowledge of trauma's impact on the body and mind. The development of such a pedagogy was described as difficult due to uneven participation from staff in the development and adoption of the TI approach. Front-facing library staff felt that managerial and male library staff were not participating in these conversations. Staff also described a need for increased educational opportunities regarding the TI approach, particularly concerning their interactions with patrons and addressing self-care for themselves by understanding the impact of vicarious trauma and burnout. This need was the impetus for the development of the trauma-informed training program at UM libraries.

Table 7.2 Front-Facing Staff Need Assessment Results

Need	Causes	Consequences	Difficulty to Correct	Criticality (1–5)
Training on how staff can better interact with patrons in trauma-informed (TI) ways.	Staff and/or patron mental health issues. Lack of empathy and self-regulation training. Lack of training regarding trauma and TI approaches.	Patron dissatisfaction. Burnout. Vicarious trauma transferred to staff or others. Referring out to other entities because staff do not know how to address trauma responses in patrons.	Moderate	5
Incorporating TI approaches into the library's organizational culture.	Trouble determining who at the library should be responsible for leading the implantation of TI initiatives. Some sectors of library staff seen as more involved with these than others, which creates stagnation in development.	Disconnect between managerial and front-facing library staff goals. Lack of support for front-facing staff, low morale, burnout, and vicarious trauma.	Difficult	5
Variety of options for serving patrons with differing needs and identities.	Lack of awareness, education, and training. Resources seen as unavailable. Overwhelming and diverse number of patrons accessing university libraries.	Lack of services and policies sensitive to the needs of nonstudent populations.	Difficult	5

(continued)

Table 7.2 (continued)

Need	Causes	Consequences	Difficulty to Correct	Criticality (1–5)
Addressing ways that the academic setting can be retraumatizing.	Cultural norm of resulting to calling police when there is danger. Lack of knowledge from staff on how to respond to a crisis or emergency.	Lack of understanding between patrons and staff. Causes some patrons and staff to feel unsafe and unprotected within the library.	Difficult	5
Increased amount of welcoming spaces.	Busy work schedule: staff too busy to connect with coworkers. Lack of managerial support for policy changes leading to increased space.	Lack of appropriate signage or spaces where patrons can rest and relax. Lack of accessible spaces for patrons with TI needs. Lack of spaces for coworkers to reach out and connect with one another.	Moderate	4
Recognizing evening staff needs.	Lack of communication with evening staff. Fewer staff that work evenings. Less resources available in evenings.	Disconnect between daytime and evening staff. Evening staff turnover.	Moderate	4
Ability to freely share resources.	Website, journal, and publishing companies access restrictions.	Discrepancies between what staff can do and what they want to do to serve patrons and provide them with accessible information.	Moderate/ Difficult	3

Staff also recognized a need for better understanding of the differing needs of patron populations, and many noted that the needs of nonstudent patrons were often ignored. The needs of homeless patrons were considered especially important, and library staff noted that recognition of the trauma responses in patrons of different cultures, races, and ethnicities was something they knew little about. Lastly, the staff identified a need for a greater amount of resources and freedom in sharing information with patrons and each other. They noted that lack of signage and available spaces for patrons to decompress was a hindrance to TI.

Implementing a Trauma-Informed Training

Based on the need identified by staff for increased TI-related educational opportunities, training sessions were piloted with UM Library staff. The purpose of these training sessions was to provide introductory information about trauma and the TI approach. The secondary goal was to provide experiential learning opportunities, allowing staff to apply these concepts to their roles. Here we list several components of the training. These activities can be used to address, understand, and work through TI-related experiences and situations that impact the staff's ability to serve patrons.

Modeling TI

Significant efforts were made to model to participants what a TI experience looks like. Through modeling, it was hoped that staff could begin to conceptualize how to modify meetings, training sessions, and spaces to be inclusive of patrons with TI needs. Modeling began at the start of the training when staff were asked to identify themselves by their name, pronouns, title, role at the library, access needs, and knowledge of TI. Asking staff about their access needs comes from the universal design approach and provides an opportunity for staff to consider what they might need to effectively engage in the training while allowing facilitators to provide the necessary accommodations. These needs are tied to identities that modify a participant's ability to engage in the meeting and could include preferring to get up and walk around during a meeting or requiring a gender-inclusive bathroom. During the training, facilitators employed techniques that conform with TI practice, including encouraging equitable sharing from participants, briefing participants on the length of time for the training, providing food and beverages, and making participants aware of any changes in the agenda ahead of time. Other examples of modeling included the provision of three- to five-minute "gentleness breaks" following each section, where staff were encouraged to stand, stretch, or participate in a prepared guided breathing or meditation activity.

Defining Trauma and TI

Once provided with initial definitions, participants were asked to provide their own examples of trauma and TI practice in their roles. Facilitated discussion began with opening questions to encourage staff to consider their perceptions of trauma, including: What comes to mind when you hear the words "trauma" and "trauma-informed"? What is trauma?, and How do you recognize it? These questions were asked to encourage participants to begin exploring their current conception of trauma and TI approaches and to draw knowledge from the experiences of those in the room. The facilitated conversation also encouraged participants to get to know each other, creating an environment where they felt safe sharing and were able to hold space for each other's perspectives.

Identifying Staff Trauma Responses

A portion of the training was dedicated to helping staff identify potentially retraumatizing situations and consider how they might respond. Activities such as What pushes your buttons? encouraged staff to reflect on their trauma responses that arise in the workplace and identify strategies for dealing with them. Staff were given time to complete the worksheet and then discuss their responses in small and large groups. Table 7.3 shows the format of this worksheet along with an example. This worksheet is an adaptation of the Hotspots worksheet developed by Trauma Informed Oregon (2019).

The process was then repeated for patrons and coworkers, with participants identifying areas that have been known to cause stress and potential trauma responses for these groups. The purpose of this activity was to encourage staff

Table 7.3   Identifying Hotspots and Strategies to Reduce Them: Participant Focus

What Pushes Your Buttons?	Why Is It Upsetting?	Is There a Reason It Happens?	Strategies to Reduce the Effect
Hearing "I need to see you" from a supervisor.	I feel I will get in trouble.	Need to share information privately.	I could ask my supervisor to instead let me know what the conversation will be about. For example, ask them to instead say, "I need to see you to tell you about an update to your project."
Reflection: Please share your feelings about this process with a partner and then with the group. Remember to be gentle with yourself.			

Table 7.4   Identifying Hotspots and Strategies to Reduce Them: Patron/ Coworker Focus

What Pushes Their Buttons?	Why Is It Upsetting?	Is There a Reason It Happens?	Strategies to Reduce the Effect
No available space for studying or working within the library.	Patrons feel they will not have a quiet place to prepare for finals or exams.	Not enough space in the library or waiting until the last minute to reserve.	Interpersonal level: Encourage patrons to reserve ahead of time, describing the process for doing this. Institutional level: Advocate to administrators to come up with creative solutions to create more space during times when more patrons visit the libraries (i.e., finals and midterms).
Reflection: Please share your feelings about this process with a partner and then with the group. Remember to be gentle with yourself.			

to walk in the shoes of their patrons and coworkers and begin considering alternative ways to interact that reduce such responses. By completing these activities in quick succession, participants were able to understand how both patrons and themselves share commonalities when it comes to stress and triggers. Table 7.4 provides the format for the patron/coworker-focused worksheet along with an example provided to prompt discussion.

Roleplay: Interacting with Patrons Using a Trauma Lens

To encourage experiential learning, facilitators composed several scenarios that may take place at the library that would require TI responses from staff. Roleplaying was conducted to give participants a chance to try out the TI skills learned during the training in scenarios relevant to their roles. Prior to the roleplaying, participants were given a trauma lens handout describing techniques for engaging with individuals in a TI manner. The handout was walked through as a large group with facilitators leading the discussion. Then, participants were given a scenario about an interaction they may encounter at the library. The scenarios were created from the composition of examples gathered from preexisting studies along with research conducted at UM libraries. Scenarios were presented by facilitators and then responded to by participants in pairs. Table 7.5 shows the trauma lens handout provided to

Table 7.5   Trauma Lens Activity

Signs of a Trauma Response

- *Hypervigilance*—On the lookout for threats that are either unlikely or exaggerated, such as shutting in to avoid an "attack," sitting near an exit to escape, or sitting with the back to the wall so that no one can sneak behind.
- *Hopelessness*—Believing nothing will ever get better and there's nothing that can improve the situation.
- *Numbing*—Having difficulty with experiencing positive or negative feelings, i.e., happiness, sadness, and anger.
- *Helplessness*—A negative view of the future, i.e., "I'm doomed" or "I'll never graduate."
- *Anger/rage*—Overreacting to situations and projecting anger onto another person, such as when a book cannot be found or there is not enough space in the library.
- *Anxiety*—Can appear as sensitivity to environmental sights, sounds, etc., lack of sleep, or overthinking.
- *Mood changes*—May go from feeling angry, to apologetic, to happy within a short time span.
- *Depression*—Can appear as a slowing down of the person's movements or speech, combined with hopeless thoughts, irregular sleep or eating patterns, and increased isolation from others or activities once enjoyed.
- *Isolation*—The individual retreats from intimate involvement with people they know or chooses to only associate with a select few.
- *Suicidality*—Individual expresses a desire to stop living verbally, or ceases engaging in the activities needed to live (eating, sleeping, tending to commitments and relationships).

Things to Say	Things to Do
Ask open-ended questions (Questions requiring a full answer rather than yes/no. Ex: Questions beginning with "what" or "how" rather than "do.") Express empathy ("I understand why you might feel that way.") Listen reflectively ("I hear you saying that you feel afraid.") Brainstorm an accommodation ("I want us to work together to make you more comfortable.")	Welcome patrons and ensure they feel supported. Ensure healthy interpersonal boundaries. Manage conflict appropriately. Keep consistent schedules and procedures Offer sufficient notice/preparation when changes are necessary. Maintain communication that is consistent, open, respectful, and compassionate.

Do	Don't
Summarize ("You're worried about not having space to complete your work in the library, and this is making you afraid of not passing your class. We're going to work together to find a space that works for you.")	Be aware of how an individual's culture affects how they perceive trauma, safety, and privacy.
Invite conversation.	Demand eye contact.
Allow for silence.	Get too close.
Allow expression of emotions.	Talk too much.
Ask, "What can I do for you now?"	Ask too many questions.
Ask, "What has brought you comfort in the past?"	Make promises you cannot keep ("I'll make sure you are safe.")
Reflect and clarify to be sure you understand.	Use platitudes ("This will make you stronger.")
Offer options to feeling better.	Touch without spoken permission.
Ask, "What should I ask you?"	Talk about your own traumatic experiences.
	Ask the person to talk about the traumatic incident(s).

TRY IT ON YOUR OWN

1. Find a partner.
2. Using an example, roleplay an interaction where one person is the patron and the other is the staff.
3. Provide feedback on how it went.
4. Switch roles and repeat steps 2–4.

LARGE GROUP SHARE-OUT?

- How did it go?
- What went well?
- What was hard?

SCENARIO

You are working at the circulation desk when a patron named Mark whom you have met with on several occasions asks to speak with you in private. Mark is a nonstudent member of the community, and you believe he may be homeless due to his appearance and the amount of time he spends in the library. Mark feels he can trust you based on conversations you've had in the past when he confided about his experience of being involved in a car crash due to a drunk driver. From the first time you met with Mark, you explained that he could call an agency number that would put him in direct contact with someone who could provide further support if he has emotional difficulty. However, when he attempted to call one night, no one was available despite what you previously described. Instead, Mark is directed by an operator to either use his local emergency room if he perceives his situation to be a crisis or wait for someone on call to contact him. The inconsistency between what you told him and what happens when he called is making Mark feel unsafe and vulnerable. He shares his frustration with you.

1. Based on the limited information provided in this illustration, how might Mark's past traumatic experience affect his reaction to not receiving the care he was told he would receive?

2. In what ways could Mark's potential homeless status impact his recovery from trauma?

Outside of the referrals you could offer, how would you respond to Mark in this moment (refer to trauma lens handout)?

participants and the text box gives an example of a scenario provided to participants along with discussion questions.

Recommendations and Next Steps

This chapter aimed at defining and describing the implementation of TI practices at the University of Michigan libraries. It is hoped that these endeavors will be continued at university libraries. Based on this research, we offer the following recommendations for the development of future TI initiatives at university libraries. These suggestions come from the collection of preexisting data from a literature search and evaluative data collected from TI training sessions, focus groups, and the research team's self-reflection.

Conduct Research and Collect Data Related to Trauma and TI within University Library Settings

Following both training sessions, participants expressed a need for more library-specific examples of the TI approach. The training sessions conducted at the University of Michigan are the first of their kind to take place at a university library. As such, little data is presently available regarding the TI-related needs and experiences of those who frequent university libraries. To better understand and address the needs of university library staff and patrons, it is imperative that data be collected regarding the TI-related experiences of patrons and staff. Collected data could include user experience surveys, key informant interviews, and further staff and patron needs assessments. Because of the sensitive nature of this work, utmost care should be taken to follow both university protocols such as IRB review, and ethical research guidelines, including protecting participants' identities and keeping data secure.

Incorporate the TI Approach into Required Training for University Library Staff

The training sessions piloted at UM were offered as additional resources for library staff. TI initiatives would be more effective if they were incorporated into current training. Additionally, library staff expressed a desire to see the TI approach reflected in library organizational policies. Incorporating TI into training could be accomplished by including an overview of the TI approach and relevant strategies in established training sessions, or by training supervisors so they may bring these approaches to their employees.

Cover Other Areas of Trauma-Informed Practice Relevant to University Library Work

These introductory training sessions did not cover more complex topics related to trauma and TI. Once a preliminary understanding of the concepts is achieved, additional training components could be incorporated. Ideas for future training were gathered from library staff. One desired training session is focused on methods of advocating for TI changes within the university setting. Another training component desired by staff involved practice organizing an event based on the TI approach. The purpose of this component would be to train staff on the steps necessary to put together a TI event, including information on how to help outside groups planning on organizing events at the libraries. Staff also expressed interest in learning how to create TI spaces within the library. Drawing from the teachings of universal design, future training sessions could educate staff on how to create library spaces that are TI and maximize accessibility for all patrons and staff.

Conclusion

Libraries have historically been places where people of all kinds gather. University libraries serve patrons with a range of identities and experiences, including students, community members, faculty, staff, and outside visitors. In this chapter, we have chosen to focus on the ways that front-facing library staff can use TI practices in their roles. However, the TI approach is not effective in a vacuum. In order to be fully effective, it is imperative that university libraries take a TI approach when developing institutional policies. Collaborating with university departments aimed at inclusivity and diversity will increase the knowledge and scope of TI initiatives. Such partnerships should also extend outside of the university, considering the unique needs and experiences of nonstudent patrons.

As one of the few remaining public institutions where visitors are not required to purchase something to spend time, libraries are essential for underserved populations (Grady 2018). With growing recognition of the diverse traumas that impact individuals comes increased knowledge on how to support such people. It is now recognized that workers in all social settings are responsible not only for being aware of the traumatic experiences of their clients, but of themselves. The TI approach is one that is being expanded and applied to a range of social institutions, and it is imperative that university libraries do not fall behind. Library staff are in a unique position to support individuals who may have experienced trauma. It is vital that the library staff be trained in practices to avoid retraumatization and the spread of trauma to others. The existence of university libraries makes the case that free and easy access to information is important and that the most underserved groups in our society deserve as much access to information as anyone. If university libraries are to continue to fulfill this role, it is essential that they create an environment sensitive to the unique traumatic experiences of their patrons. In doing so, university libraries can continue to serve patrons as spaces providing a comfortable learning environment where patrons feel safe to not only learn, but convene to share culture, knowledge, and community.

References

Burns, Eric, and Kristin E. C. Green. 2019. "Academic Librarians' Experiences and Perceptions on Mental Illness Stigma and the Workplace." *College and Research Libraries* 80, no. 5: 1–30.

Dahlberg, Linda L., and James A. Mercy. 2009. "History of Violence as a Public Health Issue." *AMA Virtual Mentor* 11, no. 2 (February): 167–172.

District of Columbia Public Library. 2014. "Pioneering a New Approach to Serving Customers without Homes." *MLK Library Modernization* (blog), October 28. https://www.dclibrary.org/node/45604.

Doktor, Alicia. 2018. "Trauma-Informed Libraries." PowerPoint, Mountain Valley Library System Youth Services Regional Meeting, Folsom Public Library, March 16. https://www.acesconnection.com/g/trauma-informed-libraries /blog/trauma-informed-libraries-presentation-folsom-public-library-03 -16-2018.

Evanston Public Library. 2017. "Justine Janis: Library Social Worker." April 19. https://evanstonroundtable.com/main.asp?SectionID=4&SubSectionID =4&ArticleID=13534.

Felitti, Vincent J., Robert F. Anda, Dale Nordenberg, David F. Williamson, Alison M. Spitz, Valerie Edwards, Mary P. Koss, and James S. Marks. 1998. "Relationship of Childhood Abuse and Household Dysfunction to Many of the Leading Causes of Death in Adults: The Adverse Childhood Experiences (ACE) Study." *American Journal of Preventive Medicine* 14, no. 4: 245–258.

Grady, Constance. 2018. "Why Public Libraries Are Still Essential in 2018." *Vox*, July 24. https://www.vox.com/culture/2018/7/24/17603692/public-libraries -essential-forbes-amazon.

Hines, Samantha G. 2017. "Connecting Individuals with Social Services: The Academic Library's Role." *Collaborative Librarianship* 9, no. 2: 109–116.

Matteson, Miriam, Sharon Chittock, and David Mease. 2015. "In Their Own Words: Stories of Emotional Labor from the Library Workforce." *The Library Quarterly* 85, no. 1: 85–105.

Moore, Alanna A., and Jaena Alabi Moore. 2018. "Racial & LGBT Microaggressions: An Introduction for Library Leaders." PowerPoint slides 14–38. http://www.ala.org/llama/sites/ala.org.llama/files/content/3-18-15%20 Revised%20slides.pdf.

Morris, Matthew C., Natalie Hellman, James L. Abelson, and Uma Rao. 2016. "Cortisol, Heart Rate, and Blood Pressure as Early Markers of PTSD Risk: A Systematic Review and Meta-Analysis." *Clinical Psychology Review* 49, 79–91.

Mullangi, Samyukta, and Reshma Jagsi. 2019. "Imposter Syndrome: Treat the Cause, Not the Symptom." *The Journal of the American Medical Association* 322, no. 5: 403–404.

Nienow, Mary C., and Sara K. Zettervall. 2018. "Whole Person Librarianship: A Collaborative Model of Social Work and Librarianship." Council on Social Work Education 64th Annual Program Meeting, Orlando, November 10. https://mlismsw.files.wordpress.com/2018/11/cswe-2018-reduced -size.pdf.

Rahal, Sarah. 2019. "Popping Balloons Prompt 3 Hours of Active Shooter Panic at University of Michigan." *The Detroit News*, March 16. https://www.detroit news.com/story/news/local/michigan/2019/03/16/ann-arbor-university -michigan-shooting-reports/3188612002.

Robinson, Jackie. 2005. "Supporting Library Users with Disabilities—A Guide for Front-Line Staff." *Library Review* 54, no. 1: 68–69.

Smullens, Sara Kay. 2015. *Burnout and Self-Care in Social Work: A Guidebook for Students and Those in Mental Health and Related Professions*. Washington, DC. NASW Press.

Substance Abuse and Mental Health Service Administration. 2017. "SAMHSA Spotlight: San Francisco, California." Brochure. HHS Publication No. (SMA) 17-5019. https://store.samhsa.gov/product/Spotlight-Building-Resilient-and -Trauma-Informed-Communities-San-Francisco-CA-Aligning-the-Work force-to-Create-a-Trauma-Informed-System/SMA17-5019.

Substance Abuse and Mental Health Service Administration. 2018. "Infographic: 6 Guiding Principles to a Trauma-Informed Approach." SAMHSA. July 9. https://www.cdc.gov/cpr/infographics/6_principles_trauma_info.htm.

Substance Abuse and Mental Health Service Administration. 2019. "Trauma and Violence." August 2. https://www.samhsa.gov/trauma-violence.

Substance Abuse and Mental Health Service Administration, Health Services Administration. 2014. *SAMHSA's Concept of Trauma and Guidance for a Trauma-Informed Approach*. HHS Publication No. (SMA) 14-4884. Rockville, MD: Substance Abuse and Mental Health Services Administration.

Trauma Informed Oregon. 2019. "Identifying Hotspots Worksheet." https://trauma informedoregon.org/resource/identifying-hotspots-worksheet.

Trippany, Robyn L., Victoria E. White, and S. Allen Wilcoxon. 2004. "Preventing Vicarious Trauma: What Counselors Should Know When Working with Trauma Survivors." *Journal of Counseling & Development*, no. 82: 31–37.

Vaccarelli, Joe. 2015. "Denver Public Library's New On-Site Social Worker Settling into Job." *The Denver Post*, June 2. https://www.denverpost.com/2015/06 /02/denver-public-librarys-new-on-site-social-worker-settling-into-job.

Van der Kolk, Bessel A. 2014. *The Body Keeps the Score: Brain, Mind, and Body in the Healing of Trauma*. New York: Viking.

Westbrook, Lynn. 2018. "'I'm Not a Social Worker': An Information Service Model for Working with Patrons in Crisis." *Library Quarterly: Information, Community, Policy* 85, no. 1: 6–25.

CHAPTER EIGHT

Assisting Students Attending School after or during Incarceration

Bobbie Bushman and Dale Monobe

Introduction

Students attending school after a period of incarceration, or during incarceration, may not only require general rehabilitative support, but also transitional support and other reasonable accommodations from a campus library. It follows that having an accurate idea of the differences and similarities between academic library resources and services and those of jail or prison libraries better facilitates the success of these students. Unfortunately, misconceptions exist about the services that prison librarians provide (Nevada librarian, personal communication, August 1, 2019). Through interviews (see Appendix: Interview Questions for California, Nevada, and Idaho Librarians) with three prison librarians and an examination of the literature, the authors hope to counter these misconceptions and provide the academic librarian with information to help facilitate the academic success of formerly incarcerated students.

Correctional facility libraries, like libraries operating elsewhere, are built to provide resources and services to a community (the inmate population) rather than a university community or a municipality; however, they face additional restrictions and unique user needs. Library standards for adult correctional institutions (outlined in more detail below) provide guidance for incarcerated populations but have been challenging to apply for a number of reasons (ALA 2006). This is due in part to limited resources for inmates. Prisoner exposure to the Internet, for example, is limited or nonexistent. In addition, there are considerable restrictions on service: reference services are generally limited, and educational programing may not exist or may be restricted in what pedagogical tools and technology can be used (California librarian, personal communication, May 10, 2019; Nevada librarian, personal communication, August 1, 2019). Therefore, compared to what a campus library can provide, the jail or prison library has significant challenges in fully providing for the academic, career, and recreational needs of prisoners. These differences can be frustrating for academic librarians collaborating with, or hoping to collaborate with, a jail or prison library. Conversely, there may be psychological barriers, such as fear, hindering collaboration by academic librarians (Millsap 2018).

Visiting the campus library, formerly incarcerated students may not fully appreciate, or know, what unrestricted library resources and services are available to them, including physical and digital resources as well as Internet access. Moreover, these students may lack basic information search skills and/or the ability to ascertain the veracity of information or an information source (Nevada librarian, personal communication, August 1, 2019).

To address these information and literacy needs, practical ideas are suggested here. When implemented, these strategies may help better facilitate the academic success of students.

Academic, Legal, Career, and Recreational Information Needs of Prisoners

Prisoners and those who have been incarcerated have distinct information needs in terms of academic, legal, career, and recreational materials. In a study of Nigerian female prisoners, for example, findings revealed "that the information needs of prisoners covered medical information (98%), education/security information (97%), life after prison, spiritual and moral (86%), financial (84%), family/friends (82%), and legal issues (72%)" (Atanda and Ojei 2018, 1).

According to the American Library Association (ALA), prison libraries should uphold certain standards, including a minimum of five hours of library access per week for general population prisoners and one hour of library access each week for limited access population prisoners (ALA 2006). In research conducted in California, a prison librarian shared that inmates at one correctional facility were allowed to access the prison library collection for two hours each week (California librarian, personal communication, May 10, 2019). In addition to dictating how many librarians and library staff should be employed for each prison inmate, the ALA's library standards (ALA 2006) also provide recommendations for correctional library collections as shown in Table 8.1. In Idaho, the prison librarian reported that the library was open from 8:00 a.m. to 5:00 p.m. seven days a week (but closed during lunch), and twice a week during the evening. Inmates were allowed to stay a half an hour to one hour during these open times (Idaho Librarian, personal communication, May 21, 2019). The Nevada correctional librarian reported, "There is no physical access [to the library] absent a court order. The courts defined 'access' broadly and largely left it up to corrections' departments" (personal communication, August 1, 2019). So, access to prison libraries varies widely from state to state and facility to facility.

Further, the ALA recommends that prison libraries should be funded in such a way as to allow as much parity as possible with public libraries (California librarian, personal communication, May 10, 2019). According to the Idaho librarian, prisons are funded through correctional agencies through the state. The Idaho Department of Correction currently only funds one full-time MLS librarian per facility. Sometimes there are additional librarians who are funded through grant money (Idaho librarian, personal communication, May 21, 2019).

Although the ALA advocates the use of prison libraries for personal use, the law only requires prisoners have the right to legal information via a library.[1, 2] Because the legal library is the primary purpose of the prison library and access to it is mandated by law, the prison librarian in California states that many of the prisoners use their time at the library to gain substantial knowledge from reading over legal cases (California librarian, personal communication, Los Angeles, May 10, 2019).

Pursuing a college degree while behind bars can provide benefits, not only for the inmate student but for prison recidivism rates. At Lansing Correctional Facility in Kansas, for example, 420 inmates have taken college courses

Table 8.1   ALA Adult Correctional Institution Library Collection Standards

Population	No. of Titles
Books	Greater of 5,000 titles or 15 titles per inmate up to a maximum of 2,500 inmates
Magazines	Greater of 50 titles or 1 per 10 inmates
Newspapers	Number based on regions represented by inmate population
Audio recordings	100 titles plus 1 per 5 inmates
Video recordings	Greater of 20 titles or 1 per 30 inmates

Source: Library Standards for Correctional Institutions 2006, Chart 3.

since 2011, and 20 have earned degrees. Findings show that allowing inmates the opportunity to pursue college while incarcerated drastically reduces recidivism rates. Among those who entered the Kansas program, recidivism rates were 2 percent compared with the national rate of 68 percent of prisoners who recommitted a crime within three years of exiting a prison ("Lansing Correctional Program" 2017). New York has a similar academic program for inmates with similar results (4 percent recidivism for participating students). New York inmates report that attending college classes in prison "gives you meaning and it gives you purpose" (Noguchi 2017, para. 30). A similar program in Georgia has served over 200 men and women, one of whom summarized the experience, "By working through rigorous academic challenges in a creative and scholarly manner, we have transformed and challenged ourselves through humanizing experiences, which in some instances has saved our lives" ("Our Students" n.d., para. 3).

Supporting academic pursuits is an important need for prisoners as inmate college students rarely have the same access to information as traditional college students. A Californian librarian explained in an interview that college courses were offered to prisoners whereby five to ten professors from a local community college came to teach a prescribed set of classes. He explained that these classes did not allow the use of computers. Nor did they allow student inmates to utilize textbooks outside of class (so, no readings could be assigned and no papers could be written requiring online research). No computer use was allowed at the institution by inmates at any time, even for college classes. Nor did the community college send a librarian or offer the assistance of one in collaboration with the prison librarian. The California librarian reported that about one hundred prisoners were college students at his library, and student status was based on whether inmates had their high school diploma (GED) and were exhibiting good behavior. Inmates who did not have their GED were encouraged to obtain it through the classes offered at the correctional facility (California librarian, personal communication, Los Angeles, May 10, 2019). Similarly, according to a Nevada prison librarian, there were county jails in Nevada that did not have LexisNexis kiosks for inmate use. Academic librarians could help facilitate inmate higher education programs by providing reference or homework assistance services for incarcerated students (Nevada librarian, personal communication, August 1, 2019).

According to Campbell, prisoners have two primary information needs: how to cope with life in prison and how to get out of it (Campbell 2005). When it comes to how prisoners seek out information, education level often determines their method and ability to gather relevant information (Campbell 2005, 5). Language barriers may also play a role in information seeking as some prisoners may not speak and read English as a first language (Campbell 2005, 23). Time restrictions on an inmate's library hours and the cost of libraries and librarians further limit a prisoner's access to information

(Campbell 2005, 7). Prisoners often have very limited library access, and budget restrictions can influence collection development, the number of librarians, the qualifications of librarians, and so forth. The Californian prison librarian noted the importance of leisure reading as a form of escapism and education for prisoners. As the sign outside the California prison library says, "If you're not reading, you're not rehabilitating" (California librarian, personal communication, Los Angeles, May 10, 2019).

Best Practice in Correctional Facility Libraries

Best practice varies within correctional facility libraries, but legal information is given priority over entertainment resources, and GED test preparation is given more prevalence than college course offerings (California librarian, personal communication, Los Angeles, May 10, 2019; Nevada librarian, personal communication, August 1, 2019). The following section examines best practices between prison libraries and public/academic libraries.

Similar to public libraries, correctional facility libraries may offer summer reading programs, nonfiction reading programs, book clubs, short story discussion groups, art contests, and GED test preparation classes (California librarian, personal communication, Los Angeles, May 10, 2019). They might also offer storytime for the children of inmates. In both the United States and the United Kingdom, public librarians are working with inmates to provide video storytimes for their children (Horton 2019; Schneider 2004). This program helps maintain a bond between inmate and child, trains inmates how to read a story effectively to their children, and allows inmates to practice reading skills. Schneider reported that the only book that one inmate had ever read was in prison (Schneider 2004). In the United Kingdom, library staff offer writing workshops where inmates are encouraged to tell their life stories and read the final product to older children and teens. This helps children understand their parent's absence, helps parents to reflect on choices, helps parents build confidence, and gives parents a way to instruct children morally (Horton 2019).

Comparable to how the community, including students, may view their public/academic libraries, inmates may consider the correctional facility libraries as places to socialize and relax, as well as being a "place of enlightenment" and a conduit to other learning opportunities by connecting inmates with educational resources and other lifelong learning programs (Brosens et al. 2015; California librarian, personal communication, Los Angeles, May 10, 2019).

However, there may be no physical correctional facility library for some to visit, either through a shortage of space or for policy reasons (Idaho librarian, personal communication, Boise, May 21, 2019; Nevada librarian, personal communication, August 1, 2019). In circumstances such as this, reference questions may be submitted by handwritten mail within a correctional facility.

When there is a physical library, inmates may ask reference questions about what is available in the stacks, and if the correctional facility library does not have what an inmate requests, the librarian may try to purchase it (Idaho librarian, personal communication, Boise, May 21, 2019). In Washington State, for example, inmates may try to access a desired book through nonprofit groups, such as Books to Prisoners who donate used books directly to prisoners who may write to the organization asking for certain titles (O'Sullivan 2019).

As for Internet access, this is restricted, but inmates may request, through the librarian, legal information via Internet searches or they may ask the librarian for unrestricted access, save criminal subject matter (California librarian, personal communication, May 10, 2019; Nevada librarian, personal communication, August 1, 2019). Additionally, a librarian may reach out to area librarians to help with inmate reference questions via the Prison-I listserv or through personal or professional connections (Idaho librarian, personal communication, August 1, 2019).

With such restricted Internet access and database searches (except when a correctional facility library has its catalog database or touchscreen Lexis-Nexis CD available), inmates preparing to take the GED test or taking college courses while incarcerated may require the assistance of a librarian to find support materials and to perform research. This model keeps inmates from building much needed firsthand research skills of the type that nonincarcerated college students routinely acquire (California librarian, personal communication, May 10, 2019).

To add to their educational challenges, inmates cannot have, or check out, hardback books for security reasons, though these books may be placed in the noncirculating reference section of the library. Thus, student inmates may not have textbooks—many of which are hardback—to study outside of the classroom setting. Unfortunately, funding to buy and place textbooks in the library's noncirculating reference section may not be available (California librarian, personal communication, May 10, 2019).

Helping alleviate the above restrictions, there is currently "a big push in the corrections industry" to transition from (if available in the correctional facility) a touchscreen LexisNexis CD that requires manual updates quarterly to a lockdown online-based tablet system—which provides up-to-date information. Inmates would check this tablet out of the library, which may have textbooks, ebooks, videos, calculators, and correctional facility handbooks on it (Nevada librarian, personal communication, August 1, 2019).

The above restrictions certainly impede information access, but other correctional facility variables may impede library service. According to a survey conducted of U.S. correctional facility librarians, "budget," and "inadequate staff," as well as a "lack of professional development" hinder library service (Shirley 2003, 73).

Overall, correctional facility libraries have similarities to public/academic library best practices, but the differences are significant. And for formerly incarcerated students, an academic library may present resources and intel-lectual freedom beyond expectations, but only if they are aware, or made aware, of these opportunities.

Restrictions/Censorship for Correctional Facility Patrons

It was not until June 2010 that the ALA developed "A Prisoner's Right to Read" to address the issue of inmates' intellectual freedom (2010). It states:

> Collection management should be governed by written policy, mutually agreed upon by librarians and correctional agency administrators, in accor-dance with the *Library Bill of Rights* and its interpretations. . . . Material with sexual content should not be banned unless it violates state and fed-eral law. . . . People who are incarcerated or detained should have the abil-ity to obtain books and materials from outside the prison for their personal use. (para. 5)

Even with regard to younger correctional patrons, the ALA states: "Age is not a sufficient reason for censorship. Incarcerated children and youth should have access to a wide range of fiction and nonfiction" ("A Prisoner's Right to Read" 2010). Despite this, collection development policies and privacy of inmate checkouts are two issues in prison libraries that have been contested by law officials (Conrad 2012). In noncorrectional libraries it is assumed that materials for adults will not be censored, but should inmates have the same privilege? Is collecting books about crimes such as rape and murder a respon-sible way for a correctional facility library to build a collection?

The Department of Corrections in Connecticut sought to revise its collec-tion development policy to exclude books of a violent nature. Critics point out that prisoners having access to television shows that include the same violent content are not present in the correctional facility library. Conrad's study found that policies vary from institution to institution with regard to the privacy of prisoner checkout records (Conrad 2012, 420). Most institu-tions have collection development policies that restrict materials that provide instruction in criminal activity. Only six of the sixteen prisons reported that patron requests were considered when ordering materials. And several librar-ians reported that even when they selected items for the collection, those selections required the additional approval of the administration, which slowed the collection acquisition rate to seven to ten months in some cases (Conrad 2012, 421). In sum, in a correctional facility library, an item that presents a security risk might be banned for content (e.g., how to commit crimes) or format (e.g., can be made into a weapon) (California librarian, personal com-munication, May 10, 2019; Conrad 2012, 415).

Given the above collection development restrictions, it should come as no surprise that reference questions are restricted as well. According to the

California librarian, inmates can come to the library in person during their two-hour time slot or they can send a librarian questions through institutional mail. Questions that demonstrate an attempt to harm another person cannot be answered, such as: "What happens if I stab my bunkmate?" And legal questions cannot be answered, although the patron can be directed to legal resources, just as a public/academic librarian would do (California librarian, personal communication, May 10, 2019).

Though directed to legal resources, inmates have limited access to information technology, including Internet access, and must ask for help from a librarian to answer reference questions (Al-heeti 2019). Moreover, without access to computers and the Internet, any college course that inmates take is likely to be vastly different than any college course they may pursue after incarceration (California librarian, personal communication, May 10, 2019).

However, there are instances when inmates can access computers and the Internet, albeit with restrictions and filters. Collaborating with the Hennipin County Library in Minnesota, a correctional facility's resource room computers "are connected to the library's network" with filters that restrict access to appropriate websites that help facilitate community reentry needs (Lilienthal 2013, 28). Also, Colorado's Institutional Library Development (ILD) "was recently credited in *Corrections Today*, the magazine of the Adult Correctional Association (ACA), "with launching 'ground-breaking initiatives' such as intranet training of prison library staff and an online library management system, providing inmates with access to an online catalog but which was customized to prevent inmates from using features such as email" (Lilienthal 2013, 29).

In sum, information restrictions abound for inmates with checkout, reference, and Internet access limitations. Moreover, physical access to the library may be limited for the above restricted services (California librarian, personal communication, May 10, 2019). Certainly, for public/academic librarians, such restrictions, except for safety issues, are anathema to the information profession's advocacy for intellectual freedom.

How Academic and Public Librarians Can Collaborate with Correctional Librarians

Collaborating with correctional libraries can bring benefits to incarcerated and formerly incarcerated patrons, to the prison librarian (which can sometimes be an isolated position), and can increase patronage at the supporting academic (or public) library. In fact, prisoners are typically avid library users and use the library to improve their knowledge. Harlow, Jenkins, and Steurer (2010) found that inmates with a GED had an average literacy score of 270, while the general public, with the equivalent education, had a literacy score of 260. One theory for the statistically significant difference is that because prisoners have more free time than the general public, inmates frequent the correctional library weekly, compared to one-tenth of the general population entering a public library during the same period (Harlow, Jenkins, and Steurer 2010). Collaborations between public or academic libraries and prison libraries may be a way to maintain this captive library audience, helping patrons who are used to making extensive use of the correctional library transfer their patronage to a public or academic library.

Building relationships with inmates does not just serve the inmate but also impacts their children and other family members. For example, Hennepin County Library (HCL) in Minnetonka, Minnesota, sends a librarian to visit the county jail once a week as part of their thirty-year partnership with the local jail. The program allows incarcerated parents to record themselves reading a story. The book and the recording are then sent to the inmate's family members to give the inmate's family a way to connect with their incarcerated relative through books, while also providing a storytime experience for children in the family (Witteveen 2017). The same library also facilitates a program called "Freedom Ticket," which promotes the public library's services to inmates so that inmates can fully utilize the free resources and services from the public library once they are released. Freedom Ticket highlights library resources, such as job search support ("Outreach Services" 2019). In addition, the library prints and distributes a brochure for exiting inmates called the "Going Home Guide" (Witteveen 2017, 33). In addition to these programs, HCL also visits two juvenile correctional facilities to offer access to public library books, and programs such as book clubs, poetry, book talks, and other literacy programs ("Outreach Services" 2019). HCL has "an online orientation video (also available on DVD)" that "assures returning offenders that they will be "treated with dignity and respect by library staff." HCL also provides correctional child and adult participants with a "Going Home" guide that lists library locations and resources to assist with issues such as employment, education, housing, health, and family matters (Lilienthal 2013, 28).

Librarians can also assist with instruction in correctional facilities. The Multnomah County Library (MCL) in Portland, Oregon, has sent a librarian to the county jail for the last sixteen years to teach GED classes and literacy classes, including offering a "National Career Readiness Certificate" for inmates (Witteveen 2017, 34). Similarly, Salt Lake County Library works with inmates in a life skills class, including highlighting the library as a community resource. At the end of the class, inmates are issued a public library card and, if they already have a card, all fines are waived (Witteveen 2017, 35). Library staff received comments of gratitude and appreciation (Witteveen 2017, 35). The Inside-Out Prison Exchange Program is an innovative educational program that brings together college students and incarcerated students into the same classroom. These semester-long courses are held in a prison, jail, or other correctional settings. In one Washington, DC, jail, advanced legal research students (outside students) and the incarcerated (inside) students were taught together and learned the same legal bibliography skills and techniques for performing legal research ("The Inside-Out Prison Exchange Program" 2019).

Another way academic and public librarians can support prison libraries is by creating a partnership to help answer prisoners' reference questions. In New York, prisons and jails around the country are invited to mail information requests to the library. These letters are distributed to librarian and student volunteers who answer them (Drabinski and Rabina 2015). Of the reference questions answered in this study, 44 percent were general reference (which was noted as being questions primarily about song lyrics, geographical information, baseball statistics, China's constitution, designer sunglasses, and Rastafarianism), 35 percent were questions about reentry (employment and social services inquiries), and 21 percent were self-help questions (such as the rights of prisoners) (Drabinski and Rabina 2015, 46). In a similar program at San Francisco Public Library, two librarians answered approximately sixty reference questions each week received via mail from prison inmates (Al-heeti 2019). According to an interview with an Idaho prison librarian, she also can contact local area academic librarians with reference questions and for interlibrary loan requests (Idaho librarian, personal communication, Boise, May 21, 2019).

When Melanie Colletti, a student in library science at the University of Denver, learned about the scarcity of library services available for postin-carcerated individuals, she helped create a resource guide for inmates returning to their communities to assist them in locating useful and necessary services (Lilienthal 2013, 31). Likewise, our interview with a California librarian suggested academic librarians could collaborate by cocreating pathfinders with prison librarians to highlight materials the two libraries could share to serve inmate patrons (California librarian, personal communication, May 10, 2019).

Another suggested opportunity for collaboration was assistance with legal inquiries. Since prison librarians do not necessarily have a legal background or access to legal training or expertise, it would be helpful to provide this as part of prison librarian professional development. Academic librarians might obtain legal training for themselves and inmates by connecting legal librarians, legal students, and law professors. Similarly, there is limited professional development for prison librarians, which academic librarians might also provide help with (California librarian, personal communication, May 10, 2019).

In California, the prison librarian reported collaboration primarily in the form of generous book donations from academic and public librarians, recalling at least 8,000 books provided in a two-year period. When asked what kind of collaborations the librarian would like to have, they stated: "I would actually encourage them to come visit, in person and see kind of what we are like, and then I think more productive ideas can come from physically visiting the location and actually sitting down and assessing" (California librarian, personal communication, May 10, 2019).

Assisting those recently released from incarceration is one way public and academic librarians could serve this community. In California, inmates and former inmates are now eligible for Pell Grants, so education is more attainable for this group, providing one more way librarians can assist an inmate's transition to life outside prison. When asked how librarians can make these initial connections, the California librarian suggested contacting the nearest parole or probation office. They would likely be happy, it was suggested, to have collaborative help in finding inmates jobs, training for job skills, and so forth. Even better, if librarians can provide the inmates a library card in hand before leaving prison through collaborations with local public libraries. Technology classes are also a huge need, as so much has often changed for the prisoners while they are in prison, and because they have had no access to technology while in prison (California librarian, personal communication, May 10, 2019). In Nevada, the prison librarian echoed these suggestions regarding ways academic librarians can work with formerly incarcerated patrons:

- Assist with computers, literacy, typing, and technology.
- Think about the barriers postincarceration.
- Provide resource lists of what the library offers (Nevada librarian, personal communication, August 1, 2019).

The California librarian reported that there are many potential collaborations as prisons:

> have such a captive audience. When people are in prison, they use the library and are excited to use the library. When we transition them outside . . . it seems like a lot of them don't turn to the library for the same kinds of support that they're so used to. (California librarian, personal communication, May 10, 2019)

This is another way that librarians can partner with prisons—by making library cards and resources available as prisoners are being released. The librarian in California continues, "I try to encourage them to go use the public library when they get out. I actually tell them, go get a library card," because the public library is "going to provide you with more opportunities than you can imagine" (California librarian, personal communication, May 10, 2019).

Millsap reported one prison librarian's hope that their inmate patrons can successfully transition to a library patron postincarceration:

> Each time a patron would come in and tell me that this would be their last time in the library because they were going home, I always remind them to visit their public library (and then I prayed silently that whoever that librarian might be they would not fear this man because of his criminal background). (Millsap 2018, 80)

Academic and public librarians can work with corrective librarians, probation officers, and other staff at correctional facilities to ensure this prison
librarian's hope becomes a reality.

Recommendations for Academic Librarians

Although the ALA suggests prison library standards, correctional libraries
are by no means standardized. Access to books, Internet resources, and a
librarian vary by state, and even location. In addition to the best practices discussed, librarians can begin collaborative efforts by reaching out to their local
prison or jail. Taking a tour of the local correctional facility is an important
first step (Nevada librarian, personal communication, August, 1, 2019). Offering reference, life skills, and literacy classes as well as legal support and academic support for college classes are other ways academic librarians can assist
incarcerated patrons. Book donations, textbook access, and programming
that helps connect inmates with family members (such as virtual storytime
sessions) are other ways to support patrons still in the correctional system.

Assisting patrons postincarceration not only provides support to a population that greatly needs it, but it transitions people who are used to making
extensive use of one library (in prison) to another library (public or academic). Librarians can do this by visiting with inmates prerelease, including
information about library resources in inmate exit packets, and collaborating
with probation and parole services. Postincarceration programming that
helps with reentry, access to community information, housing information,
employment information, social services, and especially technology would
be ways to further support this population. Partnerships, such as those mentioned in this chapter, not only expand a public or academic library's patron
base, but support fellow prison libraries and librarians, help vulnerable
members of our community, promote the ALA's mission, keep patrons who
are used to utilizing libraries engaged in libraries, and strengthen the communities we serve.

Notes

1. Younger v. Gilmore, 404 U.S. 15 (1971).
2. Bounds v. Smith, 430 U.S. 817 (1978).

References

Al-heeti, Abrar. 2019. "Without Google, People behind Bars Pen Their Questions
    to Librarians." *CNET*, April 9. https://www.cnet.com/news/without-google
    -people-behind-bars-pen-their-questions-to-librarians/?fbclid=IwAR1
    wTJYniw64r9C2Lqg3lFA85-v-GV_vZG-dYb-zgpuc09etYuRbaf_dWEI.

Brosens, Dorien, Liesbeth De Donder, Sarah Dury, Tom Vanwing, and Domi-
    nique Verté. 2015. "Life-Long Learning: The Prison Library as a Bridge to
    Participation." *Procedia—Social and Behavioral Sciences* 191: 1496–1500.
    https://doi.org/10.1016/j.sbspro.2015.04.434.
Campbell, Diane K. 2005. "The Context of the Information Behavior of Prison
    Inmates." *Progressive Librarian* 26, no. 1 (Winter): 18–32.
Conrad, Suzanna. 2012. "Collection Development and Circulation Policies in
    Prison Libraries: An Exploratory Survey of Librarians in US Correctional
    Institutions." *The Library Quarterly* 82, no. 4 (October): 407–427. https://
    doi.org/10.1086/667435.
Drabinski, Emily, and Debbie Rabina, 2015. "Reference Services to Incarcerated
    People, Part I: Themes Emerging from Answering Reference Questions from
    Prisons and Jails." *Reference & User Services Quarterly* 55, no. 1 (Fall): 42–48.
Harlow, Caroline Wolf, H. David Jenkins, and Stephen Steurer. 2010. "GED
    Holders in Prison Read Better Than Those in the Household Population:
    Why?" *Journal of Correctional Education* 61, no. 1: 74, 80.
Horton, Clare. 2019. "It's Not Just You Who Does the Jail Sentence, It's the Whole
    Family." *The Guardian,* March 19. https://www.theguardian.com/society
    /2019/mar/19/prisoners-stories-reconnect-children.
"The Inside-Out Prison Exchange Program." 2019. Website. https://www.inside
    outcenter.org/index.html.
"Lansing Correctional Program." 2017. Donnelly College. https://www.donnelly
    .edu/academics/college-in-prison-program.
"Library Standards for Adult Correctional Institutions." 2006. American Library
    Association. http://www.ala.org/asgcla/resources/librarystandards.
Lilienthal, Stephen M. 2013. "Prison and Public Libraries." *Library Journal* 138,
    no. 2: 26–32.
Millsap, Katie. 2018. "Building Partnerships with Correctional Libraries." *Texas
    Library Journal* 94, no. 3: 79–80.
Noguchi, Yuki. 2017. "College Classes in Maximum Security: 'It Gives You Mean-
    ing.'" *National Public Radio,* March 27. https://www.npr.org/2017/03/27
    /518135204/college-classes-in-maximum-security-it-gives-you-meaning.
O'Sullivan, Joseph. 2019. "Washington Officials Reverse Ban, Will Allow Prisoners
    to Get Used Books in the Mail." *The Seattle Times,* April 10. https://www
    .seattletimes.com/seattle-news/politics/washington-corrections-officials
    -reverse-ban-will-allow-prisoners-to-get-used-books-in-the-mail/?fbclid
    =IwAR2VnmNsSEdUxFMXprVIhJezPUUY4EtkGzmnMkT8fVaL0Xhjuw
    6WFHAoddc.
"Our Students." n.d. Common Good Atlanta. Retrieved January 11, 2020, from
    http://www.commongoodatlanta.com.
"Outreach Services." 2019. Hennepin County Library. https://www.hclib.org/about
    /outreach.
"A Prisoner's Right to Read: An Interpretation of the Library Bill of Rights." 2010.
    American Library Association. http://www.ala.org/advocacy/intfreedom
    /librarybill/interpretations/prisonersrightoread.

Sambo, Atanda, and Nnebuogor L. Ojei. 2018. "Women in Prison and Their Information Needs: South—South Prison Libraries Perspective." *Library Philosophy and Practice (e-journal)* 1. https://digitalcommons.unl.edu/cgi /viewcontent.cgi?article=4691&context=libphilprac.

Schneider, Julie. 2004. "Has Your Public Librarian Been in Prison? A Report from the Library Services to Prisoners Forum." *ALA Newsletter* 26, no. 4 (Winter). http://web.archive.org/web/20090423230314/http://www.ala .org/ala/mgrps/divs/ascla/asclapubs/interface/archives/contentlistingby /volume26/publiclibrarianinprison/LibrariansinPrison.cfm.

Shirley, Glennor L. 2003. "Correctional Libraries, Library Standards, and Diversity." *Journal of Correctional Education* 54, no. 2 (June): 70–74.

Witteveen, April. 2017. "Prisons & Publics." *Journal of Correctional Education* 61, no. 3: 33–36.

Appendix: Interview Questions for California, Nevada, and Idaho Librarians

1. Have you ever provided library services for a college student or students in your jail or prison? If so, how many? Can you tell me some details about those experiences?
2. What services, including computer access, do you provide for prisoners in your library? Is that different for prisoners taking classes or enrolled in continuing education, or do you have different levels of access for different prisoners?
3. What services would you like to provide, but aren't able to due to time, financial reasons, or other constraints?
4. Can you tell me about collaborations you've participated in with other libraries/librarians or collaborations you've heard/known about?
5. If an academic or other library contacted you for collaboration, what would you suggest?
6. What services can academic libraries provide to support incarcerated students/prisoners taking classes?
7. What services can other libraries provide to support prisoners after incarceration?
8. What would you want academic librarians to know about incarcerated or formerly incarcerated patrons?
9. What else would you like to share about being a prison librarian/ working in a prison library? What else do you wish I would've asked you today?

CHAPTER NINE

Academic Libraries Supporting Students Experiencing Homelessness and Housing and Basic Needs Insecurity

Vikki C. Terrile

Introduction

There is a growing body of scholarship around student homelessness in higher education, part of a larger and growing concern for meeting students' basic needs. Within the context of educational institutions, students' basic needs security generally means ensuring that students have safe and adequate housing and reliable access to adequate and nutritious food (Goldrick-Rab 2017). Understanding that students cannot learn if they have not slept or eaten, if their mental and physical energy is geared toward planning at a survival level, and/or if they are or have experienced trauma from unmet needs, colleges and universities have begun to address basic needs security. Although most of these efforts have focused on food insecurity, there is growing awareness that students may also be dealing with inadequate, dangerous, or unstable housing situations. Recent studies indicate that between 30 and 52 percent of students experience housing insecurity, with 5 to 14 percent experiencing (or having experienced) homelessness (Hallett,

Crutchfield, and Maguire 2019, 4). Although the role of public libraries in the lives of people experiencing homelessness has been well documented, albeit still highly conflicted (Zulkey 2019), much less has been said about how academic librarians can support students experiencing housing instability or homelessness and the associated stress and trauma.

Perhaps not surprisingly, the literature specific to academic libraries and homelessness tends toward the security and problem patron narratives that are still common within the broader field of libraries and homelessness. For example, William H. Weare Jr. (2013) describes how some of the community members who use his urban university library are homeless and that "a few appear to have behavioral issues, and some have hygiene issues" (3). Similarly, Scott E. Muir (2011) stresses that universities which allow community use may see users "who are homeless which can result in situations and concerns that college and university libraries may not have experienced before" (1). Steve Albrecht (2018) lists "aggressive homeless people who are suffering from mental illness and dealing with substance abuse problems" (5) as his number one security concern for both academic and public libraries. Rachael Cathcart (2008) describes having little experience with "obvious homelessness or serious mental illness" (87) in her academic library. These articles tend to conflate homelessness and mental illness without any discussion of the traumatic nature of homelessness and housing insecurity, while also ignoring the reality that the colleges and universities being discussed likely enroll students who have previously experienced or are currently experiencing housing insecurity or homelessness. To these authors, students and "the homeless" are two separate and mutually exclusive populations.

There is a dearth of scholarship detailing how academic libraries support people experiencing homelessness. Mary Kelleher (2009) describes how her private, religious college library serves teens from a local shelter (who are not students of her institution). Lydia N. Collins, Francis Howard, and Angie Miraflor (2009) describe the services to patrons experiencing homelessness served through outreach and programming at a joint public-university library in San Jose, California. Here again, there seems to be a lack of awareness at the time this article was written that students may also be experiencing homelessness. More recently, academic and public librarians at this library have become actively involved in the campus's efforts at meeting students' basic needs and addressing housing insecurity. Recent studies about homelessness in higher education (Gupton 2017; Hallett and Crutchfield 2017; Klitzman 2017) do not mention academic libraries or librarians.

Sara Goldrick-Rab, Jeb Richardson, Joel Schneider, Anthony Hernandez, and Clare Cady (2018), in their national study of college students' housing and food insecurity, mention librarians as staff members who should be included in training and task forces but do not describe in any detail why or what this should look like. Rashida M. Crutchfield and Jennifer J. Maguire

(2018), in their study of students' basic needs at the California State University, describe how many housing insecure students use college libraries as places "where they could arrive early and leave late without disruption and feel safe" (25), but do not detail any specific involvement of academic library faculty and staff.

Thus, while academic libraries are certainly serving students who are experiencing homelessness, housing insecurity, and other basic needs insecurity, there has been limited discussion within the profession about how we can best meet student needs. One exception is an Institute of Museum and Library Services (IMLS) funded research project conducted by Ithaka S+R and Northern Virginia Community College (Blankstein, Wolff-Eisenberg, and Braddlee 2019). Through surveys and interviews with almost 11,000 students at seven community colleges in New York, Washington, and Virginia, the Community College Libraries and Academic Support for Student Success (CCLASSS) project found that students describe how "many of their most significant challenges take place outside of the classroom" (3) and that "students who have been historically underserved or disadvantaged . . . often report encountering greater challenges . . . than their peers" (3). Most significantly, as the project report's title states, "student needs are academic needs" (Blankstein, Wolff-Eisenberg, and Braddlee 2019).

Homelessness and Trauma

Homelessness is defined in a number of ways within government agencies; at its most inclusive it denotes "lack[ing] a fixed, regular, and adequate nighttime residence" (McKinney-Vento Act), specifically when applied to children and youth. In their study of students' basic needs at California State University, Crutchfield and Maguire (2018) use this definition as the basis of their measurement survey, since "this broader definition was used as the foundation for homelessness determinations for K–12 students and therefore allows for comparison of data with elementary and secondary educational studies, which have been shown to be more commonly descriptive of youth or young adult homelessness" (17). Within this definition, homelessness will include living in a car, shelter, motel/hotel, campground, or on the street, as well as "couch surfing" (staying with friends or family for short stays without a promise of long-term housing). Additionally, the nature of homelessness for college students can vary dramatically. Some students may still reside with their families and have experienced housing instability as part of a family unit. Others may have been considered unaccompanied homeless youth as minors, meaning that they left or were told to leave their families and were surviving on their own. Finally, some students may be heads of their own households, including spouses/partners and dependent children. Housing insecurity is more prevalent than homelessness and may include precarious rental situations, such as renting without a lease, or residing where the mortgage is at risk of foreclosure. Homelessness can have long-term negative effects; for example, basic needs insecurity in young children has been linked to delays in cognitive development (Manfra 2019) and brain architecture (Craig 2016), as well as to challenges with social-emotional development (Haskett, Armstrong, and Tisdale 2016). Additionally, school-age children who experience homelessness are more likely to be chronically absent than their stably housed peers, to experience serious health issues, and subsequently, often perform below their peers academically, although there are some questions around whether homelessness leads to worse outcomes than extreme poverty (Pavlakis, Goff, and Miller 2017). Thus, even if students are currently securely housed, there may be past experiences and traumas related to basic needs insecurity that impact their learning.

The experience of homelessness is itself traumatic, and is often preceded by and concurrent with other traumatic life experiences for students and their families, including home foreclosure or eviction, or serious medical conditions. It is important to understand how and why basic needs insecurity can be traumatic. First, as Susan E. Craig (2016) explains, "trauma depends not only on the event, but also on the absent or limited resources available to help a person respond to the situation, manage, and return to a sense of calmness and control" (16). Thus, extraordinary events, as well as long-term stressors, may become traumatic experiences depending on the circumstances and individuals involved. With this in mind, it is important to understand that not all stressors become traumatic; some can become the basis for personal development, but as Ronald E. Hallett, Rashida M. Crutchfield, and Jennifer Maguire (2019) point out, "not having basic needs met is *never* positive for one's growth and development . . . lacking access to food and housing can create significant traumas that may negatively impact a student's ability to remain engaged with school" (45). The stress of worrying about where they will sleep and how they will get their next meal is extremely distracting and damaging to students, making it difficult to concentrate on schoolwork or have the physical and mental energy to participate actively in their education. In addition, the toxic stress of generational poverty and systemic racism is also deeply correlated with both trauma and homelessness (Hallett, Crutchfield, and Maguire 2019) and can compound the struggles of many students. The trauma created by basic needs insecurity does not disappear as soon as needs are met; for example, Sara Goldrick-Rab, at a speaking event in May 2019, described working with an adult student who had been homeless and noted that it was months after she was stably housed before the student felt she could truly concentrate on her schoolwork.

The nature and prevalence of trauma are essential to consider when we examine prevailing assumptions about students and student success. In the last decade, conversations around hard work, character, and perseverance—often lumped into the folksy term "grit"—have been ubiquitous in education research and policy (Tefera, Hernández-Saca, and Lester 2019). By focusing on student-level actions and choices, these narratives remove responsibility from unjust and unequal schools and systems and support the illusion that any student can succeed if they just have enough grit. Therefore, Steven Goodman (2018) argues, "it's not about grit. Sure, hard work, determination, practice, and perseverance make a difference, and might even be a determining factor if all things were equal. But they're not" (5). Further, Adai A. Tefera, David Hernández-Saca, and Ashlee M. Lester (2019) define the use of grit within educational contexts as a master narrative. According to Molly Andrews (2004), "one of the key functions of master narratives is that they offer people a way of identifying what is assumed to be a normative experience" (1). In this way, researchers and policy makers reify that academic success and performance is only and always about individual effort, and not influenced by outside factors. Tefera, Hernández-Saca, and Lester (2019) argue that by focusing on grit, "the educational gaze is on the student as opposed to a more holistic approach that considers the multiplicity of factors that maintain power, privilege, and oppression" (6–7). Julie Ann Winkelstein and Vikki Terrile (2017) note that "in education, resilience and grit are held up as something we should teach our kids (especially low income children and children of color) so they can be successful regardless of their environment." Thus, any work to support students' basic needs in higher education will also have to contend with biases and assumptions about students, their families and communities, and how these assumptions may impede progress. There may also be administrative or institutional reluctance to admit that students are struggling. With declining enrollment a concern for most colleges, fears around how admitting to student basic needs insecurity will impact enrollment may need to be addressed. It is worth noting, however, that robust student services may influence students' enrollment decisions in positive ways. For example, the Campus Awareness, Resource & Empowerment (CARE) Services offered at CARE program at Kennesaw State University in Georgia are so strong that they act as an incentive for students to apply to and enroll at the university (Marcy Stidum, director of CARE Center, in discussion with author, February 7, 2019).

Trauma, homelessness, and other basic needs insecurity may be less visible in academic settings than in public libraries, where, for example, it is not unusual to see people who are experiencing homelessness using the library with all of their belongings in tow. Hallett et al. (2019) note that it can be difficult to identify students experiencing trauma and/or basic needs insecurity because their need is often not visible and can manifest in varied ways. Additionally, they explain that "within the higher education context, students may have limited interactions with institutional agents" (Hallett, Crutchfield, and Maguire 2019, 45). At the same time, colleges and universities do not exist in a bubble and are clearly impacted by challenges being experienced in surrounding communities as well as the struggles students bring with them, regardless of whether they commute or live on campus. For librarians and other library staff, interactions with students in need may be more or less frequent than for other campus staff. For example, we may see students who spend long hours in the library, fall asleep, use the library restrooms for bathing, or who stash their belongings in the library. However, we may not have the direct relationships that teaching faculty have with their students, so while we may see behaviors that are troubling, we may not recognize a pattern that allows us to support a student who is struggling. Additionally, it is likely that there are other departments or agents on campus that "deal with" student homelessness and food insecurity. There may even be territorialism around providing services to students, especially if these departments are funded based on the number of students they serve. In this regard, it seems sensible for academic libraries and librarians to focus on how their specific skills and services can support students, rather than trying to take on roles that are outside their purview.

Supporting Students' Basic Needs

The academic librarians who shared their experiences for this chapter described providing similar types of services for supporting students' basic needs, most often tied to campus antihunger efforts. These services tend to be a mix of existing, traditional library services that can be highlighted and/or adapted to better support students experiencing housing or food insecurity, as well as more innovative efforts. It is worth noting that many of these ideas are being shared across and among multiple departments on campuses, and are also being used in public libraries to serve people experiencing homelessness.

Several librarians described how books sparked their work on student food and housing insecurity. For example, seeing Sara Goldrick-Rab speak or reading her book, *Paying the Price: College Costs, Financial Aid, and the Betrayal of the American Dream*, either on their own, or as part of a campus-wide event, increased their awareness of the challenges being faced by students on their campuses. Celia Rabinowitz, dean of the library at Keene State College in Keene, New Hampshire, describes that Goldrick-Rab visited their campus and spent a great deal of time speaking with students and faculty about concerns around student basic needs. Part of a broad open pedagogy initiative at Keene State College that goes beyond open educational resources (OER) to looking holistically at all of the factors that impact student learning and success, the visit by Goldrick-Rab launched student-led initiatives around food insecurity. Similarly, after Elizabeth Dill, director of library services at Troy University's Dothan Campus in Alabama, read *Paying the Price: College*

Costs, Financial Aid, and the Betrayal of the American Dream, she created a library display based on the book, which further led to her posting on Twitter to see what other academic libraries were doing in this arena. Alyse McKeal, librarian/professor 1 at Palm Beach State College's Lake Worth Campus in Florida (who is also a social worker), explains that in 2015, the college used the book *Breaking Night: A Memoir of Forgiveness, Survival, and My Journey from Homeless to Harvard* by Liz Murray for their common read title, following her 2014 visit to the campus. During that visit, at least a dozen students came forward and self-identified as experiencing homelessness, which led to Alyse rereading the book and exploring how the library could support students.

As noted in the published research on student homelessness and higher education (Crutchfield and Maguire 2018; Goldrick-Rab et al. 2018), college libraries are often used by housing insecure students as safe, comfortable spaces. Frequently, the library is the building on campus that opens earliest and closes latest; many libraries, especially those at large universities, are open twenty-four hours. Libraries also generally have ample seating, including soft-seating and private study carrels, as well as restrooms, outlets for charging phones and other devices, and computers and printers for student use. Textbook and technology loans (including laptops and calculators) are common academic library services that benefit all students, especially those struggling financially. Amy Beth, chief librarian at Guttman Community College, the City University of New York (CUNY), notes that the library space on the college's leased midtown Manhattan campus has the most open hours of any other campus space and may even be open on days the school is closed for inclement weather. Since most Guttman Community College students commute from the outer boroughs of New York City, having a space they can spend time around classes is essential. Additionally, because the college, which opened in 2012, was founded with specific goals and requirements to increase the likelihood of student completion, supporting students' basic needs has been integral to all aspects of the student experience. Beth and her staff offer food and referrals to support services to students they see dozing in the library; Guttman, like all of the CUNY community colleges, has a campus Single Stop office (https://singlestopusa.org) to assist students in applying for public benefits, fight eviction, and access services. At Guttman Community College, the Single Stop office is also where the campus food pantry is located, as well as areas where students can find clothes, sanitary pads/tampons, and school supplies. When library faculty and staff identify students in the library who may need services, they walk the students into Single Stop and make the referral in person.

There are a number of academic libraries that are closely affiliated with campus food pantries in a number of ways, as noted in a May 2019 article in *American Libraries*. The Tiger Food Exchange at Fort Hays State University in

Kansas is located at the entrance to the Forsyth Library, and because of the high levels of institutional support, is a featured stop on tours for prospective and new students. In addition, the library also provides storage space for donated canned and dry goods, and librarians include information about the Tiger Food Exchange in their outreach to students and faculty. According to Deborah Ludwig, Dean of the Forsyth Library, the Tiger Food exchange is highly visible to students through its prime location in the library, which serves to reduce stigma and barriers around its use; this location has not created problems one might expect in a library setting (such as vermin or additional pressure on library staff).

Ludwig works closely with Robert Duffy, the coordinator of the Drug and Alcohol Wellness Network at Fort Hays State University, who also coordinates the Tiger Food Exchange. Ludwig and Duffy agree that partnerships are essential to meeting students' basic needs in higher education. For libraries especially, identifying other departments on campus with whom to work can magnify efforts to support students' food and housing security.

At Keene State College in New Hampshire, the library became involved with the Hungry Owl, the student-initiated campus food pantry, when students approached Dean Rabinowitz about giving out prepackaged pantry food bags through the library once they realized that the limited hours the Hungry Owl was open were preventing student access. The Hungry Owl provided large plastic tubs and keeps them stocked with bags; students go to the circulation desk and show their library cards to request the bags. Rabinowitz explains that students are used to borrowing nonbook materials (including bicycles!) from the library, so being able to "check out" bags of food was an easy way to lower barriers to access. Since these initial efforts, food availability at Keene State College has become even lower-barrier; open shelves with canned goods and bins of wrapped snacks are available across campus. Dill, at Troy University Dothan, initiated conversations on her commuter campus around starting a food pantry, learning firsthand the challenges involved in this endeavor.

Securing long-term funding, resolving issues around data collection (e.g., how to notify students in case of a food recall), and determining eligibility for nonprofit status, are all issues Dill and her colleagues are trying to address. While they are working out how to implement much-needed food resources on campus, the challenges they have faced are providing impetus for larger discussions around students' basic needs, as well as providing opportunities to involve multiple stakeholders, especially students, in planning and consideration.

Making food and other resources available on campus is a common approach for addressing students' basic needs. At Guttman Community College faculty are encouraged to collect swag at conferences to bring back for students, and any leftover food from meetings or events on campus are brought to a common area outside the library for students to eat. Guttman faculty also will buy or bring food for students to eat during class, and at Fort Hays, faculty are asked to bring a canned food item to donate to the Tiger Food Exchange as their entry ticket to the fall convocation ceremony.

Librarians at San Jose State University collect clothing and toiletry donations for a local nonprofit that finds housing for students and community members, and the librarians interviewed for this chapter describe seeing more and more librarians and other faculty making donations and "doing the hard work" around supporting students' basic needs. However, as Beth at Guttman observes, members of her library staff have needed to take advantage of the free food available on campus because they are struggling to meet their own basic needs. This is a key point: many colleges rely on faculty and staff to donate food and/or money to food pantries and other support services. In the age of rampant contingent staffing on campuses, however, it is likely that many faculty, particularly adjuncts (Quart 2018), and other staff are themselves food and housing insecure.

Meeting student needs through charity is a dangerous neoliberal slippery slope; it is common in K–12 education for (underpaid) teachers to pay out of pocket for classroom supplies or for materials students' families cannot afford. This seems to be the case in higher education as well, as most food pantries are funded through grants and donations. Increasingly, there is recognition that other methods, including changes to benefit eligibility, may be better able to address the causes of food insecurity and provide longer-term solutions that do not rely on charity (Laterman 2019).

Academic libraries are also leveraging traditional services including LibGuides and in-person displays to provide current information and resources to students in need. Dill created a LibGuide that explains food insecurity and provides local resources for students experiencing other basic needs insecurity at Troy University Dothan (see Appendix). In a previous position at a four-year public college, Stephanie Noell, currently research and instruction librarian at Savannah College of Art and Design, created a display in the library with local resources, including transportation resources and food resources within walking distance of the campus. Later, as a community college librarian noticing even greater levels of student need, she converted an unused newspaper cabinet into a display housing resources in English and Spanish. She then replicated that same information on the library's website with a LibGuide; this guide is still being updated by other librarians (see Appendix).

Following a workshop from her university's center for teaching and learning on student poverty, Leslie Poljak, outreach and engagement librarian at the University of Pittsburgh in Pennsylvania, created a LibGuide highlighting campus and local food and housing resources for students (see Appendix). Poljak updates the LibGuide regularly, and works closely with the staff of the Pitt Pantry (the school's food pantry) to swap resource lists, attend each other's events, and share resources wherever possible. The students and poverty workshop also led to a student safety net discussion group of faculty and staff on campus that shares ideas and opportunities to look holistically at student support services and what actions the campus community can take. McKeal at Palm Beach State College created a LibGuide on community resources after Liz Murray's visit to campus revealed high levels of basic needs insecurity. Originally developed in support of the book as the college's Common Read selection, the guide currently focuses on community resources for housing, food, mental and physical health, and transportation (see Appendix). Several of the librarians have marketed their LibGuides through print postcards with the URL that are given out at outreach events and made available around the library and other campus settings. Additionally, these cards (or the URL link) are shared directly with other departments, including counseling, veterans' affairs, and disability services, and/or are forwarded to faculty and staff across the campus to share with students.

In some cases, proximity to and relationships with the local public library have increased the services academic libraries can offer to students in need. Perhaps the most notable example of this is the San Jose State University, whose library is colocated with the main branch of the San Jose Public Library. The San Jose area has experienced a dramatic rise in homelessness fueled by skyrocketing housing costs, and the university is seeing staggering numbers of students who are homeless. According to media reports from early 2019, 13 percent, or over 4,300 of the schools' 32,828 FTE, were "couch surfing, sleeping out of their cars, on benches or even inside the campus library" (Woudenberg 2019).

With this level of need among students and community members, Adriana Poo and Peggy Cabrera, academic liaison librarians (San Jose State University) and Deborah Estreicher, reference librarian (San Jose Public Library) work closely together at the King Library to provide services, and to make sure the library is included in larger campus conversations around students' basic needs. Students from San Jose State University's School of Social Work volunteer in the library to work with students and community members; the librarians also refer students to social workers, counseling services, and other campus resources. Similarly, Poljak at the University of Pittsburgh explains that the main library of the Carnegie Library of Pittsburgh is across the street from the campus and provides a wide range of services and access to resources for the public, including students.

Recommendations

From a practical standpoint, there is little need to reinvent the wheel when considering the role academic libraries can play in supporting students' basic needs, as the combined history of libraries' services with people experiencing homelessness and higher education's support for student basic needs initiatives provide an ample roadmap for establishing services. There are, however, a number of important points to consider before adding or changing services to support students' basic needs.

First, as Hallett, Crutchfield, and Maguire (2019) emphasize, when developing programs or services to support students' basic needs, students should be involved. They note that "a collective campus approach that includes all students is essential to reducing stigma and creating a trauma-informed approach" (Hallett, Crutchfield, and Maguire 2019, 87). This can be challenging in libraries, where things like displays and LibGuides may not intuitively lend themselves to student inclusion.

Additionally, a number of librarians replied to my request to interview practitioners with anecdotal stories about students revealing their homelessness. For many academic librarians, this may be the first indication that students' basic needs are not being met. This ties into a point made by Jorge Matos, assistant professor and reference librarian at Hostos Community College CUNY. He notes that as the only Spanish-speaking librarian on a campus with a predominantly Latinx student population, Matos often hears of students' personal challenges along with their research and academic concerns. In his work with students, Jorge has been witness to the impact trauma, including sexual and domestic violence, and food and housing insecurity, can have on students and their learning. Matos notes that establishing trusting relationships with students, especially those with histories of trauma, is essential to helping them access services, and supporting them in their academic work. Similarly, Beth at Guttman Community College and Rabinowitz at Keene State College both emphasize the important roles library public service staff play in building relationships with students. These relationships become key to noticing when something is wrong with students, and creating a safe space for referring students in need to services on campus.

With these ideas in mind and based on what academic libraries are currently doing or planning, recommendations for getting started in supporting students' basic needs are:

- Find potential allies on campus, including students, to start conversations around students' needs;

- Do your research about what is going on in the local community and what services are available outside campus;

- See what is already in place on campus—talk to peers in student services, counseling, and academic departments about what they see and what they are doing;

- Consider what role the library can have that makes long-term sense—what can you reasonably do and sustain, especially what no one else is doing for students;

- Use traditional library services—displays, LibGuides, programming—to introduce student basic needs as a topic worth attention, and build from there;
- Focus on students and your interactions with them—build relationships while also reexamining your assumptions about student behaviors in the library;
- Take inspiration from the work that public libraries and librarians are doing to serve underserved populations;
- Understand that basic needs insecurity also impacts college faculty and staff, and be careful about assuming what employees are able to give or share.

Given staffing and budgetary worries across colleges and universities and specifically academic libraries, taking on additional roles and responsibilities could be a double-edged sword. That being said, as the campus hub for information and resources, being able to provide relevant, timely, and needed information on all aspects of students' college experiences is essential. Libraries and librarians are still trusted sources, and students are using our physical spaces for academic, personal, and basic needs. Providing displays and programs for students who are using the library on campus, combined with making resources available online, along with leveraging campus and community partnerships to offer the widest range of resources takes advantage of the types of services academic libraries already do well. Being deliberate and intentional in our engagement and interactions with students is ultimately the best thing we can do as individuals so that students know they have a trusted contact within the college community to turn when their struggles become more than they alone can handle.

References

Albrecht, Steve. 2018. "Top 10 Security Risk Factors for Public and Academic Libraries." *Computers in Libraries* 38, no. 5: 4–7.

Andrews, Molly. 2004. "Opening to the Original Contributions: Counter-Narratives and the Power to Oppose." In *Considering Counter-Narratives: Narrating, Resisting, Making Sense,* edited by M. Bamberg and M. Andrews, 1–6. Amsterdam: John Benjamins Publishing.

Blankstein, Melissa, Christine Wolff-Eisenberg, and Braddlee. 2019. "Student Needs Are Academic Needs: Community College Libraries and Academic Support for Student Success." September 30. https://doi.org/10.18665/sr.311913.

Cathcart, Rachael. 2008. "Librarian or Social Worker: Time to Look at the Blurring Line?" *The Reference Librarian* 49, no. 1: 87–91.

Collins, Lydia N., Francis Howard, and Angie Miraflor. 2009. "Addressing the Needs of the Homeless: A San José Library Partnership Approach." *The Reference Librarian* 50, no. 1: 109–116.

Craig, Susan E. 2016. *Trauma-Sensitive Schools: Learning Communities Transforming Children's Lives, K–5*. New York: Teachers College Press.

Crutchfield, Rashida M., and Jennifer J. Maguire. 2018. *California State University Office of the Chancellor Study of Student Basic Needs*. http://www.calstate.edu/basicneeds.

Goldrick-Rab, Sara. 2017. "Basic Needs Security and the Syllabus." August 7. https://medium.com/@saragoldrickrab/basic-needs-security-and-the-syllabus-d24cc7afe8c9.

Goldrick-Rab, Sara. 2019. "Paying the Price: College Costs, Financial Aid, and the Betrayal of the American Dream." *ACERT/Sociology Department Special Event*. Hunter College, May 13. CUNY, New York.

Goldrick-Rab, Sara, Jeb Richardson, Joel Schneider, Anthony Hernandez, and Clare Cady. 2018. *Still Hungry and Homeless in College*. Wisconsin HOPE Lab. https://hope4college.com/wp-content/uploads/2018/09/Wisconsin-HOPE-Lab-Still-Hungry-and-Homeless.pdf.

Goodman, Steven. 2018. *It's Not about Grit: Trauma, Inequity, and the Power of Transformative Teaching*. New York: Teachers College Press.

Gupton, Jarrett T. 2017. "Campus of Opportunity: A Qualitative Analysis of Homeless Students in Community College." *Community College Review* 45, no. 3: 190–214.

Hallett, Ronald E., and Rashida Crutchfield. 2017. "Homelessness and Housing Insecurity in Higher Education: A Trauma-Informed Approach to Research, Policy, and Practice." *ASHE Higher Education Report* 43: 7–118.

Hallett, Ronald E., Rashida M. Crutchfield, and Jennifer J. Maguire. 2019. *Addressing Homelessness and Housing Insecurity in Higher Education: Strategies for Educational Leaders*. New York: Teachers College Press.

Haskett, Mary E., Jenna Montgomery Armstrong, and Jennifer Tisdale. 2016. "Developmental Status and Social–Emotional Functioning of Young Children Experiencing Homelessness." *Early Childhood Education Journal* 44, no. 2: 119–125.

Kelleher, Mary. 2009. "We Must All Serve the Disconnected." *Library Journal* 134, no. 17: 44.

Klitzman, Chad. 2017. "College Student Homelessness: A Hidden Epidemic." *Columbia Journal of Law and Social Problems* 51, no. 4: 587–619.

Laterman, Kaya. 2019. "Tuition or Dinner? Nearly Half of College Students Surveyed in a New Report Are Going Hungry." *The New York Times,* May 2. https://www.nytimes.com/2019/05/02/nyregion/hunger-college-food-insecurity.html.

Manfra, Louis. 2019. "Impact of Homelessness on School Readiness Skills and Early Academic Achievement: A Systematic Review of the Literature." *Early Childhood Education Journal* 47, no. 2: 239–249.

"McKinney-Vento Act: Two-Page Summary." 2018. SchoolHouse Connection. August 1. https://www.schoolhouseconnection.org/mckinney-vento-act-two-page-summary.

Muir, Scott E. 2011. "Security Issues with Community Users in an Urban University Library." *Library Leadership & Management* 25, no. 2: 1–12.

Pavlakis, Alexandra E., Peter Goff, and Peter M. Miller. 2017. "Contextualizing the Impacts of Homelessness on Academic Growth." *Teachers College Record* 119, no. 10: 1–23.

Quart, Alissa. 2018. *Squeezed: Why Our Families Can't Afford America*. New York: Ecco.

Tefera, Adai A., David Hernández-Saca, and Ashlee M. Lester. 2019. "Troubling the Master Narrative of 'Grit': Counterstories of Black and Latinx Students with Dis/Abilities during an Era of 'High-Stakes' Testing." *Education Policy Analysis Archives* 27, no. 1: 1–34.

Udell, Emily. 2019. "Food for Thought: Academic Libraries Are Fighting Campus Food Insecurity with Onsite Pantries." *American Libraries* 50, no. 5: 12–15.

Weare, William H. 2013. "'What Open to the Public' Means at IUPUI." *Library Issues* 34, no. 1: 3.

Winkelstein, Julie Ann, and Vikki Terrile. 2017. "Resilience—What's in a Word?" *SRRT Newsletter Social Responsibilities Round Table* 199 (June): 5.

Woudenberg, Carina. 2019. "SJSU President Denies Students' Requests for Homeless Support." March 4. https://sanjosespotlight.com/sjsu-students-rally-for-homeless-students-rights.

Zulkey, Claire. 2019. "Give Them Shelter? Libraries Face Tough Choices When Homeless Patrons Set Up Permanent Residence." *American Libraries* 50, no. 6: 38–42.

Appendix: Academic Library Basic Needs LibGuides

Food insecurity guide created by Elizabeth Dill at Troy University in Dothan, Alabama. https://troy.libguides.com/c.php?g=979456.

Community resource guide originally developed by Stephanie Noell at Mountain View Community College in Dallas, Texas. https://libguides.mountainviewcollege.edu/community.

Pitt and local resources guide maintained by Leslie Poljak at University of Pittsburgh in Pennsylvania. https://pitt.libguides.com/assistanceresources.

Community resource guide created by Alyse McKeal and maintained by Raychell Harris at Palm Beach State College, in Lake Worth, Florida. https://palmbeachstate.libguides.com/HousingInsecurity2019-2030.

CHAPTER TEN

Academic Library Services and Communication with Patrons with Communication Disorders

Brady D. Lund

Introduction

It is easy for individuals who lack a communication disorder to underestimate the complexity of the process of communication that comes so easy to them. For example (and I promise we will not spend too much time on this), just the process of speaking the word "hello" and having a listener understand it is a process that can only be understood through an advanced study of neurology, psychology, anatomy, linguistics, communication science, chemistry, and physics.

Producing and hearing a sound involves the process of planning to make a sound; posturing of the vocal system (tongue, teeth, lips, vocal folds/cords, lungs, diaphragm) to produce a specific change in frequency that can be conveyed as pressure changes in the particles that comprise the atmosphere; the capability of the imperfect air medium to transfer sound waves over a distance; a receptacle (ear) to funnel in sound waves; a surface (eardrum) to transfer sound energy into mechanical energy (that travels via tiny bones in your ear); a set of receptors (cochlea and auditory nerve) to transfer the mechanical energy to chemical energy; and a control center (your central nervous system/brain stem and brain) to turn that energy—that little fluctuation of change—into meaning.

It is a remarkably complex process, and any minute problem with any one part of this process will cause communication to break down. Depending on where the breakdown occurs, the resulting communication disorder will manifest differently and have different effects on the individual. This is the most important thing to remember when working with individuals with communication disorders/differences: no two are alike and no one strategy will necessarily work for all.

Here is one practical example of hearing loss. Everyone has worked with a patron or coworker with hearing loss, and many have probably thought the best thing to do to make sure that the individual hears you is to just speak louder. In some cases, that might be true. In most cases, not so much. It depends on where the hearing breakdown is occurring and why. The nerve endings in the inner ear are very sensitive and prone to damage with overexposure to sound and with age. Generally, this damage does not just affect how loud sound needs to be for it to be heard and understood. It also affects the quality of the sound, meaning the sound can be very loud but, because of the damage to the nerve receptors, "ship" will still sound like "chip." In this case, it is more important to annunciate and use nonverbals (gestures/facial expressions) than to speak louder. Similarly, if the breakdown is severe damage or deformity in the cochlea or auditory nerve/processing system (resulting in deafness or auditory processing disorder), nothing you can do with your voice will make things significantly better.

This chapter is split into two parts. The first part will focus on specific communication disorders and what it would mean for you as an academic library employee in communicating with a patron. Part two will focus on some general communication strategies (informed by evidence-based research and theory) that will help you as a library employee become a more effective communicator with all patrons with which you interact.

What Is a Communication Disorder?

This section will focus on describing specific communication disorders (keeping in mind that, as stated in the introduction, each individual is unique and the disorder will vary in its manifestation), how the disorder may affect interactions in the academic library, and some common questions. There are many different communication disorders, so only a few, representative examples will be used: autism spectrum disorders, disfluency/stuttering, deaf/hard-of-hearing, social anxiety/mutism, and aphasia.

Communication Disorder Defined

A communication disorder is an impairment in the ability to formulate, send, perceive, interpret, make meaning, and use *information*, affecting areas of speech, auditory, visual, or cognitive processing. For those who work with individuals with a communication disorder (special education instructors, speech pathologists), the process of treating the disorder is not too unlike the work of an information professional remediating information literacy and search strategy, except at a *much* more fundamental and problematic level. Communication disorders most commonly develop during early childhood, when language is first acquired; however, some communication disorders occur later in life, such as aphasia, which is frequently caused by a stroke in one of the auditory/speech processing centers of the brain. Some communication disorders are treated in early childhood and disappear or are strongly mitigated by adulthood (as sometimes occurs with stuttering and social anxiety); however, there are many communication disorders that last a long time or throughout one's life. The factors that make it possible to overcome a communication disorder are usually outside an individual's control (it's not something to just "get over").

Communication disorders do not necessarily have a comorbidity (co-occur) with intellectual disability (van Hattum 1980, 4–8). This means that a large number of individuals with a communication disorder have average or above average intelligence. These are individuals that library employees are likely to come across both as patrons and as coworkers. Several of these disorders are classified as invisible disorders/disabilities (Santuzzi et al. 2014). These are disabilities that, unlike paralysis or vision loss for instance, are not necessarily perceivable to the naked eye. In some instances, the fact that the disability is invisible can lead to even greater challenges, as individuals with communication disorders struggle to decide whether to reveal their condition. This may lead to anxiety and depression, or to individuals not disclosing their disorder and then being discriminated against for being/acting/talking "weird" (this is especially true of individuals with high-functioning autism and social anxiety, who are often accused of "hiding something").

A depressing fact and cruel irony for an individual with a communication challenge is that trust is tightly related to communication; criminals with sociopathic tendencies are often characterized as some of the nicest and most trustworthy people you will meet, while individuals with a communication challenge can be branded as hiding something, untrustworthy, someone to keep a close watch on, angry, scheming, violent, and abrupt. If someone is not talking, it is almost never because they are hiding something, it is simply a difference in personality (Cain 2013).

Autism

A lot is said about autism, due to its high level of incidence, but few people really know much about it. The fact is that there is no one way to describe what autism is because it varies in symptoms so greatly from individual to individual and has no clear etiology (cause). Even among the medical community, definitions and understanding of autism are rapidly evolving (Nazeer et al. 2019).

Autism is more accurately (fully) referred to as autism spectrum disorder. Some common features/symptoms of autism include deficits in social communication (reciprocity and empathy), and restrictive and repetitive patterns of behavior and interests (American Psychiatric Association 2013). However, autism truly is a spectrum. At one end of the spectrum, there is autism with intellectual disability. Individuals with autism and intellectual disability will have difficulty living independently or gaining employment (though, depending on the severity of the intellectual disability, some excellent job services like Goodwill—and hopefully someday, libraries—are a possibility) (Lund 2018).

On the other end of the spectrum, there is high-functioning autism. High-functioning autism is often misunderstood by those who have no understanding of autism and autism advocates alike. If a normal distribution of the IQ of individuals with autism was created, high-functioning autism would be the 16–30 percent on the high end of the scale. There is still a large range, however. There are individuals with high-functioning autism who are able to get a job and function well and independently, but are by no means a genius. There are also a few with very high intelligence. These are the examples that advocates often pick out—fictional figures like Sheldon Cooper on the *Big Bang Theory* or real celebrities like Anthony Hopkins. These individuals do exist. However, painting all individuals with high-functioning autism as geniuses can actually do a disservice by creating unrealistic expectations.

Depending on the severity of autism, it may or may not be "invisible." Others will almost certainly notice someone is different (those who have been around individuals with autism long enough are often able to identify it in a stranger from just a glance), but it may not be pronounced enough for the average person to realize it is autism. This can lead to a challenging situation for the individuals with the invisible disorder, because people may label them as "weird," not realizing that they have a developmental disorder. This is why it is important to treat everyone with a high level of respect, no matter their behavior. If someone's behavior is peculiar, it is much more likely it is a disability/mental health condition than that the person is evil or dangerous.

As there is no one way to describe an individual with autism, there too is no one way to describe the library/information behavior, information needs, and optimal services for this population either. Anyone describing library services for this population as though it is one homogeneous group is, as with most populations, a deeply flawed perspective. That does not mean there are not strategies to improve services to individuals with autism or potential understandings of how these individuals interact with information, but that these models are not a simple ingredient list or universal path. Rather, services for individuals with autism should result from an assessment of library resources and needs analysis, as environment is key.

Consider the major symptomology of autism (sensory, emotional, and communication) and how your specific library presents environmental risks for these symptoms. Endeavor to find a balance between what the needs, service, and space demands of library patrons without communication disorders and those of patrons with communication disorders and other impairments/disabilities. For instance, if there is an area of the library that is rife with flashing lights and noises, loud conversations, constant movement, cramped sitting quarters, etc., ensure that there is also an area of the library that is devoid of this sensory overload with soft lighting, no or very low noise, and open space or independent study areas. If the library is considering dropping chat reference, in favor of only in-person or phone calls, due to a low number of requests, think again. For an individual with any of the communication disorders discussed in this chapter, chat reference may be the only format that the individual can or is willing to use. Librarians should consider the range of barriers to information access and seeking that deviate from the majority—democracy should not trump equity.

Disfluency/Stuttering

Disfluency is a disruption in the normal flow of speech. This includes the repeated use of fillers like *um*, *uh*, *er*, especially when they are used at a rate that disrupts or detracts from the quality of speech. A severe type of disfluency is stuttering, which is when the production of speech is disrupted by repeated syllables or stops, often due to some disconnect between cognitive and speech motor processes (how we think about what we want to say and how we move our mouths, vocal cords, etc., to actually say it) (Tichenor and Yaruss 2018). Both fillers and stuttering are more likely to occur in early childhood and reduce dramatically or vanish before adolescence, but this is not always the case, and a sizable group of individuals continues to stutter or engage in excessive use of fillers into adulthood. While the cause of stuttering is not entirely psychological, counseling can help in some cases (Dalton 2018). Speech pathology also often helps both children and adults with stuttering and excessive filler usage.

For library employees, it is important to recognize that this condition is likely not something that can be controlled by the individual (they cannot just "stop it"). Generally, it would be considered disrespectful to finish a sentence for an individual who is stuttering. Rather, it is appropriate to be patient and let the individual finish. There is no need to feel awkward about someone who stutters speaking with you. In fact, if you, as a library employee and an "authority figure" feel awkward, this will likely be reflected in your nonverbal expression, perceived by the patron, and the embarrassment will result in even worse stuttering. The ideal response would be to treat the individual no differently than anyone else. Okay, so it takes a few stops before they finish their statements—so what? If you show that you do not care about it, then it is likely to allow the individual to relax more, which in turn will likely reduce the frequency of the stops.

Deaf/Hard-of-Hearing

Hearing loss or deafness is a unique "communication disorder," one that many who are deaf may not necessarily consider a disorder, but just a difference (Leigh, Andrews, and Harris 2018). Although it affects the ability to hear, it does not affect cognition, intellect, or the ability to communicate in general. Many (but not all) individuals who are deaf identify with Deaf culture (note that Deaf culture is a proper noun, while deafness is not), which consists of a unique language (American Sign Language, in the United States), beliefs and behaviors, and networks of support and advocacy (community). Deaf culture generally pushes back against the idea that deafness is a condition that should be treated by surgery (cochlear implants). Regardless of personal views as to whether deafness is a disorder or a difference, library employees should respect the culture to which these individuals belong.

One question that might be on the minds of library employees is how to communicate with someone who cannot hear. Is it rude to write notes? Can they read lips? The answer depends on the individual, not the deafness. Most patrons who are deaf will likely have no problem exchanging notes if it gets them the information they need, but some may prefer to communicate via lip reading or using an interpreter. It is best not to make assumptions. Pass them a note to ask what they would prefer. In uncomfortable situations, well-intentioned people tend to forget the Golden Rule: How would you want someone to communicate with you? Probably ask you first, right?

In an academic library environment, it is possible the student will have an interpreter with him/her. However, depending on the college/university, the interpreter may only be present during classes (or if in an online program, maybe not at all). Deafness is one condition, in particular, where highlighting specific services or employing individuals who are deaf can send an important message to the Deaf community on campus and reduce library anxiety for this population. If the student does not have an interpreter with them, imagine the delight s/he might have if one was on staff.

Bushman (2018a; 2018b) and Bushman and Fagan (2018) have authored several articles on the topic of library services to children who are deaf. Though the population in academic libraries will be a bit older, the advice offered in these articles pertaining to inclusive services are beneficial for all librarians to read as a way to orient themselves to promoting a positive environment for library users with communications disorders.

Aphasia

Although it is less likely in an academic library than a public one, it is still possible that patrons with aphasia will use the academic library. Aphasia results from specific damage to the speech-language centers of the brain. The most common causes of aphasia are stroke, trauma, and tumors (Purdy 2016). Individuals with aphasia have normal intelligence, but are unable to find the words they want to say. They may be able to picture perfectly what they want to say, and have said thousands of times before in their lives, but the damage in the language center prevents them from connecting the concept to the word and speaking it. It is not difficult to imagine that this condition would be incredibly frustrating.

Aphasia may be the most difficult condition for a patron to have and still engage in communication exchanges. Often, pointing and symbols/images are used in place of representative (words/sign language) communication (this depends on severity). Conducting a reference interview, or even providing directions to the restroom, may prove incredibly difficult. What matters (and this is true for any interactions with individuals with any communication disorder) is that you, as a library faculty/staff member, are putting your full effort forward (actually trying). That is the most that anyone can ask or expect. If the barriers are too great, ask for help—do not push the patron away. Although it is frustrating for everyone involved, there is nothing wrong about trying your hardest and then accepting you simply cannot understand what the patron is trying to communicate and seeking assistance.

Social Anxiety/Mutism

All of the communication disorders on this list can co-occur/produce social anxiety. When individuals cannot speak well and have received ridicule for it, they can decide to just speak very little or not at all. Social anxiety can also occur separately from any of the other disorders discussed. It may be caused by a combination of environmental and neurological factors and generally is not something that the affected individual can "just get over," without counseling and/or pharmaceutical intervention. There is a significant difference between being "shy," "slow to warm up," or having stage fright, and having true social anxiety. True social anxiety affects an individual's ability to function normally in society—hold a job, perform well in classes, and live independently (Wang et al. 2016).

Forcing individuals with social anxiety into uncomfortable positions should not be the goal of any library, whether or not it could help them "get over it." That is the responsibility of the individuals and those close to them. Often barriers to information access and seeking of individuals with social anxiety can be inadvertently constructed based on administrative and personal decisions and preferences that lack forethought and empathy. For instance, a reference librarian might decide that "I do not like to answer the chat reference. If it is important enough, they will come to speak to me in person." While the reference librarian does not like chat reference, the individual with social anxiety may be absolutely petrified of asking for help, leading to an information need being unsatisfied due to the inability of the librarian to perform the full assigned duties. It is extraordinarily common that laziness, apathy, personal preferences, and failure to perform job duties to the full extent possible on the part of individuals/employees results in tremendous frustration, anxiety, depression, and failure on the part of the individual with a communication disorder who must communicate with them.

Approaches to Communicating with Those with a Communication Disorder (and Everyone)

The purpose of this section is to "bring theory to practice." There are some well-stated theories of communication and information exchange that are valuable starting points for discussion of how we as information professionals should seek to communicate with all people (including those with communication disorders). These theories originate in linguistics, communication, and information theory and show how the complexity of the biological communication system, like that discussed in the introduction of this chapter, can be understood and treated.

Claude Shannon and Information Theory

Claude Shannon was a genius. If you are not familiar with him as a library and information professional, you should really make an effort to familiarize yourself with his work. His greater contribution was probably his description of sending messages through a noisy channel (Shannon 1948). Here are a few examples of how you can think about Shannon's description (in a nutshell):

- You are driving your car listening to AM radio. You pass under a utility wire and hear static—what happened? The current flowing through the utility wire disrupted the frequency of the radio signal and blurred out the message.

- You and a friend stand on opposite ends of an empty auditorium and can have a conversation. You then stand on opposite ends of a crowded auditorium and cannot make out anything each other is saying over the crowd noise.

In both cases, there is a message (radio signal, conversation) trying to be sent through a noisy (or busy) channel. Traditionally, the thought was that, to overcome this problem, you simply needed to make your signal louder. And that technically may work, but it takes an extreme amount of additional energy. On the other hand, if you change how the signal is sent so that the noise makes less interference, you can effectively send the message without expending much additional energy.

Shannon worked for Bell Systems (part of AT&T) and his work helped create virtually all efficient systems of the second half of the twentieth century, including computer and Internet communications. His mathematical principles and findings about redundancy in sending a message through a noisy channel were vital. His findings, however, are applicable far beyond network communications. They are relevant to how we communicate in general.

You will recall in the introduction of this chapter the discussion of communication with individuals who are hard-of-hearing. Generally, if this individual is wearing a hearing aid, loudness is not the problem if they cannot hear you. It is noise. Noise that is occurring when you speak too fast and slur your speech, use a heavy accent, speak from too far away, or while not facing the listener. All of these factors reduce the quality of the message. It does not matter how loud the message is if it makes no sense.

So what would this suggest about improving communication? To make changes to the signal rather than changes to its intensity. Here are a few ways to improve the quality of a message to improve your communication with individuals with communication differences:

- Maintain eye contact—the eyes and face give clues (communicate) as to what you are saying, even if the whole message does not get through.
- Annunciate, do not overdo it, and talk in 0.1X speed, just be conscientious of how you are speaking.
- Use visuals, like gesturing and pointing, to supplement what you are saying.
- Repeat what you say—redundancy may be annoying to you, but can be extremely helpful to the listener.

Mr. Rogers' Method

I cannot claim credit for this method. All credit goes to an undergraduate professor of mine, Dr. Raymond Hull at Wichita State University (Stovall and Hull 2016). He developed these ideas while studying the auditory processing capacity of individuals at different stages of life (and would lecture about it, old-fashioned, chalk-and-blackboard style, all the time). I am simply taking these ideas and making them relevant to library service.

The central nervous system of a human being is designed to comprehend language spoken at a speed of approximately 124–126 words per minute (Stovall and Hull 2016). Anything faster than that and part of the message is going to be lost. That, actually, is the peak of the bell curve on hearing comprehension across the life span. The number is even smaller among children and older adults and, of course, for individuals with communication disorders. The average person (including many professional speakers, professors, and—yes—librarians) speak at a rate of 160–180 words per minute—or even more! So, if someone is speaking at a normal speed (as Dr. Hull has measured) (Hull 2011; Hull 2013), about 25 percent of the message is being obscured. Adults without a communication disorder can do an okay job deciphering meaning, because the brain can use context to make educated guesses about what is said that often are imperceptible to the individual. Many listeners, however, fail to get an accurate picture of what was said.

Mr. Rogers was not just some actor; he studied child psychology with some of the most renowned psychologists of the time. He also studied in Seminary. He understood how to communicate with people on a highly scientific level. He was aware of how children (and really everyone) process language. His characteristic slow, calm, measured speech was intentionally used so that all of his listeners could actually understand what he was saying. Mr. Rogers was measured at speaking, almost precisely and consistently, at 124–126 words per minute. Additionally, he made sure to repeat and rephrase important things he would say and always maintain eye contact with the camera/listener. Together, this made Mr. Rogers, scientifically speaking, one of the most effective communicators of the television era—and this, combined with his caring and sincere demeanor, made him one of the most beloved people of all time.

So, the Mr. Rogers method boils down to a very simple precept: "Do as Mr. Rogers did." Be conscientious of how you are speaking. Make an effort to speak more slowly. Very often the trouble is not how loud you are speaking, but how quickly. Repetition makes sure you are understood. Nonverbals, like eye contact, provide vital context to fill in the obscurities.

Linguistic Ambiguity

Linguistic ambiguity is what we are really talking about very frequently when misunderstandings occur in the library world. Librarianship has so many words that mean so many different things—ten words that mean the same thing, one word that means five different things (Dow, Lund, and Douhit 2019). It is insider language, and it is fine if you are in the know. If not, then it is tremendously confusing.

I once spoke about simplifying our language we use as professionals at a conference and had an attendee accuse me of being an authoritarian socialist à la George Orwell's *1984*. That—somewhat ironically—really oversimplifies what I am suggesting. Having a rich language is great and useful in many situations, but in conversing with a diverse population of patrons, with different understandings of our language, we should always aim to converse in a way they understand—not at a level that either goes over their head or demeans them. It is really not difficult to figure out the communication ability of a patron. We can often easily judge it based on the questions they ask and how they ask them (meaning what vocabulary they are using). Ideally, you should never talk at a level that is higher than the level of the patron talking to you. You should form a reactive process of communication. Let them guide the conversation, not you.

Do What Librarians Do

The earlier allusion to working with individuals with disabilities being similar to library work was intentional. The reality is that much of what librarians already learn and do can be used to create a conducive environment for individuals with communication disorders. Although a communication disorder is much more complex and impactful than a lack of information literacy, using LIS thought processes to produce meaningful interactions with individuals with communication disorders is possible.

Consider the ways in which we engage in reference service. We make no assumptions about what the individual across from us knows about a topic or their information needs. It is through clear communication and inquiry that we understand this knowledge and need and can then curate information to satisfy this need. In the same way, assumptions should not be made about the individual with a communication disorder. Do not assume anyone can communicate at a highly advanced, jargon-heavy level, but also do not assume they cannot communicate at a level higher than a typical ten-year-old. Engage in a back-and-forth exchange, and come to understand the level at which an individual can communicate and the level in which they would like to communicate.

Additional Guidance for Creating Supportive Environments

One action academic libraries can take that will improve the comfort of individuals with communication disorders who visit the library is to hire a diverse staff, especially employees with disabilities. This is not always up to the organization, as they may have no qualified individuals apply. Under no circumstances should a library hire an unqualified individual just to artificially increase diversity. However, if libraries take a close view at some of the hiring and cultural practices, there are several practical changes that might make employment more enticing and possible for individuals with communication disorders.

Clear, direct communications, from library policy to job descriptions, is important for demonstrating cognizance of challenges that individuals with communication disorders face. This includes avoiding ambiguous terminology and library jargon (information resources, information literacy, etc.) in interactions/materials for patrons or being as clear as possible in defining these terms (for everyone, including employees). This is an immediate, no-cost step that can be taken to create a more conducive culture for patrons and employees with communication disorders and related disabilities.

Other changes may not directly affect individuals with communication disorders, but show that the library is concerned about equal access and diversity. For example, improving accessibility in library spaces, providing access to resource officers, counselors, social workers in the library, and promoting special collections services like "Talking Books," communicates that the library is considered about mental health, accessibility, diversity, and equity. This will likely make the patron feel more comfortable in the environment, reduce library anxiety, and increase the likelihood that she or he asks for assistance from library employees and/or has a more fulfilling library experience.

Conclusion

The most important thing to remember when interacting with patrons with communication disorders is that their disorder does not prevent them from being important members of their communities, including the campus community. Individuals with communication disorders bring perspective, growth, and diversity that benefit the community as a whole. There is no reason to be intimidated, and not knowing all the answers is okay. Show that you care, that you are trying to help, and that, one way or another, you will find them the assistance they need. Rely on the community of stakeholders—coworkers, campus support services, the individuals themselves—for assistance; plan for situations and alternative means of communication.

References

American Psychiatric Association. 2013. *Diagnostic and Statistical Manual of Mental Disorders* (DSM-5). Chicago: American Psychiatric Publications.

Bushman, Bobbie. 2018a. "Library Services and Early Literacy Approaches in Public Libraries for Deaf and Hard of Hearing Children." *The International Journal of Information, Diversity, & Inclusion (IJIDI)* 2, no. 1/2: 89–93.

Bushman, Bobbie. 2018b. "Serving Underserved Populations: Implications from a Model of Successful Services for Deaf Children in Public Libraries." *The International Journal of Information, Diversity, & Inclusion (IJIDI)* 2, no. 3: 59–90.

Bushman, Bobbie, and Mary K. Fagan. 2018. "Public Library Programs and Accommodations for Deaf and Hard-of-Hearing Children in the United States." *The Journal of Deaf Studies and Deaf Education* 24, no. 2: 74–83.

Cain, Susan. 2013. *Quiet: The Power of Introverts in a World That Can't Stop Talking.* New York: Broadway Paperbacks.

Dalton, Peggy, ed. 2018. *Approaches to the Treatment of Stuttering.* New York: Routledge.

Dow, Mirah J., Brady D. Lund, and William Douhit. 2020. "Investigating the Link between Unemployment and Disability: Lexically Ambiguous Words and Fixed Formulaic Sequences in Job Ads for Academic Reference Librarians." *The International Journal of Information, Diversity, & Inclusion (IJIDI)* 4, no. 1: 42–59. https://doi.org/10.33137/ijidi.v4i1.32369.

Hull, Raymond H. 2011. "A Brief Treatise on the Service of Aural Rehabilitation." *The Hearing Journal* 64, no. 4: 14–16.

Hull, Raymond H. 2013. *Introduction to Aural Rehabilitation.* San Diego: Plural Publishing.

Leigh, Irene, Jean F. Andrews, and Raychelle Harris. 2018. *Deaf Culture: Exploring Deaf Communities in the United States.* San Diego: Plural Publishing.

Lund, Brady D. 2018. "Redefining Opportunity for the Library Employee with Autism: A Model of Positive Behavioral Support for Library Management." *Journal of Library Administration* 58, no. 5: 434–448.

Nazeer, Ahsan, Nehdia Hashemi, Nazish Imran, and Muhammad Waqar Azeem. 2019. "Autism Spectrum Disorder: A Concept in Evolution." *Psychiatric Annals* 49, no. 3: 103–108.

Purdy, Mary H. 2016. "Aphasia, Alexia, and Agraphia." In *Encyclopedia of Mental Health*, edited by Howard S. Friedman, 81–88. Waltman, MA: Elsevier.

Santuzzi, Alecia M., Pamela R. Waltz, Lisa M. Finkelstein, and Deborah E. Rupp. 2014. "Invisible Disabilities: Unique Challenges for Employees and Organizations." *Industrial and Organizational Psychology* 7, no. 2: 204–219.

Shannon, Claude E. 1948. "A Mathematical Theory of Communication." *Bell System Technical Journal* 27, no. 3: 379–423.

Stovall, Jim, and Raymond H. Hull. 2016. *The Art of Communication: Your Competitive Edge.* Shippensburg, PA: Sound Wisdom Publishing.

Tichenor, Seth, and J. Scott Yaruss. 2018. "A Phenomenological Analysis of the Experience of Stuttering." *American Journal of Speech-Language Pathology* 27, no. 3S: 1180–1194.

Van Hattum, Rolland J. 1980. *Communication Disorders: An Introduction.* New York: MacMillan Publishing.

Wang, Jikun, Yuhao Chen, Cuicui Tan, and Xudong Zhao. 2016. "Family Functioning, Social Support, and Quality of Life for Patients with Anxiety Disorder." *International Journal of Social Psychiatry* 62, no. 1: 5–11.

CHAPTER ELEVEN

Information Services for Students with Anxiety Disorders and Depression

Angel Sloss

Introduction

This chapter engages with information services for students with anxiety disorders and depression. Much of the available/current literature discusses the origin, duration, and psychosis of anxiety disorders and depression, but little research covers how noninstructional faculty and staff should support students outside the classroom. Dr. Christy Oslundd (2014), who wrote the book *Supporting College and University Students with Invisible Disabilities: A Guide for Faculty and Staff Working with Students with Autism, ADHD, Language Processing Disorders, Anxiety, and Mental Illness,* provides a practical framework of support that could be useful to library practitioners. By employing her framework, library practitioners can collaborate in the design and implementation of support services and programming that fit the psychological needs of diverse student/user populations.

This framework is the first of its design to engage library staff and faculty with assistance in understanding anxiety disorders and depression, and bridge the information literacy gaps that exist for those who may avoid or deem the library as a challenging space. This chapter will provide information about and context around mental health–related factors such as background, group identity, physiology, comorbid disorders, presentation, support, and programming while attempting to dispel myths about these disorders. This can help librarians understand what types of services those with depression and anxiety need, what can be provided within the specific context of the library, and facilitate informed decision making as to when/how to reach out or suggest counseling services to students and other users, providing them with access to library resources and programming along with our traditional academic support roles and functions.

Background

Mental health diagnoses have been around for centuries, but the diagnoses themselves have changed over time. The diagnosis of anxiety as an illness was hardly known before the nineteenth century, and the American Psychiatric Association did not recognize anxiety disorders until the 1980s (Crocq 2017, 107). Anxiety is characterized by more than just normal feelings of fear or worry. The Mayo Clinic (Mayo Clinic Staff 2018) defines anxiety as intense, excessive, and persistent worry and fear about everyday situations, with associating symptoms such as fast heart rate, rapid breathing, sweating, and feeling of tiredness.

Furthermore, anxiety is challenging to define due to the different causes and potential degrees of severity. "Although anxiety is related to fear, it is not the same thing. Fear is a direct, focused response to a specific event or object, and the person is consciously aware of it. Anxiety, on the other hand, is often vague and unfocused" (Mitchell 2013, sec. 2, para.1). College-aged students are more susceptible to anxiety due to major life transitions such as moving away from home for the first time, being solely responsible for financing their education, or adapting to a community where they will assume more responsibility for themselves than in their adolescence.

The World Health Organization (WHO) defines depression as different from mood fluctuations and short-lived emotional responses to challenges from everyday life. Instead, depression includes long-lasting, severe changes in feelings that affect work, school, and familial relationships (WHO 2018). Furthermore, WHO stated that more than 264 million people are affected worldwide with depression and barriers such as lack of transportation, monies, and trained health care providers prevent affected individuals from being treated (2018). Depression can result from adverse life events that impact one's social, psychological, and biological well-being. These life events can be associated with trauma such as death, unemployment, abuse, or any other distressing event. Students experiencing mental health challenges on campus may not know how to seek counseling or, more importantly, want to seek counseling. A study conducted by the Harris Poll, The JED Foundation, and other organizations discovered that minority students were less likely to seek counseling services than White students (Steve Fund and JED 2018); thus it is imperative to assist in breaking down the barriers that keep students from seeking counseling.

Myths behind Anxiety and Depression

In order for academic libraries to successfully support students with anxiety or depression, faculty and staff must be aware of the myths surrounding both disorders. The goal of the library is to assist and support patrons, and to do so equitably rather than stereotyping patrons, including those who may suffer from anxiety or depression. Part of performing this work effectively is learning about the patrons' lived experiences to the extent one can, and to use knowledge rather than myths to inform the thoughtful provision of information services. Anxiety and depression affect each patron differently, and treatment does not have a one-size-fits-all approach. The Anxiety and Depression Association of America (2018) interviewed Sally Winston, a psychologist, in 2013 about myths that those with anxiety or depression may endure. One myth associated with anxiety and depression is that some people are natural worriers or naturally obsessive, and therefore treatment would not help the affected individual. However, the reality is that therapy can help longtime sufferers and assist with reducing certain behaviors that exasperate anxiety and depression.

In particular, cognitive behavior therapy (CBT) is showing long-term beneficial effects for those people affected by anxiety/depression. CBT is a type of treatment that allows affected persons to understand the thoughts and feelings that influence their behaviors.

Campus partnerships are a critical way to help patrons access resources that they may find useful. For example, a partnership with the university counseling center to host events about mental health awareness allows the library to provide a safe space for counseling during stressful times in the semester, such as midterms and finals, to assist university students. By working in partnership with the counseling center, this creates more straightforward access to mental health professionals within the university and streamlines student access to treatment.

Another myth about anxiety disorder is that anxiety affects all or no one. As Oslund (2014) expresses, "The biggest misinformation related to anxiety disorder grows from the practice of using similar words to mean very different things" (23). Many people express feeling anxious when taking a critical test or speaking in front of a large group of people. However, this type of anxiety is much different from the obtrusive and worrisome thoughts associated with the disorder. The acute anxiety that is associated with test taking dissipates once the activity has ended. Those with anxiety, however, may feel their well-being is being threatened, that their life is out of order, or may become easily overstimulated, unlike those who experience bouts of anx-iousness. Therefore, it is imperative not to diminish any feelings that a stu-dent may share surrounding their experiences with anxiety. Instead, it is vital to understand their perspective and to understand how we can assist them in our role as librarians, or how we can critically examine existing pro-grams and services to be more inclusive. For example, schedule smaller events on the weekends for those who do not want to come to sizable events during the weekdays, or schedule frequent but small workshops to encour-age more participation from the student body.

Now, let us look at a couple of myths surrounding depression. Interest-ingly, one myth is that depression does not affect students. Students may believe that everyone else can become depressed, but it will not happen to them (Back to Campus 2019). The truth is that nearly half of all college stu-dents feel they have been depressed at one point, with 15 percent diagnosed with clinical depression (Back to Campus 2019). There is a misconception surrounding depression that insists that it is only temporary, and even that it is not a real medical problem. However, depression can last for a very long time and in some cases requires medical treatment. This particular miscon-ception may lead students to not seek help because they believe they will eventually get better with time, or they worry that their feelings of sadness may not be taken seriously by a clinical professional. By talking more about depression on campus through forums or campaigns, the campus commu-nity can help destigmatize the illness and prevent tragedies, such as suicide, which is, the third leading cause of death for eighteen- to twenty-four-year-olds from happening (Center for Disease Control and Prevention 2019).

Related to this is the perception that talking about depression only makes it worse. A therapist, such as a psychiatrist, a psychologist, a social worker, or counselor can help students understand how to manage their mood and feel-ings. Students can talk about their emotions to someone who understands and supports them, gives them tools to shift their thought processes, as well as other treatments. Therapy will help the student build confidence and feel better about him or herself as he or she begins to work with the therapist to find solutions to problems that may have seemed insurmountable when he or she was feeling depressed and maybe even hopeless. Overall, talking can assist students in dealing with their issues at hand and help provide them with the emotional support they need (Smith, Robinson, and Segal 2019).

Group Identity

There is much literature in print and online that reflects an increase in anxiety and depression among college-aged students. College life is engulfed in uncertainty and stress as students encounter new educational and social experiences. Weaver (2016) emphasized that 80 percent of students felt overwhelmed by responsibilities, and 50 percent felt anxious because they struggled with school (27). Additionally, Weaver interviewed Victor Schwartz, medical director of The JED Foundation in New York, who expressed that many college-aged students are worried about the economy, the debt they will accrue while in college, and job prospects later on down the road (26).

Another cause contributing to the rise of anxiety and depression is racism. Racism is a prevalent issue on college campuses today. "Often minority students are told that their racialized experiences on campus are figments of their imagination" (Weaver 2016, 26). When counselors, staff, or faculty become dismissive of complaints of racism by students of color, it adds to the painful experience that one faces being a person of color in America, particularly during a tense time when racism, in part fueled by the presidential administration, appears to be on the rise. "Students identified experiencing a nexus of multiple forms of racism broken down into six parts: individual racism, institutional racism, cultural racism, structural racism, police violence, and racial micro-aggressions" (Ingram and Wallace 2019, 84).

- Individual racism—the student is facing disparaging remarks about his/her beliefs, attitudes, and his/her actions.
- Institutional racism—racism students face on the university level itself, often seen in public institutions with a large majority population.
- Cultural racism—social interactions students encounter that only reflect the needs of one ethnic group while demeaning or ignoring the needs of another ethnic group.
- Police violence—students being racially profiled while engaging in academic or extracurricular activities.
- Structural racism—for example, colleges and universities participating in programming that promotes diversity, but limit the number of diverse applicants who can apply (e.g., racial exclusivity in obtaining elite university internships).

Weaver conveyed that the multiple facets of racism that students of color can face during college increase their chances of experiencing anxiety and depression much more than white students might (2016). Also, high-achieving African American students enrolled in the fields of science, technology, engineering, and mathematics (STEM) not only face the six types of racism but often face mental stress as well, as they feel pushed to prove they are the best and the brightest among their peer groups (Weaver 2016, 26). Thus, it is imperative to have an ethnically diverse group of counselors on campus, or those trained in ethnicity inclusion and cultural sensitivity to assist students with mental health issues linked to racism. Librarians being aware of how racism, as well as other forms of discrimination like homophobia, can impact students' mental health, and having resources available to direct them toward, is an important part of our work in helping students find the assistance they need.

Physiology

One of the major themes found in research on anxiety and depression is that persons with a family history of mental disorders are more likely to have inherited the disorder (Mayo Clinic Staff 2018). Also, particularly with anxiety, it does not need to show up within family history as it can occur due to environmental factors (Mayo Clinic Staff 2018). These can include the stress of living within a growing city, traffic, pollution, climate, residing within an area with lots of noise, job-related stress, or the stress of attending college.

In today's climate, many citizens go to great lengths to secure spots at prestigious universities, in order to increase their likelihood of having a bright future that includes a prosperous career and high earnings. In this environment, it is no wonder that there has been a spike in students suffering from the unabashed emotional turmoil of crushing anxiety, hopelessness, and despair. College admission today is more competitive than it has ever been (Hoffower 2018) with some wealthy families offering bribes for their children to be admitted to top schools (Medina 2019), whereas lower-income citizens may be studying more or taking an overload of classes to secure a spot at the university of their choice.

The significant pressure to be admitted and do well in college has resulted in an increase in mental health issues among millennials and Generation Z. Once these issues start to surface, students may seek out mental health services to assist them. Therefore, academic libraries must find innovative ways to provide services that help ease the stress of such a life-changing moment. These can include anything from meditation workshops to partnering with campus and community mental health organizations or building up robust collections of resources related to anxiety and depression. Most of all, being educated about mental health and offering our time, patience, and thoughtful services to those with anxiety and depression can help reduce stigma for those seeking referrals to counseling or other resources within the campus environment.

Comorbid Disorder(s) and Presentation

Hranov expresses that

Depression and anxiety frequently coexist in the same individual, either concurrently or at different times, and numerous studies show that the presence of an anxiety disorder is the single strongest risk factor for the development of depression. When the two coexist simultaneously, either as diagnosed disorders or subsyndromal states, they may view as mixed anxiety–depression or as comorbid syndromes, i.e., separate disorders occurring concurrently. (2007, 171)

Unique behavioral characteristics associated with anxiety and depression were mentioned previously in the chapter, such as a pervasive feeling of worry or changes in mood. The National Institute of Mental Health (2018) states that other symptoms may include heart palpitations, trembling or shaking, and shortness of breath. A student may exhibit all signs during a crisis or just a couple of signs. Those with anxiety may feel out of control or experience a constant fear of impending doom. Students who have depression or solely suffer from depression may display signs of hopelessness, decreased energy, isolation from student activities or hobbies, and suffer from physical pain like stomachaches and headaches, in addition to having difficulty making choices or attending classes. Students may overeat or not eat at all and appear to be very irritable (NIMH 2018). Although anxiety and depression can be present within a person, other mental health conditions like obsessive-compulsive disorder (OCD) marked by uncontrollable reoccurring thoughts and actions, or agoraphobia, a fear of places and crowds, may also be present.

Support and Programming

Often, students may not feel comfortable initially seeking help or inquiring about resources on anxiety and depression. This is why libraries must offer resources that address such issues, and provide a bridge to connect patrons with available support within the library and, most importantly, across the campus community.

There are several things the library can provide to students to assist with access to mental health services within the academic library environment. For starters, the library can consult with counseling services to bring initiatives into the library during peak events such as midterms and finals to check in with students. Providing a quiet space for counseling services to operate within the library assists with making counseling more accessible to students. The library can allocate areas where display boards and handouts are given to provide free information about mental health awareness and university counseling services so that students can independently make a choice to take information as needed, rather than feel that the library or staff are pressuring them into services or asking them to self-identify as someone with anxiety or depression.

Lastly, expand collection development related to mental health. When selecting titles on mental health–related issues, ensure that these titles focus on community needs and requests: as the Association of Specialized and Cooperative Library Agencies (ASCLA) points out, never assume (2019). A great addition to any library collection would be Graphic Medicine (https://www.graphicmedicine.org). Graphic Medicine combines visual storytelling and medicine to offer its readers a unique experience by providing insight on mental illnesses, treatments, and available health care services via comics. Furthermore, it would be in the best interest of the student to work with staff to display sufficient signage to allow students to navigate independently. It is imperative to note that as library professionals, we do not want to put ourselves in a position where we are acting as counselors or health care professionals. The goal is to fast-track services for students by establishing a rapport with the university counseling center and other relevant resources. As some colleges and universities may not have counseling centers, partnering with public health services in the community is vital.

Many public libraries and a few academic libraries are buying new furniture to help students stay fit mentally and physically by purchasing study cycles (stationary bicycle desks), which can ease stress through exercise. Some are also purchasing cots to create nap rooms for their students. A study called "Sleep and Mental Health" on neuroimaging and neurochemistry suggests that a good night's sleep helps foster both mental and emotional resilience (2019). Academic libraries can learn from public libraries when deciding what type of programming would be appropriate for their student body.

For example, Colorado's Longmont Public Library began circulating Well-Being Bags, stocked with books, movies, music, and articles designed to spark conversations about mental health (Peet 2019, 52). The bags can be checked out to patrons who need to spark meaningful conversations about mental health with their loved ones. They have also added additional bags called Experience Bags to promote healthier and happy lives. Experience Bags contain popular movies and books on subjects like dogs, cats, chocolate, and how to take care of a loved one suffering from a mental health issue. This initiative, in partnership with the organization Supporting Action for Mental Health, has allowed the library to curate useful and relatable material for the community they serve. Students and faculty can benefit from such bags in helping spark open conversations about mental health on campus, especially during midterm and finals weeks.

Memorial University Libraries (MUL) in Canada is taking a step commonly seen at public libraries by providing pet therapy. Volunteers were sent to the library from a nearby therapy dog program to help alleviate psychological stress. MUL librarians received positive feedback from students, with many students expressing thoughts about their own animals back home. Not only do they have therapy dogs available, but the library now provides students the opportunity to interact with guinea pigs as well. MUL also provides other mental health initiatives to help students, such as meditation classes to teach students about mindfulness (moment-to-moment awareness), and coloring to reduce anxiety.

Continuing Education: National Network of Libraries of Medicine

Academic staff can also support mental health in libraries by taking courses administered by the National Network of Libraries of Medicine (NNLM). NNLM in conjunction with the National Institutes of Health (NIH) and the National Library of Medicine (NLM) provide a plethora of courses and information resources to support mental health within the academic community. The most sought out course under this program is "Caring for the Mind: Providing Mental Health Information at Your Library" (https://nnlm.gov/class /caring_2020), which provides detailed information on how to disseminate health information within the library setting. Participants learn about the most effective electronic resources to consult and offer ways to improve their collection. Some of the resources covered within the class are Medline Plus, Drug Information Portal, DailyMed, and Pillbox, to name a few.

The course "Caring for the Mind: Providing Mental Health Information at Your Library" will help one gain awareness about mental health issues affecting the community, and learn how to respond to tough reference questions posed by the student body. In addition, it covers the latest collection development tools, websites, and resources that focus on mental health. Often academic libraries are left out of the discussion of mental health, leaving the library unprepared to interact with students seeking mental health services. Courses like those offered through NNLM are valuable to the academic library unit because they often fulfill training that staff does not receive on the university level.

Library professionals who work for a historically Black colleges and universities (HBCU) may find it challenging to know what programming works best for the library as students of color are less likely to seek out mental health services (Primm 2019). Dr. Charnequa Austin Kennedy, director of Tennessee State University's Counseling Services, says that she sees an increase in students needing basic social skills, so having programming to address those needs is very appropriate (Charnequa Austin Kennedy,personal communication, October 29, 2019). Dr. Kennedy mentioned that some students suffering from mental health challenges simply may be lonely and are unaware of how to make friends. Students are in an age of social media, and they know how to connect to people but not necessarily how to build friendships, so having programming that encourages socialization one-on-one is essential.

She further adds that students can be assisted not only by adding furniture but by having items to check out for low-level need-of-care students. For example, fidget spinners, slinkies, yo-yos, light therapy lamps, and a blanket would allow students to independently self-soothe and allow employees to show nonverbal support while promoting mental health wellness within the academic library setting. The goal is to keep the student from escalating to a higher level need of care, and items like this could possibly prevent the student from escalating.

Other initiatives that Tennessee State University hosts include the Let's Talk Program. The Let's Talk Program is a nonclinical line of care and service that allows students to meet with a counseling specialist outside of the actual counseling center. They have set up numerous locations within the library, residence halls, and student athletics to lessen the stigma for students seeking help. The program is a national initiative that all colleges and universities can participate in. Additionally, if faculty and staff are not feeling confident about how to effectively engage with students who are suffering with anxiety or depression, the library can contact counseling services for assistance. Counseling staff is available for consultation with faculty and staff regarding student well-being and outreach presentations. For those students who may not be ready to seek help or talk with a counselor, they may contact the TSU Counseling Center for access to a confidential online screening tool that is available 24/7 to complete a check-in about mental health wellness in the areas of stress, depression, anxiety, eating concerns, mood, alcohol use, and substance use. Students may take more than one of these screeners or complete a screener more than once to monitor any changes.

Lastly, another initiative that the counseling center is working on is mental health first aid training. The Tennessee State University counseling staff is undergoing training to become certified as instructors of mental health, in order to assist in the training of faculty/staff around campus. Their goal is to inform university personnel of what to do and the universal language needed to talk with students suffering from mental health disorders. The training consists of faculty and staff doing a personal assessment before they engage in dialogue with a student, as well as how to access immediate assistance when a student is in a crisis. The most important thing to remember is that librarians and staff should only enter a dialogue after assessing whether they are themselves emotionally able to assist a student who may be in a mental health crisis. From there, the library should seek out immediate assistance from the counseling center and any other appropriate departments (such as emergency services if the student expresses suicidal thoughts) while ensuring the student is safe.

Academic libraries may receive some pushback about accommodating students with mental health challenges (Peet 2019). In addition, Peet explains that staff may also object to being asked to engage with students who display symptoms of mental health crisis because it makes them feel uncomfortable, or they feel unprepared to assist (2019). It is critical to balance staff concerns for safety with the need to get the student immediate assistance from qualified professionals, and to have clear plans in place to care for both. Mental health on campus is not an issue that is going away, so preparing employees to keep their role in engagement to a minimum while servicing the student's needs is essential. In addition, encouraging staff to support and encourage one another can boost confidence in caring for students with depression and anxiety. Asking library staff in what ways they are willing to engage or assist a student in distress may yield a reasonable solution that will benefit all.

Conclusion

Dr. Christy Oslund's framework of understanding the background, myths, group identity, physiology, comorbidity, and presentation of anxiety and depression allows practitioners of the library field to understand the origin of these disorders and what resources are needed to help such students. Not only does this framework help provide us with a perspective of what types of resources libraries must allocate to assist affected students but the framework allows professionals to reflect on appropriate programming for impacted students.

While reviewing the research, it was evident that more needs to be done for students who need counseling services. The research allowed me to reflect on my own experiences assisting students with anxiety and depression, as well as my own personal struggles with dealing with anxiety and depression, giving me the chance to think about how to show sympathy and compassion when providing services for students with mental illnesses. The most important conclusion that I came to was that academic librarians need to remember that each student exhibits anxiety or depression in their own way. The signs may be subtle or pronounced, chronic or short term. No matter how students present these signs, it is important to remember that they are human beings who need to be served and supported just like any other student. Furthermore, it is important to acknowledge that the students you encounter may be facing mental health struggles, whether or not those have been explicitly self-disclosed by the student.

A student will encounter good days as well as bad days, so it is imperative to not take any negative reactions personally when interacting with students displaying symptoms of anxiety and depression. Anxiety and depression can affect relationships, and those facing anxiety and depression may be more sensitive to verbal responses in conversations. They might view what others are telling them with greater suspicion and give passive-aggressive responses. In these moments, there are a couple of things staff can do to connect with the patron. Try to use mindful listening. Focus on what the student is trying to express, clarify by asking the student questions (if needed), and then try sharing your response. This helps ensure that you are hearing what the student needs correctly and that you are on the same communication path. If the student needs support, the other thing to do is to ask the student what type of support they prefer. The student might just need a listening ear or positive words of affirmation. An affirmation can be essential as some sufferers may feel isolated, abandoned, or that no one cares for them. By taking the affirmation approach, library professionals can affirm that they are here to help the student get the services they need.

The library field is a service-oriented profession, making it critical for employees to take care of themselves as well. Interacting with students who suffer with anxiety and depression can take a toll emotionally and physically. Taking on too much responsibility during interactions can have an adverse effect, and it is important to set boundaries around what help you are able to offer (e.g., referrals to counselors rather than counseling itself or limiting the amount of time spent helping the patron). It is also important to practice self-care. Try de-stressing by engaging in physical or creative activites—for example, taking a yoga class or utilizing an adult coloring book for relaxation.

Helping students with mental illness can be challenging, and often staff may feel as if they are getting it wrong; whether or not that is the case, it is vital for library practitioners to remember that they are doing their best to help, and having training as well as a clear sense of what resources and services are available can help. In time, staff will become more comfortable with their skills and abilities to assist those with distress disorders. The continuing increase of mental health disorders across college campuses does not seem to be going away. Therefore, the more faculty and staff become involved in promoting mental wellness, the more prepared they are to make mental health resources more accessible.

References

"Back to Campus: Do You Know the Facts? Breaking Down the Myths about Depression." n.d. Retrieved October 25, 2019, from https://roar.nevadaprc .org/system/documents/3392/original/NPRC.1185.BreakingDownThe MythsAboutDepression.pdf?1436890089.

Centers for Disease Control and Prevention. 2019. "Gateway to Health Communication." Retrieved August 12, 2019, from https://www.cdc.gov/health communication/toolstemplates/entertainmented/index.html?CDC_AA _refVal=https://www.cdc.gov/healthcommunication/toolstemplates /entertainmented/tips/SuicideYouth.html.

Crocq, M.-A. 2017. "The History of Generalized Anxiety Disorder as a Diagnostic Category." *Dialogues in Clinical Neuroscience* 19, no. 2: 107–116.

Hoffower, Hillary. 2018. "9 Ways College Is Different for Millennials than It Was for Previous Generations." *Business Insider*, September 24. https://www .businessinsider.com/how-college-is-different-now-then-millennials-vs -baby-boomers-2018-9#college-is-more-expensive.

Hranov, Luchezar G. 2007. "Comorbid Anxiety and Depression: Illumination of a Controversy." *International Journal of Psychiatry in Clinical Practice* 11, no. 3: 171–189. doi:10.1080/13651500601127180.

Ingram, LaDrea, and Barbara Wallace. 2019. "'It Creates Fear and Divides Us:' Minority College Students' Experiences of Stress from Racism, Coping Responses, and Recommendations for Colleges." *Journal of Health Disparities Research & Practice* 12, no. 1: 80–112.

Mayo Clinic Staff. 2018. "Anxiety Disorders." May 4. https://www.mayoclinic .org/diseases-conditions/anxiety/symptoms-causes/syc-20350961.

Medina, Jennifer. 2019. "Actresses, Business Leaders and Other Wealthy Parents Charged in U.S. College Entry Fraud." *The New York Times*, March 14. https://nyti.ms/2F8Km15.

Mitchell, Mark A. 2013. "Anxiety." In *The Gale Encyclopedia of Nursing and Allied Health,* 3rd ed., edited by Brigham Narins. Farmington, MI: Gale.

"Myths and Misconceptions about Anxiety." n.d. Retrieved January 11, 2020, from https://adaa.org/understanding-anxiety/myth-conceptions.

National Institute of Mental Health. U.S. 2018. "Anxiety Disorders." Last revised July 2018. https://www.nimh.nih.gov/health/topics/anxiety-disorders /index.shtml.

National Institute of Mental Health. 2018. "Depression." Last revised February 2018. https://www.nimh.nih.gov/health/topics/depression/index.shtml.

National Network of Libraries of Medicine. n.d. "About MAR." Retrieved October 25, 2019, from https://nnlm.gov/mar/about.

Oslund, Christy. 2014. *Supporting College and University Students with Invisible Disabilities: A Guide for Faculty and Staff Working with Students with Autism, AD/HD, Language Processing Disorders, Anxiety, and Mental Illness.* London: Jessica Kingsley Publishers.

Peet, Lisa. 2019. "Mental Wellness: Libraries across the Country Are Finding New Ways to Support Patrons Experiencing Mental Health Challenges—as Well as the Staff Who Serve Them." *Library Journal* 144, no. 5: 48–53.

Primm, Annelle B. 2018. "College Students of Color: Overcoming Mental Health Challenges." National Aliance of Mental Illness. July 16. https://www.nami .org/Blogs/NAMI-Blog/July-2018/College-Students-of-Color-Overcoming -Mental-Health.

"Sleep and Mental Health." 2019. *Harvard Mental Health Letter.* Updated March 18, 2019. https://www.health.harvard.edu/newsletter_article/sleep -and-mental-health.

Smith, Melinda, Lawrence Robinson, and Jeanne Segal. n.d. "Helping Someone with Depression." Last updated November 5, 2019. https://www.helpguide .org/articles/depression/helping-someone-with-depression.htm.

"The Steve Fund and JED Launch Equity in Mental Health Framework to Support College Students of Color." 2017. The JED Foundation. November 9. https:// www.jedfoundation.org/steve-fund-jed-launch-equity-mental-health -framework-support-college-students-color.

Weaver, Sandra Long. 2016. "High Anxiety: Colleges Are Seeing an Increase in the Number of Students with Diagnosable Mental Illness, Anxiety and Depression." *Diverse Issues in Higher Education. Gale Academic Onefile.* Database.

World Health Organization. 2019. "Depression." December 4. https://www.who .int/news-room/fact-sheets/detail/depression.

CHAPTER TWELVE

Secrecy, Avoidance, Shame, and Misunderstanding

Where University Libraries Are Struggling to Support Mentally Ill Students and Opportunities for Change

Abigail L. Phillips

Introduction

There is an established and dynamic dialogue about various facets of disability within library and information science (LIS) research (Guder 2010; Hill 2013). However, discussing mental illness as a disability and identifying ways to support students are often neglected. This could be a result of mental illness being incorrectly identified and thus overlooked as a disability, the intense prejudice and shame attached to mental illness, or misunderstanding by faculty, instructors, university administrators, and other students (Reilly 2018; Storrie, Ahern, and Tuckett 2010). Whatever the combination of factors, mentally ill students are at a disadvantage when striving to complete a degree.

This chapter will draw on literature from nursing and behavioral health and include the discourse within the accessibility and disability justice movements (Kumbier and Starkey 2016). By pulling from outside, but adjacent, fields, this chapter will provide practical insights into ways mentally ill students can be better served by librarians and possibilities for advancing the current research within LIS surrounding mental illness and mental health.

University and college students are uniquely underserved when considering mental health care (Reilly 2018). Although many higher education institutions provide mental health services (e.g., therapy sessions, group therapy, psychiatric clinics) on campus, students may be either unaware of these resources, fear reaching out to advisors or instructors for help, struggle with stigma and shame, unable to recognize the severity of their mental struggles, or endure long waitlist for services (Reilly 2018). Seeking out local resources is often unworkable due to lack of insurance, financial challenges, and/or perceived or actual lack of support from family and friends. As a result, mentally ill students suffer in silence, being both stigmatized and isolated by peers, which impacts their educational experience (Eisenberg et al. 2009).

For this chapter, the author uses the American Psychiatric Association (APA) *Diagnostic and Statistical Manual of Mental Disorders: DSM-V* definitions of mental illness and mental health. Mental illnesses are defined as "health conditions involving changes in emotion, thinking or behavior (or a combination of these). Mental illnesses are associated with distress and/or problems functioning in social, work, or family activities" (APA 2013, 20).

Mental health is an umbrella term under which a variety of mental concerns fall, from an individual experiencing a milder, although still profoundly impactful, mental health issue such as grief over the end of a relationship to severe, lifelong mental illness such as schizophrenia (APA 2013, 22). This chapter will focus on mental illness advocacy in a way that treats assistance and awareness not as simply an important service to students, but as a plea for equity of access to education for disabled students. Although the author conducts research on mental illness and mental health, she is not a medical professional and does not possess the training of a therapist, social worker, or psychiatrist.

In articles from *The Atlantic, The New York Times,* and *The Chronicle of Higher Education*, the high demand for counseling services by university students is detailed, as well as the inability at times for these centers to meet student needs due to the overwhelming demand ("Campus Mental Health" n.d.; Kwai 2016; Wolverton 2019). In a 2018 report from the American College Health Association (ACHA), 53.4 percent of students responded that they have felt hopeless within the last twelve months. Forty-two percent felt so depressed that they found it hard to function. Twelve percent responded that they had seriously considered suicide. These are black and white, difficult numbers to comprehend and distill what are the helpful and practical ways to support these students.

Grassroots Efforts

Across the broader library and information landscape, libraries, including public, academic, and school libraries, have made efforts to connect services and resources with patrons in need as seen through the growing inclusion of social workers as library staff, outreach to homeless youth, and a growing interest by administrators in providing training for working with mentally ill patrons (see Johnson n.d.; Westbrook 2015). Libraries are not alone in this effort. Museums have held special afternoon sessions or days for children, youth, and adults on the spectrum as well as those with related spectrum disorders (Colangelo 2018). These separate and tailored experiential periods provide library access to those who might otherwise avoid this environment due to cognitive limitations and emotional challenges.

Other efforts have been made within the LIS community, including a mental health zine focusing on mental health experiences among LIS professionals from MLIS students, librarians, archivists, museum workers, faculty, and others (Phillips et al. 2019; Pho et al. 2018) as well as instructor policies regarding student mental health and wellness included in syllabi. For example, the author of this chapter includes a "Mental Health and Well-Being" instructor policy in her syllabi, along with local and national mental health resources. Another assistant professor at a Midwestern iSchool makes it clear from the start of the semester that mental health and wellness of students is a priority and an aspect of her teaching she is constantly reworking to help students where they are.

Two librarians, Cecily Walker and Kelly McElroy, in 2016 began LIS Mental Health Week (*#LISMentalHealth*) largely through the medium of Twitter, typically held during mid-February (McElory 2018; Smale 2016). During this week, those within the LIS community blog about experiences with mental illness, a Twitter chat is held providing an avenue for discussion in a platform that supports this form of quick exchange of thoughts and reflections, and libraries are encouraged to host programming that raise awareness and help demystify mental illness (Waryan 2018). Although promising and exciting, these are still on the fringe of LIS and everyday work in university libraries. Additionally, how does internal LIS mental health advocacy translate to the front desk work of a librarian working with a distressed student? How can librarians and library staff, working within their professional capacity, without the training of a therapist or social worker, but still in the role of service professionals, be of assistance?

When considering librarianship as a field, and academic library work in particular, which is intricately linked to supporting patrons by connecting them with information, some questions arise: How can more be done to train information professionals to be aware of mental health and better serve patrons? What support is needed and desired? What support can be provided that is lacking, including within the classrooms of LIS instructors? What connections can be made across campuses to improve the provision of critical mental health information?

What Is Currently Provided in University Libraries?

Many university libraries offer wellness and mental health–geared interactive passive programming, events, speakers, and other activities during finals week, midterms, and throughout the semester for students, sometimes casually in the common spaces. For example, a midwestern university's library provided a passive program in which students could anonymously add tips, reflections, and comments on dealing with stress using a large white board as a medium.

Other libraries invite therapy dogs, host yoga classes, hold meditation, and/or mindfulness sessions, book clubs, and coloring activities as a source of anxiety and stress relief (Jalongo and McDevitt 2015). As complementary therapies in the library, although the research is in early stages, these types of activities have been shown to help decrease student stress and anxiety as well as enhance student engagement (Ramsey and Aagard 2018; Rose, Godfrey, and Rose 2016; Sparks 2017).

Another example, similar to the above paragraph, in a central meeting space within a university library, shows a popular form of passive programming using a whiteboard. In this library, the question changes weekly depending on what is going on around campus (e.g., finals, Spring Break), questions about health and well-being, and random silly requests.

The flyer shown in Figure 12.1 promotes a mental health awareness week occurring within the library of School of Clinical Medicine around the topic of mental health

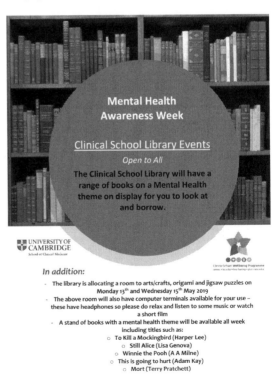

Figure 12.1 Mental Health Awareness Week: Clinical School Library Events

as well as selected books that highlight mental health. This library staff not only offer an activity, but also a quiet space for those in need, and a collection of books all focused on mental health as an overarching theme.

Much like public libraries, McGill University Library created a display of books available for check out following the theme of well-being. Although not mental health or mental illness specific, this type of display helps promote the importance of taking care of one s mind and body.

The additional benefit of hosting mental health and wellness initiatives within the library is the opportunity for collaboration with the university's student health center (Ramsey and Aagard 2018). As a number of studies have highlighted students' lack of awareness regarding the health services available to them on campus and within the larger community, a partnership between a university library and other support services has the potential to encourage information sharing and build opportunities for library staff mental health training (Jalongo and McDevitt 2015).

However, these activities and programs are momentary in nature, only appearing around specific events or periods during a semester. For example, bringing in therapy dogs and yoga instructors is geared toward anxiety and stress reduction during midterms or finals week (Jalongo and McDevitt 2015), a time when students would understandably feel anxiety and stress about prepping for an exam, project, or final grades. However, this type of stress and anxiety is, while difficult, attached to an exam, graduating, or finishing a project. Generalized anxiety disorder, panic disorder, and post-traumatic stress disorder (PTSD) are diagnosable mental illnesses that can last months, years, or a lifetime ("Psychology Topics" 2019).

The mental health and wellness care demonstrated in some of the above examples demonstrate a surface level of mental health understanding. Is this how university libraries view advocacy for mental illness? A broad spectrum of self-care, meditation, and crafting activities are helpful to some but may be a weak cure-all for someone with a chronic, persistent illness. A combination of destressing activities (e.g., therapy dogs in the library), collaborative work with a university's counseling center (e.g., programs on stress management tips), and, as mentioned earlier, training for librarians and library staff, particularly frontline workers, on basic mental health resources and techniques for getting students the help they need.

What *They* May Not Understand

They encompasses university staff, faculty, teaching staff, library administrators, librarians/library workers, and other employees within the university system who engage with undergraduate, graduate, and doctoral students in some way. It is critical to think beyond the library: the library does not exist in a silo. Research has indicated that university staff lack the proper mental health literacy or the training to appropriately support mentally ill students (Gulliver et al. 2017).

What training is available is met with skepticism toward efficacy and unease about the standards of the training, particularly when considering online health interventions and mental resources for students (Farrer et al. 2015). Although the research focuses largely on mental health services for on-campus students, as more and more students choose an online educational avenue either entirely or in a hybrid program, there is a need to explore how online students' mental health needs can be supported even at a distance. As online students' engagement with instructors, staff, and university resources lack the face-to-face element, there are small additions, such as incorporating relevant mental health support and crisis contact information into libraries' websites, introductory information about making it through graduate school as a distance student, and sharing national and regional resources with instructors who teach online, encouraging them to take the proactive step of sharing with students. More information is better, particularly when considering mental health resources. Easily findable and regularly updated information on national and regional media health organizations would help reduce the felt embarrassment or stigma regarding mental illness, and it would demonstrate a commitment to student health.

Training and Guidance

Faculty, staff, and administrators' lack of knowledge regarding depression, generalized anxiety disorders, eating disorders, self-harm, suicidal ideation, and other mental illnesses speaks to a larger misunderstanding of not only what students are experiencing, but the degree to which students are struggling from the undergraduate to the doctoral level. Substantial, university-wide training is a critical need to recognize signs, engage, and respond when help is needed (Gulliver et al. 2018). University librarians must be a part of this discussion alongside other university staff, faculty, and administration.

Without training or knowledge sharing, librarians and library staff run this risk of further enhancing a feeling of otherness in students with a mental illness. Otherness is a term used in sociological research but is infrequently applied within psychology and other health sciences fields (Appelqvist-Schmidlechner et al. 2016). For some individuals who are mentally ill, otherness is an intense feeling "of being perceived as abnormal or different" (39). Preexisting stigma, shame, and stereotypes of the mentally ill are factors contributing to the experience of otherness (Leavey 2009).

Although this chapter is a part of a book focusing on university libraries, it is impossible to ignore the systemic problems regarding the mental health of students at the university level. In 2010, Storrie, Ahern, and Tuckett conducted a review of the literature regarding "emotional and or mental health problems of university students worldwide" (1). The authors provide several recommendations for universities, including offering improved connections between the university and external mental health providers and growing students' awareness of supportive services both within the university and community mental health providers. A notable takeaway from the work of these researchers is the call for "policies and personnel with expertise in mental health" (1). Not all university staff should be expected to have expertise in mental health and mental illness (it simply is not practical or realistic), but guidance from policies and personnel with this experience is a leap in a hopeful direction.

Potential Roadblocks

Roadblocks to adequate and consistent mental health care are a problem beyond libraries and universities, but within the LIS community there are unique barriers (Pescosolido 2020; Schnyder et al. 2020). The customer service–driven nature of librarianship and library work can have negative impacts on those library workers working day-to-day with patrons. Additionally, as previously mentioned, a lack of training by librarians and library staff alongside the possibility of a lack of awareness of mental health as a lived experience by students and university staff is a concern.

Compassion Fatigue and Emotional Labor

Two topics of frequent discussion within the library community are compassion fatigue and emotional labor (Shuler and Morgan 2013; Westbrook 2015). Shared stories of these experiences often include references to burnout and can be seen through practitioner articles, blog posts, tweets, Facebook private groups, and shares on other social media platforms (Geary and Hickey 2019). One of the many calls within the LIS community is for self-care and self-awareness when feeling overwhelmed, much the same call within other professions such as nursing (Eberle 2018; Hector, Paige, Hector, and Bonifas 2019).

The empathy work acted on a day-to-day basis with university students, student workers, faculty, university administration, and more, along with the inherent customer service nature of librarianship, can lead to intense emotional labor. This type of labor requires an individual to "to induce or suppress feelings to sustain the outward countenance that produces the proper state of mind in others" (Shuler and Morgan 2013, 120). Along with all the other stressors a librarian or library staff member may experience, emotional labor is one more factor that can contribute to burnout. Burnout can lead to apathy toward the job, depression, a feeling of helplessness, and potentially leaving the librarianship profession (Geary and Hickey 2019).

For university libraries to successfully serve mentally ill students, there is a need for empathy from library administrators regarding the mental health of their employees, including education about mental health and mental illness, initiating strong internal changes to reduce the stigma surrounding mental illness, and a venue for librarians and library staff members to share their experience with colleagues (Burns and Green 2019). If library employees themselves do not feel comfortable or understood sharing and acknowledging personal mental health concerns in the workplace, their ability to support a patron in need is diminished, particularly if they are experiencing a substantial amount of emotional labor and compassion fatigue (Eberle 2018).

Barriers to Seeking Help

Students may not understand the terminology used in the mental health care system (Appelqvist-Schmidlechner et al. 2016). They may also not understand the signs of major depression, generalized anxiety disorder, bipolar disorder, or other disorders (Schomerus et al. 2019). This reflects back to the earlier discussed challenges of mental health literacy among students, librarians and library staff, instructors, and university staff (Campbell et al. 2019).

Again, students' lack of awareness about mental health resources, both those within the university and externally, is a substantial problem that must be addressed on a wider university level (Storrie, Ahern, and Tuckett 2010). Lyndon, Crowe, Wuensch, McCammon, and Davis (2019) found educational campaigns that highlight the similarities between mentally ill students and nondiagnosed students may be one way to help destigmatize mental illness among undergraduate students. A campaign of this nature and others that "normalize" mental illness and mental health concerns could be shared via social media, university websites, listservs, and more—encouraging to students undiagnosed to reach out for help and treatment.

What Lies Ahead for University Library Support of Students?

Libraries are a stopping point for individuals in need of finding information whether a specific book or a referral to another organization within their community for further assistance is needed. University libraries serve as multiple points of support as well. Students receive technology support, research consultations, and an environment that encourages study and gathering.

Librarians and Library Staff as Gatekeepers

With universities offering counseling, psychiatric, and other mental health services to students, sharing this information broadly by making a point to highlight what is available to students is one pathway for libraries to reinforce their established information role (Ramsey and Aagard 2018). As information providers and connectors, librarians and library staff are gatekeepers to mental health resources and a starting place for students to find information easily.

Another simple practice could be the creation of readily available print documents containing mental health resources including those university based, national level, and available assistance within the off-campus community alongside library marketing materials. By doing so, students would not need to ask librarians or library staff questions that may be difficult. Similar information on the library's website and a collaboration with the university's health center and counseling center would be an added benefit for students either as online distance students or those who infrequently visit the library (Smale 2016). However, it is vital for the resources and websites to be clearly visible, identifiable, and easy to find. Undergoing training through organizations, such as Mental Health First Aid, can be a benefit to the professional development of librarians and staff who engage with students on a regular basis and relieve some of the discrimination, prejudice, and shame attached to mental illness (Throgmorton 2017).

Possibilities for Programming, Events, and Library Support

When considering more active involvement with students dealing with mental illness, regularly scheduled, collaborative, and targeted programming could fill a clear need. This would include programs featured throughout the school year and potentially ongoing, evolving projects. These library programs help to develop a sense of community among students through participation and collaboration. Programming ideas that could be tailored to mental health support include zines making events, small maker activities, and one-shot art classes (Gulliver et al. 2019).

Zines are "self-published, non-commercial print-work that is typically produced in small, limited batches" ("What Exactly Is a Zine?" n.d., para. 3). These highly personal and passionate creations offer the artist a venue for self-expression, honesty, and creativity. Zines can focus on a variety of topics such as gender identity, sexuality, feminism, everyday life, and mental health struggles. Much like *Reserve and Renew: The LIS Mental Health Zine* (Pho et al. 2018), zine making is an outlet for shared connection with zinesters and readers.

Maker activities, small-scale projects such as e-textiles and paper circuits, are another outlet for self-expression but with the added component of the maker mind-set. Failure and mistakes are embraced and even celebrated (Martin 2015). For those struggling with mental health issues, an environment of this kind can support the mental well-being of participants who may struggle with mental illness. Consistent, inclusive, and nonableist programming can be created by university librarians and library staff, ideally in collaboration with the health center and counseling center. There is a promise and achievable hope of developing a library environment in which students who live with a mental illness can feel supported, recognized, and (perhaps slightly) understood.

Conclusion

This chapter drew attention to the need for university libraries to make improvements to the ways in which they support mentally ill students. Although not trained as therapists or psychiatrists, librarians, through their MLIS education and professional development, are uniquely placed to serve as connection points between students and mental health resources. Collaborative programming with the counseling center, widely shared information about on- and off-campus support systems, and some degree of basic mental health training for library workers would help further reinforce the library as a space and welcoming space for all.

References

American College Health Association. 2018. "NCHA II Spring 2018 Reference Group Executive Summary." Silver Spring, MD: American College Health Association.

American Psychiatric Association. 2013. *Diagnostic and Statistical Manual of Mental Disorders: DSM-5.* 5th ed. Washington, DC: Author.

Campbell, Laurie O., Jamie Stickl Haugen, Claudia C. Sutter, and Glenn W. Lambie. 2019. "Building Capacity for Mental Health Literacy of Suicidality and Self-Injurious Behaviors: A Formative Design Investigation." *Journal of Formative Design in Learning* 3, no. 1: 53–61.

"Campus Mental Health." n.d. *American Psychological Association.* Retrieved January 21, 2020, from http://www.apa.org/advocacy/higher-education/mental -health/index.aspx.

Colangelo, B. J. 2018. "Cleveland Museum of Natural History Hosting 'Sensory Friendly Sunday' for Patrons on the Autism Spectrum." *Clevescene,* July 10. https://www.clevescene.com/scene-and-heard/archives/2018/07/10 /cleveland-museum-of-natural-history-hosting-sensory-friendly-sunday -for-patrons-on-the-autism-spectrum.

Eisenberg, Daniel, Ezra Golberstein, and Justin B. Hunt. 2009. "Mental Health and Academic Success in College." *The BE Journal of Economic Analysis & Policy* 9, no. 1: 1–35.

Farrer, Louise, Amelia Gulliver, Kylie Bennett, and Kathleen M. Griffiths. 2015. "Exploring the Acceptability of Online Mental Health Interventions among University Teaching Staff: Implications for Intervention Dissemination and Uptake." *Internet Interventions* 2, no. 3: 359–365.

Geary, Jade, and Brittany Hickey. 2019. "When Does Burnout Begin? The Relationship between Graduate School Employment and Burnout amongst

> Librarians." *In the Library with the Lead Pipe*, October 16. http://www.in
> thelibrarywiththeleadpipe.org/2019/when-does-burnout-begin.

Guder, Christopher. 2010. "Equality through Access: Embedding Library Services for Patrons with Disabilities." *Public Services Quarterly* 6, no. 2–3: 315–322.

Gulliver, Amelia, Louise Farrer, Kylie Bennett, and Kathleen M. Griffiths. 2019. "University Staff Mental Health Literacy, Stigma and Their Experience of Students with Mental Health Problems." *Journal of Further and Higher Education* 43, no. 3: 434–442.

Hector, Paige, P. Hector, and R. Bonifas. 2019. "Nursing Home Employee Self-Reflection on Life Stressors and Compassion Fatigue." *Journal of the American Medical Directors Association* 20, no. 3: B30–B31.

Hill, Heather. 2013. "Disability and Accessibility in the Library and Information Science Literature: A Content Analysis." *Library & Information Science Research* 35, no. 2: 137–142.

Jalongo, Mary Renck, and Theresa McDevitt. 2015. "Therapy Dogs in Academic Libraries: A Way to Foster Student Engagement and Mitigate Self-Reported Stress during Finals." *Public Services Quarterly* 11, no. 4: 254–269.

Kumbier, Alana, and Julia Starkey. 2016. "Access Is Not Problem Solving: Disability Justice and Libraries." *Library Trends* 64, no. 3: 468–491.

Kwai, Isabella. 2016. "Today's College Students Are Not Less Resilient." *The Atlantic*, October 19. https://www.theatlantic.com/education/archive/2016/10/the-most-popular-office-on-campus/504701.

Leavey, JoAnn Elizabeth. 2009. "Youth Experiences of Living with Mental Health Problems: Emergence, Loss, Adaptation and Recovery (ELAR)." *Canadian Journal of Community Mental Health* 24, no. 2: 109–126.

Lyndon, Amy E., Allison Crowe, Karl L. Wuensch, Susan L. McCammon, and Karen B. Davis. 2019. "College Students' Stigmatization of People with Mental Illness: Familiarity, Implicit Person Theory, and Attribution." *Journal of Mental Health* 28, no. 3: 255–259.

Martin, Lee. 2015. "The Promise of the Maker Movement for Education." *Journal of Pre-College Engineering Education Research (J-PEER)* 5, no. 1: 4.

McElroy, Kelly. 2018. "LIS Mental Health Week 2018." February 19. http://www.kellymce.info/bloggy/2018/2/19/lis-mental-health-week-2018.

Pescosolido, Bernice A. 2020. "Stigma as a Mental Health Policy Controversy: Positions, Options, and Strategies for Change." In *The Palgrave Handbook of American Mental Health Policy*, edited by H. H. Goldman, R. G. Frank, and J. P. Morrissey, 543–572. Cham, Switzerland: Palgrave Macmillan.

Phillips, A., A. Pho, K. McElroy, N. Gustavsen, K. Deibel, and V. Fox, eds. 2019. *Reserve and Renew: The LIS Mental Health Zine*, 2.

Pho, A., K. McElroy, N. Gustavsen, A. Phillips, K. Deibel, and V. Fox, eds. 2018. *Reserve and Renew: The LIS Mental Health Zine*, 1.

"Psychology Topics." n.d. *American Psychological Association*. Retrieved November 21, 2019, from https://www.apa.org/topics/index.

Ramsey, Elizabeth, and Mary C. Aagard. 2018. "Academic Libraries as Active Contributors to Student Wellness." *College & Undergraduate Libraries* 25, no. 4: 328–334.

Reilly, Katie. 2018. "Anxiety and Depression: More College Students Seeking Help." *Time*, March 19. http://time.com/5190291/anxiety-depression-college-university-students.

Schnyder, N., D. Lawrence, R. Panczak, M. G. Sawyer, H. A. Whiteford, P. M. Burgess, and M. G. Harris. 2020. "Perceived Need and Barriers to Adolescent Mental Health Care: Agreement between Adolescents and Their Parents." *Epidemiology and Psychiatric Sciences* 29: 1–9.

Schomerus, Georg, Susanne Stolzenburg, Simone Freitag, Sven Speerforck, Deborah Janowitz, Sara Evans-Lacko, Holger Muehlan, and Silke Schmidt. 2019. "Stigma as a Barrier to Recognizing Personal Mental Illness and Seeking Help: A Prospective Study among Untreated Persons with Mental Illness." *European Archives of Psychiatry and Clinical Neuroscience* 269, no. 4: 469–479.

Smale, Maura. 2016. "Academic Libraries and Mental Health: LIS Mental Health Week." *ACRLog*, January 18. https://acrlog.org/2016/01/18/academic-libraries-and-mental-health-lis-mental-health-week.

Storrie, Kim, Kathy Ahern, and Anthony Tuckett. 2010. "A Systematic Review: Students with Mental Health Problems—a Growing Problem." *International Journal of Nursing Practice* 16, no. 1: 1–6.

Throgmorton, Kaitlin. 2017. "Mental Health First Aid." *American Libraries Magazine* (blog), March 1. https://americanlibrariesmagazine.org/2017/03/01/mental-health-first-aid.

Walker, Cecily. 2014. "Library Mental Help Week." *Cecily Walker* (blog), October 27. https://cecily.info/2014/10/27/library-mental-help-week.

Waryan, Chloe. 2018. "LIS Mental Health Week 2018: A Roundup of Student Support." *Hack Library School*, March 27. https://hacklibraryschool.com/2018/03/27/lis-mental-health-week-2018-a-roundup-of-student-support.

"What Is a Zine?" n.d. *The Bindery*. Retrieved January 20, 2020, from https://www.binderymke.com/what-is-a-zine.

Wolverton, Brad. 2019. "As Students Struggle with Stress and Depression, Colleges Act as Counselors." *The New York Times*, February 21. https://www.nytimes.com/2019/02/21/education/learning/mental-health-counseling-on-campus.html.

CHAPTER THIRTEEN

How Interpersonal Violence Impacts Our Patrons, Our Library, Our Campus

Racine L. Amos

Foundations

The words Title IX and *#MeToo* have become national idioms for sexual assault, fostering reflection on the traditional role of today's academic libraries in having the potential to shift the paradigm of response and support for an individual's experiences of interpersonal violence (IPV). By the deliberate development of systemic and employee capacities demonstrating conscious efforts of support and safety, the potential to positively impact an individual's well-being and academic success increases. Incontrovertibly, IPV, defined here to include sexual assault, dating violence, and stalking, has often been considered an ineffable topic. Unspoken or whispers in my mother's generation, as a member of Generation X, the topics of consent and IPV prevention were nonexistent within my personal and educational experiences. My daughter, a millennial, and her peers had the subject of IPV infused into their lived experience, along with the tangible expectation of proactively addressing the prevention of IPV, embedded in family dialogues and curriculums.

First, it is necessary to acknowledge that those victimized and perpetrators of IPV can be any gender identity, orientation, ethnicity, etc. Research has shown that IPV is especially predominant and pervasive in women's lives when compared with victimization across other groups (Kennedy et al. 2012). For that reason, this chapter often may infer or refer to data related to woman-identified persons. Second, while respecting the self-actualization and empowerment of individuals negatively impacted by the choice and action of others to harm them that choose to self-identify as "victim," it is with the deliberate intention that the term "survivor" will be used. This is in recognition of individuals' strength in navigating interpersonal trauma responses, which often include a nonstatic and nonlinear spectrum of victimization, survival, and healing.

The current undulating legislative landscape of the United States Department of Education, Office of Civil Rights, overseers of Title IX, has resulted in iterative interpretations and implications for not only primary through postsecondary educational institutions but for individuals and communities nationwide. In 2011, the "Dear Colleague Letter" issued federal guidance to K–12 school districts, colleges, and universities and prompted sweeping changes in response and resources regarding IPV. This included requirements for prevention education, employee training, and designation of Title IX coordinators, individuals responsible for institutional compliance regarding reports of IPV.

Subsequent federal edicts, the 2015 "Dear Colleague Letter" bolstered by the April 2014 "Not Alone: The First Report of the White House Task Force to Protect Students from Sexual Assault," made it clear that sexual assault and other IPV on campuses remains a long-hidden crisis that deserves critical response at every institutional level. Current efforts, while attempting to create systemic "equity" between survivors and the accused, created impending Title IX legislation that contains drastic changes that may result in the disempowerment of those violated by acts of IPV. Among the proposed changes is the redefinition of "sexual harassment," a term that includes sexual assault, specifying that it must be severe and pervasive in nature. This has the potential to exclude, by language, a broad spectrum of sexual misconduct and assault that occurs on campuses. A second change is that during adjudication processes, parties can be directly cross-examined by the other party. Cross-examination is a catastrophic departure from the established practice of questioning via the adjudication officer(s). Conceivably, this shift eliminates safeguards to limit irrelevant questions that can influence decision makers and create barriers for survivor participation due to feasible perceptions of decreased emotional safety.

In envisaging sexual assault, dating/domestic violence, and stalking within an inclusive framework of IPV, a salient platform for the interconnectedness of the unique dynamics of each crime is provided. For example, it is not atypical within incidents of dating/domestic violence to encounter acts of sexual assault and stalking.

Perpetrators of IPV and society often attempt to "victimize" the offender's behavior and/or cast blame on the survivor for what has occurred—for example, by focusing on a survivor's choice of dress or behavior in order to deflect from the harmful acts the perpetrator chose to engage in against the survivor. Too often, survivors are forced to defend actions preceding and during the incident (such as "Why didn't you fight back?") as well as contend with skepticism. Within a pervasive context reports of IPV often are met by immediate questions of veracity, concurrent with an allegation. This victim-blaming culture has been demonstrated as an instrument of shame and silencing against many survivors.

Each person that a survivor interacts with after an incident of IPV becomes a key element of that individual's healing and recovering process. Negative reactions to sexual violence disclosure are associated with poorer psychological functioning (Sabina and Ho 2014). Influenced by culture and personal perspectives, individuals receiving a disclosure of IPV victimization may unconsciously perpetuate "secondary victimization." In sharing subjective perspectives, these individuals can convey messages to survivors that what happened was "their fault," that they will not be believed, and/or that the survivor must report what happened to prevent the perpetrator from doing it to another person. Ultimately, these and similar communications can have a cascading effect impacting a survivor's decision to pursue any further course of action. Often upon disclosure, survivors are fearful of judgment and blame that results in an aversion of reporting and help seeking. According to the 2011 College Dating Violence and Abuse Poll, more than half (57 percent) of college students who report having been in an abusive dating relationship said it occurred in college (Break the Cycle n.d.). In 2015, research conducted by the National Sexual Violence Resource Center cites more than 90 percent of campus sexual assault victims, regardless of gender identity or sexual orientation, do not report the crime (Taylor 2018).

A critical challenge in comprehending the scope of IPV is the historical prevalence of shame and stigma that fosters a culture of underreporting. This results in research that demonstrates high prevalence rates of IPV that is contraindicated within official reporting structures and reports. Based on historical statistical data, it is irrefutable that IPV is happening at higher education institutions. In 2015, educational institutions were required to begin collecting additional annual crime statistics specific to IPV as Violence Against Women Act (VAWA) offenses (includes sex offenses, dating/domestic violence, and stalking). According to the United States Department of Education Campus Safety and Security website (n.d.), 2017 cumulative data represented 6,339 postsecondary institutions that reported via the Clery Act Annual Security Report 16,977 VAWA offenses. Of those incidents, 14,994 occurred on campus, 702 were noncampus, 1,274 occurred on public property, and 7 were reported by local law enforcement.

For some people, this reported number of offenses may appear high, but in reality this number represents a truncated illusion of the reality of victimization experienced by survivors on college and university campuses. Validated by personal experience and simple math, the current method of annual security reporting creates a false narrative of "safety" that is illogical due to the exclusion of off-campus incidents and because incidents are grossly underreported. According to Westat (2019), in spring 2019, the Association of American Universities (AAU) embarked on collecting data on the prevalence of IPV during enrollment at public and private postsecondary institutions, in an effort to refine and update previous survey data collected in 2015. The largest survey of its kind, the resulting study represented data from 108,221 undergraduate respondents and 73,531 graduate and professional respondents (Cantor et al. 2020, vii).

> As contained in the Report on the AAU Campus Climate Survey on Sexual Assault and Misconduct, the prevalence rate of nonconsensual sexual contact by force or inability to consent for women undergraduates is nearly three times higher than for women graduate and professional students (25.9% vs. 9.7%). Undergraduate men are twice as likely to report sexual contact by physical force or inability to consent as men graduate/professional students (6.8% vs. 2.5%) and among transgender, genderqueer, gender questioning, or gender non-conforming (TGQN) students, 22.8 percent of undergraduates and 14.5 percent of graduate and professional students reported this type of victimization. The prevalence rate of intimate partner violence was 10.1 percent among all students who had been in a partnered relationship since entering college. Additionally, among all students, 5.8 percent reported experiencing stalking.

From a statistical perspective consider that according to a division of the Institute of Education Sciences, during fall 2017 there were 16.8 million undergraduate students enrolled in degree-granting postsecondary institutions. Within this total, female students made up 56 percent of total undergraduate enrollment (9.4 million students), and 7.3 million male students of the remaining 44 percent (National Center for Education Statistics 2019).

Based on this data, of the estimated 9.4 million female-identified students enrolled in 2017, statistically, approximately 2.4 million incidents of nonconsensual sexual contact by force or inability to consent by female undergraduate students and 532,900 male students would have occurred at postsecondary institutions over a four-year period. Additionally, approximately 1.7 million incidents of dating/domestic violence and 974,400 incidents of stalking may have transpired over a four-year period, for a statistical projection of approximately 5.6 million total VAWA offenses. In comparison, a four-year projection utilizing the 16,977 *actual* VAWA offenses reported for 2017 as the annual average, results in a projected total of 67,908 VAWA offenses that would be reported to postsecondary institutions. This projection reflects a 1.2 percent reporting rate of IPV by survivors to formal reporting postsecondary structures.

There is limited data available regarding incidents of IPV that occur in academic libraries. Typical survey metrics are developed and interpreted to include campus libraries as "other non-residential" or "academic" buildings. According to the Report on the AAU Campus Climate Survey on Sexual Assault and Misconduct (Westat 2019), 7.7 percent of women, 5.5 percent of men, and 1.2 percent of TGQN persons indicated that penetration with physical force or inability to give consent occurred in "other non-residential building," with 15.9 percent of respondents declining to state an incident location. Additionally, 5.4 percent of women, 4.0 percent of men, and 5.6 percent of TGQN persons indicated that sexual touching with physical force or inability to consent occurred in "other non-residential building."

Academic libraries are not immune to acts of crime and violence. Even with current data limitations, incidents specific to academic library locations are becoming a more frequent actuality. In July 2015, a Hunter College male student attempted to rape a female student while she was reading in a private study room she had reserved in the campus library ("Hunter College Student" 2015). In September 2019, a group of female students was sexually harassed by a man who ran from the University of North Carolina–Chapel Hill Library after one of the women displayed pepper spray (WRAL 2019). In October 2019, a woman was sexually assaulted in the bathroom at Clemson University's Robert Muldrow Cooper Library ("CUPD: Sexual Assault Investigation Continues" 2019). In November 2019, a Kingsborough College female student was sexually assaulted in the library bathroom ("Police: Kingsborough College" 2019).

The implications of campus safety research and data reach beyond current campus community members as this information is encouraged to be critically reviewed by students and parents prior to selecting an institution as suggested by websites of organizations like College Parents America ("5 Questions Every" 2017).

Serving as a campus-based victims' advocate and prevention educator for twelve years, often the first institutional contact for survivors, a critical philosophy was to offer information and foster transparency. This philosophy is both critical for the well-being of the student-survivor and potentially impacted the decision making, academics, and social experience of that student. With institutionalized multiple opportunities for trauma-informed support, each survivor is enabled to navigate their unique healing journey at their own level of resilience and individual pace. While attempting to process and reframe their postincident physical and emotional self, survivors as patrons, in desiring to self-actualize any "next step," may utilize academic libraries to better discern the scope and impact of their experience and choices for further action. Survivor engagement with the academic library can manifest in a variety of platforms, online messaging systems, utilizing catalog to access collection resources, research inquiry, events, the instruction classroom, etc.

In conducting IRB-exempt qualitative research for this writing project during fall 2019, an anonymous survey was distributed and interviews conducted with campus-based IPV prevention education and/or advocate professionals and academic librarians. As the yet to be published Survey of Academic Library Support of Interpersonal Violence Survivors (SALS-IPVS) included, academic librarian respondents represented (75 percent) and campus-based advocacy/prevention professionals (25 percent) from Association of American Universities (AAU) member institutions. One respondent when asked to "describe current and potential opportunities for academic librarians to engage with patrons that are a survivor of interpersonal violence," an academic librarian very astutely replied, "the potential exists anytime you are interacting with patrons." According to Westbrook, "Intimate partner violence (IPV) exemplifies a deeply personal crisis in which information services can make a significant difference in the life choices that people make" (2015, 8).

Navigating the Environment

Being centralized repositories of information, academic libraries are equitable spaces for patron knowledge development. Academic libraries experience high volumes of people, extended hours, and typically limited on-site security presence. This combined with the nature of collaborative academic work in public yet, isolating workspaces can make libraries attractive venues for those seeking to commit acts of IPV. With a founding tenet of open accessibility, regardless of a patron's history of behavior, unless it includes a violation of institutional policy that bars access, those individuals retain privilege, right, and use of academic library spaces and services. When SALS-IPVS respondents were asked, "Would you describe academic libraries as "safe spaces" for patrons that are survivors of interpersonal violence?" 62.50 percent of respondents were "neutral." One respondent shared, "I can see the potential for academic libraries to be this kind of space, but I'm not sure if they are in reality." Within this context exists a tenuous landscape for libraries and librarians to navigate between issues of equity and safety for employees and patrons.

Facility

It is the responsibility of academic libraries to contextualize security needs into best practices within building design and the specific student, staff, and faculty needs at that institution (Henrich and Stoddart 2016). The facility design concept of crime prevention through environmental design (CPTED) is intended to reduce victimization and the opportunity for crime perpetration by deliberate design, management, and use of physical environments. There exists limited information regarding the intentional utilization of CPTED in academic library construction or renovation. Due to the common increased need to renovate academic libraries, the use of CPTED has the potential for adoption and utilization at many institutions. As the ability to retrofit to meet safety needs can be spatially or cost-prohibitive for many institutions, it is suggested that academic library employees tasked with participating in designing processes, employ a "victim-centered" framework during initial processes. Although academic libraries with impending construction may be encouraged to consider adopting principles of CPTED to prevent violence perpetration by individuals and groups, they should also be inclusive of the needs of survivors of IPV.

An assessment by several members of the library should be undertaken prior to any intended environment changes or in the absence of changes, an embedded task for individuals or committees addressing health and safety concerns. Any such assessment should include evaluating sightlines, lighting, concealed or isolated routes, entrapment areas, isolation, areas for activity generation to discourage crime perpetration, impediments to cell phone reception, location and proximity of internal and external emergency "blue light" phones/call buttons, signage, and overall design (Henrich and Stoddart 2016). It is suggested that design team members experience their library individually from multiple perspectives, during and after daylight. The intent is for each committee member to consider safety and associated impacts and consequences when occupying physical spaces of their library environment. For example, if existing carrels and stacks have dim lighting and no emergency phones, it is critical to consider potential harms that can occur in that space, how to limit vulnerability, and how an individual may escape or get help, with the objective of improving patron safety.

Rarely does dating/domestic violence and stalking spontaneously cease. The escalation of behaviors and potential violence is prevalent especially when perpetrators feel a loss of control over or access to the survivor. This increased risk for harm and lethality is not mitigated by the issue of a protective order, which is difficult to enforce in environments that are subject to and promote vulnerability due to spatial, policy, and resource limitations. For example, a patron reported that unwanted gifts are being left in their assigned carrel from an alleged stalker, but there are no witnesses or video evidence of the behavior that would enable the patron to file for violation of the existing protection order. Academic libraries must consider how to balance the ethics of librarianship, principles of equitable access, and First Amendment rights with personal safety.

Promoting Safety for Patrons

Although librarians are neither first responders nor trained counselors, there is a profound opportunity for academic libraries to serve as a safe and welcoming space and for library employees to have appropriate skills to support the immediate information needs of survivors in an environment that fosters safety and access to resources. This includes dedicated "safe space," providing privacy and protection without proximity to other patrons and employees. SALS-IPVS respondents were asked their opinion of the level of preparedness of academic libraries as a system, and of academic librarians in regard to IPV. Regarding the preparedness of both academic libraries and academic librarians to appropriately respond to a disclosure of abuse/violence, refer a survivor to appropriate resources, and respond to an incident of dating/domestic violence in the library, on a five-point scale, 50 percent of respondents indicated at most, a moderate level of preparedness across all three survey items.

This supports the idea that, in addition to any annual compliance training (such as Title IX training), librarians and library employees would benefit from trauma-informed training that reflects components of "whole-person librarianship," a multidimensional collaborative model informed by social work that reflects the intentional inclusion of the full spectrum of the lived experience of patrons outside the library to address the needs, impacts of trauma, and navigation of the experience of vulnerable populations (Zettervall and Nienow 2019). The same authors provide inspiration for academic libraries, "Every person is greater than the trauma they experienced, and libraries benefit from the positive influences patrons bring as whole people . . . as well as having the chance to respond with empathy to challenges arising from negative experiences" (Zettervall and Nienow 2019, 27).

Curating Safety and Resources

Libraries, whether for academic, employment, or community purposes are inclusive spaces serving a diverse spectrum of patrons, including survivors. Although some individuals impacted by IPV will seek direct and personal engagement with library resources, due to the private and personal nature of IPV, a multifaceted design of survivor resources manifests basic principles of universal design and access. The generational norms of "silence" surrounding the issue of IPV reinforce information barriers, which can additionally be fostered by limitations and/or exclusions of IPV topic materials and programs in libraries.

Collections

Collections inherently incorporate the ability to inform survivors of IPV of pragmatic knowledge and inform the scholarly knowledge base. These existing catalogs of information resources represent a gateway to discovery for survivors that hinges on collection development decisions that serve to positively impact or create information barriers for survivors by the exclusion of resources. Academic libraries should consider critical reflection in regards to auditing collections to determine the volume of materials available for survivors and researchers. For example, scanning catalogs utilizing current taxonomy related to topics of IPV and include expanding the survey scope to include violence against traditionally marginalized identities such as racial and ethnic minorities, LGBTQ, differently-abled, men, etc. This effort will provide a holistic needs assessment that can determine potential collection limitations and/or exclusions and inform future acquisition decisions that will extend survivors' access to resources and promotion of research.

Outreach

Libraries are mutual spaces of use by survivors and perpetrators, which means that the ability to overtly advertise programs and resources is complicated by the inherent mutual notification of perpetrators of the same information. In seeking to provide support, there is a need to be mindful, as broad advertising of resources may inadvertently put survivors at risk, for example, by sharing the time and location of support groups. An example of a possible safety promotion initiative, providing access to resources without disclosure of victimization, academic libraries can utilize passive marketing techniques such as bathroom stall/carrel stickers or by establishing a LibGuide to create awareness, outline potential cyber-safety concerns, and offer resources.

When librarians are trained in awareness of IPV, the services provided to survivors is strengthened (Benson 2016). The reality is that while it may not be written within the scope of job descriptions, collective responsibility supports patrons within library environments regardless of the impetus of distress and/or trauma, and should be a humanistic incentive for each employee of academic libraries to positively impact the individual and campus community.

How Engagement and Disclosure Intersect with Policy and Self

The issue of IPV can infringe on the ethos of individuals and institutions. With diligent reflection on the role and emergent nature of academic libraries as patron-centered repositories of information, considerations for adaptability to meet survivor needs is obtainable and reflective of a commitment to social justice. Institutional doctrines surrounding IPV have the potential to vicariously impact libraries and librarians by sustaining cultures of inconsistent or absent training on policies, exclusion of libraries from strategic IPV planning, and maintaining environments of situational reactivity. A patron disclosure of IPV is a deviation from the paradigm of libraries and patron interaction, resulting in the need for library professionals to contemplate the needs of survivors within traditional user service models.

Engagement

The engagement role of academic libraries includes the cultivation of internal and external relationships that support and encourage personal and scholarly growth of campus and greater community members. Engaging with patrons, through reference work, information sessions, or other means is one of the core aspects of our work as librarians. When presented with an inquiry regarding IPV, a librarian should always assume the patron may be a survivor (Wilmoth 2008).

There exists potential with many academic libraries to interact with survivors in person and online via "Ask a Librarian" or similar technologies. In virtual spaces, it is important to recognize that unless there is an authentication process, patrons can be located worldwide necessitating that academic librarians are prepared to utilize research skills to locate resources based on locale—for example, a patron survivor studying abroad who is seeking local IPV agencies or other resources. Online and in-person exchanges about IPV can be challenging for both parties, including the potential impact of personal significance and/or triggering for one or both parties.

Librarians have long recognized the tendency of library users to pose their initial questions in incomplete, often unclear, and sometimes apparently covert manners (Dewdney and Michell 1997). Survivors may be anxious due to possible inability to define what happened as IPV, hesitation over potential disclosure, and/or the perpetrator may be in proximity and there is a safety concern. It is critical that academic library staff understand the many barriers that can impact survivors at any point during an in-person or virtual engagement with patrons.

> *Patron:* "I want information on domestic violence."
> *Librarian:* "What would you like to know about domestic violence?"
> *Patron:* "I want to know what resources are available."

At this juncture, the librarian has options. The librarian can share any existing LibGuide of resources available that could be beneficial for survivors or researchers. After sharing and requesting the patron review the LibGuide, the librarian can ask if the patron's needs have been met or require additional assistance. Alternatively, if no LibGuide or electronic resource exists:

> *Librarian:* "It would help me to find the best information for you if you could tell me a little more about how you plan to use the information."
> *Patron:* "For personal use."

As the patron is further defining their needs, while ambiguous, inquiring within this context allows the patron control over the degree of self-disclosure

(Dewdney and Michell 2016) without the academic librarian appearing intrusive. Librarians should avoid the potential for the patron to disengage from the conversation, seeking privacy from disclosing during an often documented and/or monitored exchange, or in the event there is an individual in proximity that the patron does not wish to possibly gain awareness of the patron's personal situation. Similarly, for employees who may feel disclosing such information may be a reflection on their professional capacity, allowing the survivor degrees of privacy does not limit the academic librarian's ability to provide the requested information.

> *Librarian:* "I have information on local resources. Are there any particular types of resources or in a specific geographical area?"

This supports the need for librarians to be trained and aware of local community resources, such as hotline numbers, and allowing the patron to self-define any other resources or geographical areas that might be helpful.

This provides the patron with confirmation that the librarian or library staff is actively listening to the patron's needs, is committed to providing help, and is not attempting to force disclosure from the patron. During each stage of interaction, academic librarians and staff should avoid using "why" questions as it may create an insurmountable barrier when it is critical for academic libraries to foster trust when engaging with survivors of IPV. The goal should be to provide enough information for the patron to make their own informed decision, encouraging survivors to retake control of their lives (Wilmoth 2008).

During all initial engagements when it is perceived that the patron may be a survivor of IPV, academic librarians and staff should convey and inform survivors of any reporting obligations of the academic library staff. Most institutions have designated individual roles as mandated campus security authorities (CSAs), individuals that are required to report incidents of IPV. Some institutions designate all employees as being "responsible" to report incidents of IPV. In many cases, the identity of the reporting individual is not required, but growing practice from an institutional liability framework is to mandate that all identifying information conveyed to responsible employees is reported to designated authorities. Libraries and librarians should confirm institutional policies regarding Title IX reporting to ensure accurate information is shared with survivors as early as possible during disclosure. For example, after escorting the survivor to a private location or initiating a private chat or email online, the librarian may state, "Thank you for having the strength to share with me and you can tell me as much or as little as you want about your experience and regardless, I will provide you whatever information you need. I must tell you that I am required to share information regarding incidents of IPV." The librarian should follow this or any similar statement to the survivor by sharing details on what information will be shared, with whom, and of any potential follow-up actions as per the institution's policies. SALS-IPVS respondents were asked, "Do you believe academic libraries understand institutional reporting and response obligations under Title IX?" Responses were 50 percent Probably yes, 37.50 percent Might or might not, and 12.50 percent Probably not. With this mediocre confidence reflected, it is apparent that academic libraries should consider committing to longitudinal training of academic library faculty and staff that fosters an innate understanding of institutional requirements for federal compliance.

The Necessary Tool for Change: Collaboration

Student retention is on the minds of senior administrators in higher education nationwide. As quoted by *Inside Higher Ed,* "College enrollment in the U.S. has decreased for the eighth consecutive year," according to new data released by the National Student Clearinghouse Research Center (Fain 2019, para. 1). With decreases in federal and state funding, institutions are critically examining student retention and, as a part of this, should employ intentionality in deconstructing the experiences of survivors, including ethically gathering information on associated impacts on academic and social success. Many advocates would concur with Mengo and Black (2015) that sexual and physical/verbal victimization is associated with decreases in GPA, which influences retention. These findings are troubling and suggest that universities must do more to address sexual and physical violence, for the well-being of the student body as well as the health of the institution. When asked in relation to academic libraries' engagement and collaboration with campus-based advocacy/prevention programs, "It doesn't seem to be a priority with our administrative leadership" (SALS-IPVS respondent).

Academic libraries as an element of the institutional ecosystem are not immune from a duty to address and support the needs of patrons that are survivors of IPV. Addressing the shortcomings of various institutional systems may positively influence the psychosocial impact of IPV for students who are considering withdrawal. Utilizing research and consultation with internal and external subject experts can assist in informing efforts to develop and improve institutional resources.

According to the SALS-IPVS data, there was no indication by either academic librarians or campus-based advocacy/prevention professionals of frequent collaboration. Data reflected that 100 percent of campus-based advocacy/prevention professionals at most "occasionally" collaborate in violence prevention programming and/or resource development with academic libraries and librarians. Among academic librarians, 66.67 percent indicate at most "occasional" collaboration with campus-based advocacy/prevention professionals, 33.33 percent at most "occasional" collaboration with campus internal subject experts, 50 percent rarely or never collaborate with community agencies, and 66.67 percent never with external subject experts. Although this can be influenced by financial barriers to compensate experts, the data suggest that by addressing these existing modest efforts to engage and utilize experts, academic libraries and librarians have the opportunity to bolster the campus knowledge base and resources.

Members of the academic library that engage with the public beyond the university community and should be deliberate in cultivating relationships with on- and off-campus organizations that promote supportive services for survivors. With a shared foundation and principles of social justice, self-determination, and protection of individual rights, collaboration with campus-based advocacy/prevention programs gives libraries access to response, training, and programming resources and partnerships built on respect and shared values. In these collaborations, the library provides the patron with information, and other resources to help the patron interpret and act on the information.

Similarly, forming relationships with external community agencies, often also serving students in addition to campus-based programs, provides an additional partner for the academic library for training and response. There exist opportunities for library employees to obtain and engage in personal development and knowledge building on the topic of IPV that can enable librarians' benefit and growth among like-minded peers. For example, there exist opportunities for librarians to develop, seek, and engage in grass-roots efforts created for and by librarians. Founded by Miranda Dube, librarian, University of New Hampshire, Librarians for Survivors (www.libraransfor survivors.com) seeks to create awareness, promote research, and provide technical assistance to libraries on the issue of IPV.

When asked what recommendations they have for academic libraries to be "safe or safer" spaces for patron victims/survivors of interpersonal violence, one SALS-LPVS respondent said:

> Partner with campus expertise and invite them to create satellite spaces in addition to staff training and programming . . . librarians are not clinically trained to do more than identify and refer. It's tempting to always be adding new hats to our professions, however, this is one clear moment when we can serve students better by collaborating instead of overstretching.

The issues and trauma of IPV in varying contexts are enmeshed within global societies, and higher education institutions will, unfortunately, remain settings for the commission of crimes as well as spaces survivors must adapt to navigate post-trauma. Academic library employees have the unique capacity to proactively define and redefine systems of knowledge that convey "truths" about what we know about the world and how that knowledge is organized and evaluated by survivors of IPV (Morales, Knowles, and Bourg 2014, 445).

Academic libraries have the ability to willingly participate and establish active standards of practice that represent commitment to social justice, community health, and promoting a "whole person" mind-set for the support and success of all patrons.

References

Break the Cycle. n.d. "College Dating Violence and Abuse Poll." Retrieved February 2, 2020, from https://www.breakthecycle.org/dating-violence-research/college-dating-violence-and-abuse-poll.

Cohen, Shawn. 2015. "Hunter College Student Bit Victim after 'Rape' Attempt Failed." *New York Post*, July 9. https://nypost.com/2015/07/08/hunter-college-student-bit-victim-after-rape-attempt-failed.

"CUPD: Sexual Assault Investigation Continues." 2019. Clemson University. October 7. https://alerts.clemson.edu/2019/10/07/cupd-sexual-assault-investigation-continues.

Dewdney, Patricia, and Gillian Michell. 1997. "Asking 'Why' Questions in the Reference Interview: A Theoretical Justification." *The Library Quarterly* 67, no. 1: 50–71. https://doi.org/10.1086/629910.

Fain, Paul. 2019. "College Enrollment Declines Continue." *Inside Higher Ed*, May 30. https://www.insidehighered.com/quicktakes/2019/05/30/college-enrollment-declines-continue.

"5 Questions Every Parent, Student Should Ask about Campus Safety." 2017. College Parents of America. November 21. https://collegeparents.org/2017/11/21/5-questions-every-parent-student-should-ask-about-campus-safety.

Henrich, Kristin J., and Richard A. Stoddart. 2016. "Library Safety through Design: Using a Checklist Approach at the University of Idaho." *Journal of Library Administration* 56, no. 7 (November): 777–789. https://doi.org/10.1080/01930826.2015.1124705.

Kennedy, Angie C., Adrienne Adams, Deborah Bybee, Rebecca Campbell, Sheryl Pimlott Kubiak, and Cris Sullivan. 2012. "A Model of Sexually and Physically Victimized Women's Process of Attaining Effective Formal Help over Time: The Role of Social Location, Context, and Intervention." *American Journal of Community Psychology* 50, no. 1–2: 217–228. https://doi.org/10.1007/s10464-012-9494-x.

Mengo, Cecilia, and Beverly M. Black. 2015. "Violence Victimization on a College Campus." *Journal of College Student Retention: Research, Theory & Practice* 18, no. 2 (November): 234–248. https://doi.org/10.1177/1521025115584750.

Morales, Myrna, Em Claire Knowles, and Chris Bourg. 2014. "Diversity, Social Justice, and the Future of Libraries." *portal: Libraries and the Academy* 14, no. 3: 439–451. doi:10.1353/pla.2014.0017.

"Police: Kingsborough College Student Sexually Assaulted in Library Bathroom." 2019. CBS New York. November 26. https://newyork.cbslocal.com/2019/11/26/kingsborough-college-sexual-assault.

Sabina, Chiara, and Lavina Y. Ho. 2014. "Campus and College Victim Responses to Sexual Assault and Dating Violence." *Trauma, Violence, & Abuse* 15, no. 3 (April): 201–226. https://doi.org/10.1177/1524838014521322.

Taylor, Zachary W. 2018. "Unreadable and Underreported: Can College Students Comprehend How to Report Sexual Assault?" *Journal of College Student Development* 59, no. 2: 248–253. https://doi.org/10.1353/csd.2018.0023.

United States Department of Education. n.d. "How Many VAWA Offenses Were Reported?" Retrieved February 5, 2020, from https://ope.ed.gov/campus safety/Trend/public/#/answer/3/301/main?row=-1&column=-1.

Westbrook, Lynn. 2015. "'I'm Not a Social Worker': An Information Service Model for Working with Patrons in Crisis." *The Library Quarterly* 85, no. 1: 6–25. https://doi.org/10.1086/679023.

Wilmoth, Wendy S. 2008. "Serving Sexual Assault Survivors in the Academic Library: Using Tools of Crises Intervention and Empowerment Counseling in the Reference Interview." *Georgia Library Quarterly* 45, no. 1: 9–13.

Zettervall, Sara K., and Mary C. Nienow. 2019. *Whole Person Librarianship: A Social Work Approach to Patron Services.* Santa Barbara, CA: Libraries Unlimited.

Beyond Theory and Practice

New Directions for Research and Service

Julia C. Skinner and Melissa Gross

When we proposed this volume, we included the title of this conclusion as a part of it, to help guide our thinking toward ever more inclusive spaces. But what does it mean to be truly inclusive?

Often, when we speak of inclusion, we consider some demographic information, and may try to bring people in the door (as presenters, employees, or students) who speak to diverse demographics. Although this is a great start, it is not an end point. To be inclusive means to start with ourselves, and to look critically at what we're offering, who it is serving, and how we can do better.

It is this continuous process of evaluation, humility, and growth as a practice rather than as a standalone activity that enacts real change. Each of us has blinders, each of us slips up, but in recognizing and learning and in making adjustments, we incrementally move toward creating more welcoming spaces that speak to our mission and to our passion to serve that drives the profession.

By doing this for our own practice, and for our institutions writ large, it is our hope that each individual act of reevaluation will be a drop in a bucket. Although it may not seem like much, those drops add up over time to a full bucket, and to an ever-expanding community of information professionals committed to elevating our field to greater heights.

In a field that struggles with diversity and retention, which exists during a time when information literacy and access to information are more critical than ever, this work is more critical than ever. Although not an exhaustive list, here are a few ideas for where we can start, informed both by our own experiences and the work of chapter authors.

Diversity in LIS Recruiting and Retention, Both for Researchers and Practitioners

In our field diversity is often thought of in terms of racial diversity, which is an important metric to consider (and one our field must address). However, we consider diversity to broadly include the entire range of identities and experiences, and encourage our colleagues to actively bring in those who are often excluded. By having a diverse field, our patrons are more likely to see themselves mirrored in the faces they see in the library, and are more likely to see it as a space where they can thrive. And, most critically, we need to not only bring in new voices, but keep them here and amplify them: this includes robust support networks within institutions and the field, considering how to include a range of perspectives in each of our professional undertakings (conference panels, committees, etc.), and the ability to truly listen and learn when concerns arise. It also means respecting the right of our colleagues to say no: tokenism does not serve underrepresented individuals nor their workplaces, and if we create a truly welcoming space (rather than one that simply seems "diverse" on its face), we will find that our field will gradually include all the voices we so desperately need to hear.

Moving beyond Just Sensitivity Training

Offering training to educate people about the experiences of others and how best to respectfully engage is a wonderful start, and offers some concrete guidance for those who may feel lost and unsure where to start when working with different communities. However, this is simply a starting point. Libraries can continue to improve patron services as well as employee relations by looking beyond traditional models to find other ways to teach: partnering with campus and community groups, finding new approaches to training (e.g., one-on-one conversations, interactive activities), ongoing mentorship for employees to become educated about diverse experiences, training in active listening and in setting aside the ego when being told of a microaggression (or beyond), etc., can help staff learn and to retain what they learn, and benefit patrons and employees alike.

Finding Blind Spots and Working to Address Them

All of us have beliefs and learned behaviors that may be hurtful to others, whether or not we mean them to be. In some cases, we may not even realize we are doing something that might be upsetting to someone else (a couple of examples include not respecting a person's pronouns or touching someone's hair without permission). Unlearning these can feel challenging, because it asks us to admit that the way we move through the world may not reflect our intentions. Listening to feedback, ingesting it, and using it to change behaviors is a great start, and there is a wealth of printed and online literature to help you do so. Some suggestions include:

- Charis Books and More. 2020. "Understanding and Dismantling Racism: A Booklist for White Readers." *Charis Books and More.* https://www.charis booksandmore.com/understanding-and-dismantling-racism-booklist-white -readers.
- Iowa State University Library. 2020. "DEI Read & Learn." *Iowa State University Library LigGuides.* https://instr.iastate.libguides.com/c.php?g=799527&p =7093246.
- Racial Equity Tools. 2020. "Book and Film Lists." *Racial Equity Tools.* https:// www.racialequitytools.org/fundamentals/resource-lists/book-and-film-lists.
- Racial Equity Resource Guide. 2020. "Resources." *Racial Equity Resource Guide.* http://www.racialequityresourceguide.org/resources/resources/filterType /Books.
- University of California Los Angeles Office of Equity, Diversity and Inclusion. 2020. "Implicit Bias." *University of California Los Angeles.* https://equity.ucla.edu /know/implicit-bias.

Similarly, there are blind spots in the field as a whole and the literature that documents professional practice. When we ask questions like "whose perspectives are being shared here?" and "whose perspectives are missing?" we can begin to fill those gaps as we publish writing, organize conferences, and build public-facing programs.

As library professionals, serving all our patrons is one of our most important and most pressing duties. As this volume shows us, meaningful work is being done in research and practice, sometimes shared publicly (as here) and sometimes quietly enacted as a part of one's daily work with patrons. In our field more than most, theory and research undergirds practice, and our practice informs theory and research, helping it become more robust, effective, and true to the world we live in. Our profession is of critical importance, now and always, and it will take all of us across the field to come together and share what we know in order to continue rising to the important call we each answered by becoming information professionals. We encourage you to continue learning, sharing, and growing together.

About the Contributors

Racine L. Amos graduated in 2019 with an MS in library and information science with a concentration in archives management, from Simmons University School of Library and Information Science, and earned a bachelor of arts in social work (minor in legal and policy studies) from Fordham University and a masters in social work (MSW) with a concentration in research from Fordham Graduate School of Social Services. A second career librarian, Racine arrives at University Libraries with twelve years of experience in Student Affairs, having served as the survivor advocate at several private and public institutions nationwide and former Gender and Women's Studies part-time faculty at University of Rhode Island. Amos's research interests include "whole person librarianship," the application of social work concepts to inform and enhance user experience, instruction, and library practice. With additional interest in genealogical research, Amos is in the process of completing individual family historical projects for skills building and her genealogy certification portfolio.

Bobbie Bushman is an assistant professor at Emporia State University. Dr. Bushman has published research about library services to children with disabilities, deaf and hard-of-hearing patrons, homeschoolers, and underserved populations. In addition to research, she speaks at library conferences across the United States about how librarians can better serve their underserved patron populations.

Marna M. Clowney-Robinson, LLMSW, MSW, MLIS, is currently a public services librarian at the University of Michigan Library in the Operations/Access Services Unit. In this role, she provides selection support for the social work and multicultural studies subject areas. She also provides instructional support for the Learning and Teaching Unit. Marna currently serves as secretary for the Librarians Forum Board at the University of Michigan Libraries. Nationally, Marna is the secretary for the Ethnic & Multicultural Information

Exchange Round Table (EMIERT), and member-at-large for the Social Responsibilities Round Tables (SRRT), both units within the American Library Association. Marna also is a licensed clinical therapist with Catholic Social Services and in private practice, where she specializes in identity issues, eating disorders, trauma issues, and mixed-race identity issues. In addition to her role as a clinician, Marna instructs other mental health professionals on the use of bibliotherapy and graphic medicine as a therapeutic modality.

Phillip Fitzsimmons is the reference and digitization librarian at Southwestern Oklahoma State University in Weatherford He earned his MLIS from the University of Oklahoma in Norman. He is the administrator of the SWOSU Digital Commons. His research interests include digital services for academic libraries with an emphasis on institutional repository administration and library reference services.

Andrew Foskey is the coordinator of library instruction at the Kolwyck Library and Information Commons at Chattanooga State Community College. His professional interests include reflective librarianship, student success, and assessment of student learning. Andy's favorite work experience was traveling to the United Kingdom as an embedded librarian for a Harry Potter study abroad course.

Melissa Gross is a professor in the School of Information at Florida State University and a past president of the Association for Library and Information Science Education (ALISE). She received her PhD from the University of California, Los Angeles, in 1998 and was awarded the prestigious American Association of University Women Recognition Award for Emerging Scholars in 2001. She teaches and does research in the areas of information-seeking behavior, resources for youth, research methods, the evaluation of library programs and services, information literacy, and teacher and librarian collaboration. She has published extensively in a variety of peer-reviewed journals including *Library and Information Science Research*, *Library Quarterly*, *Journal of the Association for Information Science and Technology*, and *College & Research Libraries*. She has authored, coauthored, or coedited ten books.

Lorin K. Jackson works as a research and instruction resident librarian at Swarthmore College, proud recipient of a 2019 Association for College and Research Libraries (ACRL) Excellence in Academic Libraries award. Before becoming an academic librarian, Lorin worked with underserved youth in the nonprofit and educational sector for a decade. During this time, she held positions as a teacher and program associate in after-school youth development programs in the Bay Area. Follow her @lorinland on Twitter. She uses she/them pronouns.

Andrea Kincaid is an academic librarian and adult educator currently serving as head of public services at Chattanooga State Community College. Andrea comes from a reference and instruction background while also working in marketing, social media, assessment, and public services. An active member of the profession since graduate school, Andrea is currently the secretary of the Access Services Roundtable of the Tennessee Library Association as well as a prolific conference presenter.

Brady D. Lund is a PhD student at Emporia (KS) State University's School of Library and Information Management. He received his MLS degree from Emporia State and his bachelor's degree in communication sciences and disorders from Wichita State University. He is the author of over two dozen peer-reviewed articles, books, and book chapters, including many on the topic of diversity and inclusion for individuals with special needs in library and information organizations.

Jinxuan Ma is an assistant professor in the School of Library and Information Management, Emporia State University. She earned her PhD in information studies from Florida State University. Her research and teaching interests focus on health information-seeking behavior and health-related social media analysis.

Bharat Mehra joined the School of Library and Information Studies at the University of Alabama as professor and EBSCO endowed chair in social justice in January 2019. From January 2005 to December 2018, he was a faculty member in the School of Information Sciences at the University of Tennessee. His research focuses on diversity and social justice in library and information science and community informatics or the use of information and communication technologies to empower minority and underserved populations to make meaningful changes in their everyday lives. He has applied action research to further engaged scholarship and community engagement while collaborating with racial/ethnic groups, international diaspora, sexual minorities, rural communities, low-income families, small businesses, and others, to represent their experiences and perspectives in the design of community-based information systems and services.

April K. Miller is the Sayre campus librarian at Southwestern Oklahoma State University in Sayre. She earned her MLIS from the University of Oklahoma in Norman. She is the leader of the Promotions Team and handles the Campus and Community Outreach for SWOSU Libraries. Her research interests include marketing academic library services with an emphasis on identifying and creating successful partnerships with the campus and community.

Dale Monobe has taught rehabilitation counseling (as well as practiced rehabilitation counseling) and library science on the graduate level and is currently the Utah/Nevada MLS regional director in the School of Library and Information Management at Emporia State University. He not only has an interest in underserved patrons at academic libraries, but also in accessible games and gamification, and in humanistic lifelong learning.

Abigail L. Phillips is an assistant professor in the School of Information Studies (SOIS) at the University of Wisconsin–Milwaukee. In 2016, Dr. Phillips received her PhD in information studies from the School of Information at Florida State University. Before joining the SOIS faculty, she held the position of postdoctoral fellow in the Department of Instructional Technology and Learning Sciences at Utah State University. Her research interests include youth, cyberbullying, empathy, mental illness, neurodiversity, and maker education. As a mental health self-advocate, Dr. Phillips has become increasingly interested in the intersection of mental illness, LIS education, and librarianship as practice. She is active on Twitter (@abigailleigh) and her website (abigailleighphillips.com).

Monte-Angel Richardson, MSW, is a social work researcher specializing in the intersection of violence, trauma, and collective resilience. She received her master's degree in social work from the University of Michigan where she was involved with the Trauma-Informed Care Librarianship initiative. In the field of social work, Monte-Angel has previously researched and published in the area of post-traumatic growth and communal response to gun violence. She presently serves as an institutional researcher at the University of New Mexico and is currently completing research from ongoing research regarding communal violence and trauma in California and Japan.

Amanda Roper is the evening and weekend librarian and Tennessee reconnect liaison for Chattanooga State Community College. She has presented at the Library Marketing and Communications Conference, Georgia Libraries Conference, and for the Carterette Webinar Series and is the vice president of marketing and branding for the Georgia Library Association. Amanda's research centers on marketing and outreach in academic libraries, library support of student parents, and critical information literacy instruction for adult learners.

Stephanie Rosen, PhD, is the accessibility specialist for the UM libraries, helping to promote equitable access to our resources for all users, regardless of ability or background. Her responsibilities include leading library-wide engagement with accessibility, developing educational materials for staff and public, and collaborating with partners to advocate for accessible scholarship, publishing, and teaching.

Danica San Juan, MSW, received her master's degree in social work from the University of Michigan and is a former research fellow for the Trauma-Informed Care Librarianship project at the University of Michigan. In the field of social work, Danica is practicing interpersonal psychotherapy with clinical populations, including clients with trauma.

Michelle Shea, MLS, MEd, is an education librarian at Texas A&M University–Central Texas. She assists with academic research, coordinates children's programming, and collaborates as a library liaison. She also enjoys writing about student-centered services, library instruction, and community connections.

Julia C. Skinner has a PhD in library and information science from Florida State, as well as graduate training in this field and from the Center for the Book at the University of Iowa. She has worked as part-time faculty, a museum director, and in a number of special collections positions. She currently runs Root, a fermentation and food history organization in Atlanta. Although she is no longer a part of the field full-time, she is still deeply passionate about libraries as a space for building community and creating a better world. You can find her on social media at @bookishjulia or @rootkitchens

Angel Sloss is an assistant professor and digital reference/embedded librarian at Tennessee State University in Nashville. She received a master of library science with a concentration in digital libraries from Drexel University, and a master of educational technology and educational media with a concentration in school librarianship from East Tennessee State University. Her professional experience has included K–12 as well as academic libraries; Angel has presented and served on panels at local educational and historical workshops. She has contributed an excerpt on Alexander Twilight to *Race and Ethnicity in America: From Pre-contact to the Present* published by ABC-CLIO, and a chapter on cultural sensitivity toward race and ethnicity in *The Library Workplace Idea Book: Proactive Steps for Positive Change* published by ALA Editions. Currently, she is a doctoral student studying higher education leadership at Tennessee State University.

Lynne Stahl is the humanities librarian at West Virginia University. She earned her PhD in English from Cornell University and her MLS from Emporia State University. Current research interests include critical information studies, feminist film theory, cultural studies, and open educational resources.

Vikki C. Terrile is an assistant professor and the public services and assessment librarian at Queensborough Community College, the City University of New York (CUNY). She earned her MS in library science from Long Island University, and her MA in urban affairs from Queens College (CUNY) where her capstone project was on arts programming for mothers experiencing homelessness. She has worked with adults, youth, and families experiencing homelessness for more than ten years through library programming and outreach, and has written and presented extensively on this work. She is currently a doctoral student in education at SUNY, the University at Buffalo, with research interests in critical library pedagogy, homeless services and information, and children's literature.

Joseph Winberry became a PhD student at the University of Tennessee's College of Communication and Information in August 2019. His research interests include social justice topics in information settings, community informatics, and qualitative research methods with thematic emphasis on older adults, LGBT+ people, and the social impact of information organizations. He received a bachelor's degree in history and political science from the University of North Carolina–Greensboro as well as a master's degree in information sciences from the University of Tennessee–Knoxville. In 2019, his paper, "Shades of Silver: Applying the Strategic Diversity Manifesto to Tennessee's Knox County Office on Aging," was named the best master's student paper by School of Information Sciences faculty. That year he also received the Gary R. Purcell Award, the single highest honor awarded to a graduating master's student.

Index